Simon & Garfunkel

The Biography

Simon & Garfunkel

The Biography

Victoria Kingston

FROMM INTERNATIONAL
NEW YORK

First Fromm International Edition, 1998

Copyright © Victoria Kingston 1996

All rights reserved under International and Pan-American Copyright Convention. Published in the United States by Fromm International Publishing Corporation, New York. First published by Sidgwick & Jackson, London 1996.

Library of Congress Cataloging-in-Publication Data

Kingston, Victoria.
    Simon and Garfunkel : the biography / Victoria Kingston.
        p. cm.
    Discography: p. ****
    Includes index.
    ISBN 0-88064-193-2
    1. Simon and Garfunkel. 2. Rock musicians—United States—
Biography.   I. Title.
ML421.S53K56 1998
782.42164'092'2—dc21
[B]
                                                                98-10558
                                                                    CIP
                                                                    MN

10 9 8 7 6 5 4 3 2 1

Manufactured in the United States

This book is dedicated to
Christopher David Kingston
1953–1984
who was my brother and my first friend

CONTENTS

CONTENTS

ACKNOWLEDGEMENTS

I began this biography in December 1981 and, as it didn't see the light of print until January 1996, I owe a debt of gratitude to a lot of people. For convenience, these are listed alphabetically within each section.

First, the institutions – and the people in them – who gave freely of their information and time. In the UK: The American Embassy Library; The British Library – Reference Division; CBS Records, London and Warner Brothers Records, London. In the USA: the Board of Education, Brooklyn Law School, Columbia University, the Jewish Information Bureau, New York Public Library – Music Division, Queens College, Louis Ricca, Principal of the Queens Valley School (Public School 164), Flushing, all in New York; the Motion Picture Association of America and Newark Public Library, New Jersey.

Journalists and writers: Roy Carr, Donald Clarke, editor of *The Penguin Encyclopedia of Popular Music* and author of *The Rise And Fall of Popular Music* (published by Viking). These two books were very useful for historical detail on music and artists. Ray Coleman, Robin Denselow, who pointed me in many right directions, Paul Gambaccini, Lon Goddard, Patrick Humphries, Norman Jopling, Spencer Leigh, Dr R. Serge-Denisoff and Penny Valentine.

A legion of people who shared with me their memories of Simon & Garfunkel: Mike Batt, Martin Carthy, Denholm Elliott, Jack Froggatt, Davi Graham, Roy Guest, Roy Halee, Alexis Korner, Jim Lloyd, Les Lowe, Graham Lyle, Daniel Massey, Ron

McCausland, Jimmy Parsons, Peter Pavey, Judith Piepe, Arthur Speed, Pam Speed, Redd Sullivan, Jimmy Webb and Wally Whyton.

In particular I should like to thank Geoff Speed, for his unstinting support and encouragement, and Robin and Chris Sherwen, for letting me stay at their house in Liverpool and recalling 1965. Robin died before this book appeared in print; he was witty, generous and very good company; my thanks and sympathy go to Chris.

My friends – who were tolerant, understanding and interested while this book was being written. I am grateful to them for being there, sometimes at crucial moments: Dr Peter Adams, Ken Atkin, David Bowman, Gerald Burgess, Catherine Chassay, Veronica Clarke, Jean, Iain & James Douglas, Dr Graham Fentiman, Alison Hutchings, Fionnuala Kenny, Beryl Kingston, Lynn Martin, Frankie McGowan, Shelia Parsons, Rob Pope, Diane & Tom Redfern, Lynne Roberts, Flora Smyth Zahra, Chris Stanbury, Mike Walker, Kathleen Wildman, Joy Wilks for all her kindness.

At Sidgwick & Jackson: Producing a book is a team effort, and I am grateful to the following people at Sidgwick & Jackson: Charlotte Greig who encouraged me to send in the manuscript; my first editor, Ingrid Connell for commissioning the book and for her patience and expertise in those early stages; Antonia Bailey, my publicity officer, for being both efficient and dynamic; my editor Carey Smith who had the uneviable task of stepping in during the later stages: I thank her for her good grace, her skill and her good humour.

My special thanks go to Art Garfunkel, for the fascinating insights he gave me into the duo.

My four-legged family, my houseful of dogs, love me with unquestioning devotion and loyalty. They give me great comfort after a long day.

Finally, my mother Dorothy, for her warmth, her absolute common sense, her unfailing support – and for the friendship we share.

PROLOGUE

It was Noël Coward who made the point that popular music has a strange potency. Ask almost anyone and they will be able to tell you where they were when they heard 'Bridge over Troubled Water' for the first time. This is more than being famous, more than being a household name. This is a kind of legendary status in which artists lodge in our consciousness, plug into our private memory bank.

I remember once being in a mini-cab when the radio was playing 'The Sound of Silence'; the cab driver told me how that song had affected him years earlier when he had first heard it. He went on to say how much he liked '7 o'Clock News/Silent Night'. 'It's more than a song,' he said. 'It's more like a piece of life as it is. It tells you what life is like now.' If that is so, I thought, then artists of this stature do indeed become a part of our history.

And I don't think that is being sentimental. I think it is a simple fact. Simon & Garfunkel were important in many ways. It was important that they were Jewish, that they presented themselves as such without adopting pseudonyms to conceal their heritage; that made it easier for others to do the same. It was important that they were American because the songs Paul Simon wrote became, in the tradition of Gershwin and Berlin, documents of their age. It was important that they were childhood friends because that generated a spirit of optimism and camaraderie that everyone loved.

I wrote this book because I wanted to chronicle the career of the duo. Granted they both have separate and solo identities, but this is about the two of them together. People will continue to speculate about whether one is more talented than the other, whether either could have existed without his partner, which one has the more significant career as a solo artist. These questions are not being addressed here.

What I wanted to explore, to get inside, was the fascinating dynamics of the friendship which produced the unique Simon & Garfunkel sound. In a letter to me, Art Garfunkel described it as 'the intertwining of the lives of these two men' which is exactly what I found intriguing. In the hours when he talked to me, I noticed that he always referred to the duo as 'Simon & Garfunkel', never as 'Simon and I'. Artie continually distanced himself from the Garfunkel half of the duo he became. There was Simon & Garfunkel; then there was also Paul and Artie. Interestingly, even when they were at their most separate, Paul and Artie's lives still seemed to run parallel as important events continued to occur simultaneously for each of them.

This book dominated my life for many years. There were days when the sheer weight of material terrified me, when I couldn't see my way through the contradictions and paradoxes that emerged as I dug deeper into their lives and careers. At times, it was exasperating and exhausting – but often it was thrilling and compulsive. I was driven to understand what motivated these two middle-class boys from Queens to become a legend, to achieve the heights of fame and wealth and to survive, in a world where rock legends often fall by the wayside. But Simon & Garfunkel never belonged exclusively in the rock world. They were a unique phenomenon.

This book, then, is about the duo. I have added a final chapter to bring the story up to date. Simon & Garfunkel came to an end just before the release of 'Hearts and Bones' in autumn 1983. The story of the duo ends there because that was the point at which we knew there would never again be a permanent reunion. Simon & Garfunkel were history.

This book is, I hope, a tribute to them, to the brilliant songs Paul Simon wrote, to the inimitable sound Simon & Garfunkel produced. Above all, to the magic of the duo, for they did become, by any standards, a legend.

Chapter One

CHILDHOOD

The opening lines of 'Baby Driver' aptly describe their writer's arrival in the world, for Paul Frederic Simon was born on 13 October 1941 in Newark, New Jersey, on what was probably a grey morning. The music in his ears described in the song came courtesy of his father, Louis Simon, a bass player in a radio band. Paul's mother, Belle, was an elementary school teacher.

On 14 December 1945, Paul's brother, Eddie, was born. The family moved to Forest Hills in the New York suburb of Queens, which lies across the Queensboro Bridge on the East Side. There they lived in a smart, two-storey brick house in a wide street lined with trees. The houses were all identical, and later Paul would describe how his father often got confused by this: 'My father used to drive into the wrong driveway all the time. He'd say, "Damn it, how do you tell one of these houses from another?"' But it was a respectable and pleasant neighbourhood. The Simons were happy there. They were only three blocks away from a little boy born just three weeks after Paul: a boy called Artie.

Arthur Ira Garfunkel was born in New York City on 5 November 1941, the second in a family of three sons. The eldest boy was three years older than Artie, and Jerry was four years younger. Jack Garfunkel, their father, was a successful business-man, a packaging and container salesman who marketed his own products; he was also an inventor. Their mother was a secretary. The stability of their family life clearly influenced Artie. He would

I

later say, 'I have self-discipline and a sense of values from my parents.'

The Garfunkels had no show-business background but they sang well. One of Art's earliest memories is of listening, at the age of four, to them harmonizing in thirds to the popular standard 'When the Red Red Robin' and recording it on their wire recorder. To young Artie it was always 'a pleasing sound'. He was thrilled when he heard his own voice played back. 'That really got me into this business more than anything in the world, singing and being able to record it.' He could hear that he had good pitch, and he would sing to himself, to the rhythm of his walk to school, 'while I was stepping over the cracks in the sidewalk, singing and sort of practising'.

Paul's earliest memory is quite different from Art's. Perhaps surprisingly, it isn't a musical memory at all. He recalls in 1947 sitting on his father's knee in the living room, listening to a baseball game on the radio and rooting for his beloved team, the Yankees. He also remembers, at the same age, going to Ebbett's Field with his father. The Dodgers were playing and Paul, not wishing to be seen supporting a rival team, wore his Lone Ranger mask, hoping no one would recognize him.

In autumn '47, Paul and Artie started in the first grade at Public School 164 in the Queens Valley, where Belle Simon taught third grade. The headmaster of the school, Louis Ricca, described her as 'a superb teacher and a wonderful person'. Paul and Artie didn't really know each other at this stage. Paul's first significant memory of Artie came in the third grade, when Artie stood up at a school concert and sang the Nat King Cole hit, 'They Tried To Tell Us We're Too Young'. The auditorium was silent while he sang, then suddenly filled with the loud applause of teachers and children. Paul was deeply impressed. A girl sitting next to him leaned over and said what a great voice Artie had. He was nine years old, and an overnight sensation. Paul was never to lose that admiration for Art's voice. 'Artie was always the best singer,' he said.

Few people would argue with that. From the beginning, Artie loved singing. By this time, he was training his voice in a remarkably mature way. When wire recorders were superseded by modern tape recorders, the Garfunkels were one of the first families to buy one. Art would sing on to the tape and then play it back, critical of any flaws in his voice, listening for ways to improve. In time, he became more ambitious. 'I said to my father, "I want to harmonize to it. Let's get a second recorder." When we got two recorders, I was off and running. Then I could overdub.'

Although Paul grew up with music around him, it was a chance remark that inspired him to take up singing seriously. One spring afternoon when he was about ten years old, he was sitting on his bed, singing along to an *Alice in Wonderland* record. He had been chosen to appear in the school graduation production in the summer and he was practising the songs. Louis Simon was getting ready for his club appearance that evening. Dressed in his tuxedo, he paused at Paul's door to listen. Then he said, 'That's nice, Paul. You have a nice voice.' That remark was the turning point in Paul's life. 'That was it. From that moment on, I thought of myself as someone who could sing.'

Paul's respect for his father was an important aspect of his early life. In some ways, Louis was a glamorous role model for his son. A successful bass player who had played on several rock 'n' roll records; he used to perform on the *Garry Moore Show* and the *Arthur Godfrey Show* on TV.

'We'd stay up and see Dad,' Paul recalls. 'I was very proud of him. I liked him and I liked him as a musician. Ultimately, I think he got bored with it. In his 40s, he got his doctorate in Education and he ended up teaching at City College. I liked that, too.'

The *Alice in Wonderland* production for which Paul had been practising was what brought Paul and Artie together. In the early summer of '53, both boys were rehearsing their roles. Art was the Cheshire Cat and Paul was the White Rabbit – late for a very important date. Art recalls his first impression of Paul. 'In May and June every day after school there'd be a rehearsal, and there was this very, very funny person named Paul Simon.' They started walking home together after rehearsals and realized how much they had in common. They shared an interest in music and sport. 'Neither of us was one of the group types,' Art says. 'I guess we were drawn together. Being outsiders, in a sense, was one reason.'

On Sunday afternoons, Paul would walk over to Art's house. If it was raining, they would stay in and record their voices on the tape recorders. 'We did a disc jockey show once. Paul was Ted Howard and I was Art Michaels.' They were eleven years old and already learning to be a team.

In autumn 1953, Paul and Artie began at Parsons Junior High School, where they would spend the next two years, as part of a special accelerated programme for bright students. They hated the school. It was in a rough neighbourhood, a twenty-minute walk from where they lived.

That first year was miserable for them. On many occasions they were attacked on the way to school by a gang of local boys who would throw their books over a fence, steal their lunch money or challenge them to fights they couldn't possibly win. Paul and Artie dreaded the confrontations. It was perhaps another factor to cement their friendship.

In autumn '54 they turned thirteen, a significant age for a Jewish boy and marked by the bar mitzvah, traditionally held on the Saturday nearest to his thirteenth birthday. It is an ordeal for a shy adolescent because he must stand up in front of relatives and friends to thank them for all they have done for him. But it's also a proud and exciting experience because he receives presents and makes a moving speech which opens with the solemn words: 'Today, I am a man.'

Art didn't enjoy being the bar mitzvah boy. 'I was acutely uncomfortable being the centre of attention, but I did like the singing part. I was even the cantor at my own service.' He also sang in the High Holiday choir, which gave him early training in harmony and breath control.

Paul, on the other hand, didn't participate much in the religious life of the community. 'My father didn't buy any of it,' he recalls. 'But my mother came from a religious house. So every year she'd go to the synagogue and come home and wail, "I'm the only one sitting alone."'

With adolescence came a new interest: rock 'n' roll. Very few white people at that time realized that 'rock 'n' roll' was a slang euphemism for sex, or that its origins lay in black rhythm and blues. Although several black artists were popular in the early '50s, there was a lot of racism in the music industry. In a sense, rock 'n' roll brought back music into the mainstream.

Alan Freed was one of the few white DJs to play black music and though he didn't invent the term 'rock 'n' roll', he certainly made it popular. Art learned the style by singing along to the hits on the radio, particularly to groups such as the Hilltoppers, the Crewcuts and the Four Aces. He always identified with them more than with popular solo artists like Frankie Laine and Eddie Fisher. Sometimes he listened to Martin Block's *Make Believe Ballroom*, 'but I didn't really feel like singing along with the McGuire Sisters'.

For Artie, rock 'n' roll began in 1954 when Alan Freed arrived in New York from Cleveland with a show called *Rock and Roll Party*, broadcast nightly over WINS from seven till eleven. It swept America that year. Artie discovered the show quite by chance: 'I opened my desk and saw a note that one of the kids in my class was passing to a girl. It said, "Listen to Alan Freed's rock 'n' roll show tonight. I have a dedication for you." That got me very curious and I listened and was hooked in right away and so was Paul.' They tuned in every night, both fascinated by the exuberance and uninhibited style.

And then Paul heard the name of the singer who would be his idol for most of his youth: Elvis Presley. He heard him on the radio of the family car, waiting in the car park of Waldbaum's Supermarket. Elvis influenced him profoundly. Like most youngsters, he wanted desperately to be like him. Later he said, 'I started playing the guitar at thirteen because of Elvis Presley.'

Of course there was a huge gap between Presley's overt, raw sexuality and the awkwardness of a thirteen-year-old boy trying to imitate him. Paul faced his limitations honestly: 'I loved Elvis Presley. And I said to myself, "I can never, never be Elvis Presley."' The adoration lingered, as 'One Trick Pony' indicates. In that film, Paul creates a protagonist, Jonah, who is haunted by Elvis and his music. According to Artie, 'Paul would probably have liked to have been Elvis Presley for most of his career. Paul does have an Elvis Presley style which he can always pull out of his back pocket.'

Coming to terms with being a gauche adolescent is always painful. Music was a form of escape for young Paul. 'I was able to sit by myself and play and dream. And I was always happy doing that.' He came to terms with what he regarded as his shortcomings, telling himself: 'I'm never going to do what Elvis Presley does. I'm going to go and find myself something else to do.' Paul's mother was a great source of strength. 'She was extremely supportive ... my mother was the first nourishing person in my life. She made me feel as if I could take my needs very seriously because she did. By the time I was twelve or thirteen, I felt that I was special because I could play the guitar and write songs.'

Rock 'n' roll was also a turning point for Art. 'I liked it all: Little Richard, Fats Domino – records that cooked. I liked the flavour those sounds had. "Earth Angel" had a terrific flavour; so did Johnny Ace's "Pledging My Love".' As he listened in teenage adulation, he also compared their performances to his own singing. 'From the earliest time we listened, I think we saw ourselves competitively. I did, anyway. I listened and I said, "I can do all that stuff, too."'

Chapter Two

TOM & JERRY

The close, nasal harmony of Don and Phil Everly was an exciting new sound. When Paul heard 'Bye Bye Love' for the first time, he rang Artie and they went to buy it. As one hit followed another into the charts, Paul and Art worked to create a similar sound. In later years, they would record more than one tribute to their idols: the famous 'Bye Bye Love' and 'Wake Up Little Susie'. For Paul, some of the fascination lay in their name. 'There was nobody named Everly in Forest Hills. Everybody's name was Steinberg or Schwarz or Weinstein.'

Still at junior high school, they started to rehearse singing in their spare time. They worked, according to Art, 'in an amazingly professional way', well equipped with Art's two tape recorders so they could overdub their harmonies, 'trying to sound like the real people'. They had intense, serious sessions in the basement of the Simon home. Art recalls: 'We'd be sitting nose to nose, looking right into each other's mouths to copy diction. I'd want to know exactly where his tongue would hit the top of his palate when he'd say a T, to know exactly how to get that T right. And I could see that you could be almost right, or even better than almost right. And that all of that really was the difference between whether or not it sounded professional.'

It was this meticulous care, this insistence on perfection that led to the unique Simon & Garfunkel sound. The split-second timing, the blending of two voices was the goal from the beginning of their partnership. Art summed up their secret, already learnt at fourteen years old: 'Once you had it precise, you cooled it out and made it seem effortless.'

Having found their style, they looked for outlets to sing – at parties, family gatherings, school functions. They did songs by the Crewcuts; 'Sh-boom' and 'Crazy 'bout You Baby' were two favourites. In spring of '55 they made their first public appearance as a duo, singing an a cappella version of 'Sh-boom' at a school assembly at Parsons Junior High. It was humble, but it was their beginning.

In June '55 Paul and Artie left Parsons, much to their relief. Paul was going away to summer camp on Long Island for the next two months. All in all, it was a happy time for him. His brother Eddie was nine and had grown into a robust companion. Their relationship was based on shared interests and a healthy competitive spirit. Although they were four years apart in age, their mannerisms and speech patterns were strikingly similar; they looked alike, except that Paul was an inch taller.

Paul remembers this particular summer very fondly, especially one afternoon in June when school had broken up and his parents were out for the day. Louis Simon had left the house early for Manhattan, where he was working with the studio orchestra, taping the *Arthur Godfrey Show* for CBS. Belle was out shopping.

Paul and Eddie were enjoying a game of baseball in the playground of Public School 165. Sudden, heavy rain interrupted play and they ran home, their dungarees and jerseys still damp, to continue their game in their bedroom. They had an imaginary batter's box at the far end but it was a cramped field, with two beds and furniture. The ball was one of a pair of foam rubber dice, the sort which hang in the windows of cars – perfect for indoor matches, bouncing off windows.

They played skilfully, neither giving an inch. Sometimes they played as many as thirty innings, maintaining a scoreless tie, and neither would concede. Over the years, they had built up physical endurance; though Eddie was younger, he was an excellent shortstop with a formidable sinking curve ball, while Paul had a superb right-handed uppercut and was a great outfielder and base-stealer, always grim in his determination to win the game.

Paul liked to act as commentator, imitating the style of delivery. He also took the role of Yankee champ, 'always coming out of retirement for one last game'. They invented names for themselves: George and Mickey Muffchatiery. Both boys had a terrific sense of audience and would pause now and then to address their imaginary crowd. The house would ring with their excited laughter and yells of triumph as one of them scored. 'My brother and I knew how to create fun,' Paul says.

They played other games, including wrestling, basketball and a strange kind of hockey in the basement. Paul was also an excellent baseball card flipper. He could land them with great precision against a wall, having practised for hours in his room. And he was the local stickball champ. 'I used to hustle stickball around Queens ... deliberately blowing the first game to fool guys and then doubling the stakes on the second.' On a good day he could make between fifteen and twenty dollars.

In autumn '55 Paul and Artie started at their new school, Forest Hills High, in the tenth grade. It was there that the friendship became a working partnership. They were inseparable at school, even sharing their detentions.

Feeling that it was important for the boys to play an instrument, Louis Simon had tried to teach Paul the piano – 'But it was no go, so he gave up on me and taught my brother.' In October '55 Louis bought Paul a $25 Stadium guitar for his fourteenth birthday, hoping he would learn that. Eddie was already playing with great skill and was being coached in classical guitar. In a rare interview, Eddie recalled his brother's first faltering attempts. 'Nobody thought Paul would be very good on guitar. The day he got it, he sat down and picked out a one-note tune ... it didn't sound too promising.' But with characteristic determination, Paul set to work and, aided by his musical background, he improved rapidly.

Louis didn't really encourage Paul in a musical career. Although he was a successful musician himself, his many years in the profession had taught him just how precarious it can be. He and Belle wanted their sons to be in secure employment – perhaps as lawyers. Paul told Lon Goddard: 'They'd say, "This is ridiculous. You play guitar six hours a day. You should be studying six hours a day. What do you want to be, a musician?"' Ironically, both Paul and Eddie became just that, following in their father's footsteps. But Louis urged his elder son to keep music in perspective. 'Sure, play the guitar,' he would tell Paul, 'but as a hobby.'

Now that Paul had some skill on the guitar, he and Artie started writing their own songs, snappy rock 'n' roll numbers in the style of the Everly Brothers. They even copyrighted their first attempt, a teenage love song called 'The Girl for Me', filling in the offical copyright form and sending it with four dollars to the Library of Congress. They meant business.

They decided to try to sell their songs. After school and on Saturdays they would go into Manhattan. Art recalls 'those really scary subway rides', Paul with his guitar, both nursing dreams of being stars. They had taken the addresses of record companies from the labels of records they liked because they thought, 'They'll be receptive to us because they make good records.'

They were wrong. The record companies didn't want to know about two fifteen-year-olds. The boys knocked on the doors of the companies clustered together in the Brill Building on 50th Street and Broadway, and the response was always discouraging. Art recalled: 'There would be this weird, freaked-out black guy. Or this very fat, cigar-smoking Jewish businessman. And they'd be gruff and you knew it was a really hard thing to get into.'

Still they went on trying, cheering each other on, giving each other courage. They called themselves Tom & Jerry because it sounded more like the pop image they aspired to. Paul was Jerry Landis, after a girl he liked named Sue Landis; Art was Tom Graph, a name chosen in honour of his favourite and most absorbing hobby – charting the progress of hit records on huge sheets of graph paper, something that reflected his early love of mathematics and design.

They carried on writing songs and trying to publish them, with no success. As Art described it: 'Getting nowhere. Nobody realizing that we were good. They were businessmen who were a generation away from the kids who were making the hits, so they just didn't trust.' Although they got a contract with one record company, they never recorded anything. It simply tied them up legally for nine months.

They were frustrated and thought about giving up. While Art recalls, 'Paul was a lot of the drive in those days,' Paul in fact had his own private source of frustration. When he reached the height of five feet two, he stopped growing. His other triumphs, though they gave him some satisfaction, were therefore tinged with some bitterness. 'I was doing well,' he says. 'I batted first on the baseball team. I had a school jacket with letters and everything on it.' He was popular at school, he had a good friendship with Artie, he had a brother and parents who were supportive of him and his talents. But like most adolescents, he was gauche and shy, and his lack of height made him more self-conscious. 'I must have been very angry, probably about not growing,' he recalls. 'I was a real angry guy. I spent a lot of time by myself, playing guitar.'

The guitar playing certainly paid off. Maybe the anger paid off, too. It was this anger which fuelled his courage to pursue their dream so single-mindedly, to turn adolescent frustration into the drive and ambition that inspired Artie. Paul was channelling his energy into a creativity.

Art and Paul decided to have one last shot at making a record. In the early months of '57 they cut a demo disc for two dollars in Sanders Recording Studio on Seventh Avenue. They didn't have much faith in it. They had two songs prepared and they performed them straight on to acetate, which meant it couldn't be erased if they made a mistake. It was strictly a one-take deal.

They sang 'Hey Schoolgirl', their own composition. During the break before the next song, a businessman named Sid Prosen approached them. He had been listening to them in the waiting room because he had booked the studio for the hour following theirs. Art described it drily to *Rolling Stone*: 'He said, "When you're finished, I want to talk to you guys." And afterwards, he came on real heavy. "Greatest thing since the Everly Brothers. I'm going to make stars out of you." And at that time, we had enough experience to separate the real offer from the phoney. We said, "We'll sign up if you'll record us and release us within sixty days." He said, for sure. We signed, recorded and released it.'

'Hey Schoolgirl' was released in autumn '57. In an exuberant song typical of its day, sung with energy and harmony, a boy declares his love for a girl in his class. On the other side was a lively number, 'Dancin' Wild'. Prosen released it on the Big Records label, actually a very small company. The disc was cut as a 78 and a 45.

Paul and Art performed locally to promote it. Prosen organized some new clothes for them: red blazers with white loafers. The image was young and fresh, and so were they. They even earned themselves a spot on the popular TV show, *American Bandstand*, hosted by Dick Clark. This was a very important step for them as teenagers all over the United States hurried home every evening just to see the programme. Its ratings were always sky-high. Natives of Philadelphia still remember the seemingly endless queues of youngsters waiting patiently outside the studio in Market Street, to be admitted to dance on the show.

Art had very mixed feelings about appearing on it. He was both nervous and thrilled. 'Here I was down there, feeling like a nobody with the stars, walking into this building in Philadelphia, seeing huge stacks of US mail bags in the hallways.' He must have hoped that one day there would be some fan mail for Tom & Jerry.

Even such dizzy success as this brings its moments of anguish – and Artie suffered some that day. 'I went to the john about a half hour before we went on the air and there were two of the kids I knew from TV in the urinals next to me. One was saying, "Who do we have today?" "Oh, somebody named Tom & Jerry." The guy says, "Who are those jerks?" It was hard for me to be the star.'

The show was seen all over America on Thanksgiving Day, 1957. They appeared right after Jerry Lee Lewis singing 'Great Balls of Fire'. Paul recalled: 'It was a tough act to follow. We didn't meet him before or after the show, though. Actually, I think we were too scared.' Scared or not, Paul loved it. 'It was a thrill, really. Every day I watched *American Bandstand* and here I was performing on the show. It made me a neighbourhood hero.'

It's very sad that we can never see this performance of 'Hey Schoolgirl'. Years later, assembling an anniversary programme, Dick Clark was dismayed to learn that this edition of *American Bandstand* had been lost. Posterity has been denied the very first TV performance of Tom & Jerry.

After the show, Artie and Paul promoted their disc with four days of record hops in Cincinnati. To their delight, they were given a proper engagement at the Hartford State Theater. There were nine acts on the bill, all of them black rhythm-and-blues artists who were well known and highly professional. Art recalls ironically: 'We were the white group, sort of the comic relief.' And Paul recalls: 'We were two white kids from Queens, playing to a completely black audience and sounding vaguely like the Everly Brothers.'

At school and in the neighbourhood, they were almost famous now, and they enjoyed every moment of it. As Paul said, 'We were big deals around Queens and in the high school.' They were now performing professionally on a fairly regular basis. They had appeared on a national television show. They had a hit record.

Their single remained in *Billboard*'s Top 100 for nine weeks, finally getting to number 59 in the early weeks of 1958 before it began to slide down again. It made the Regional Top 10, though not number 1. Altogether, they sold one hundred thousand copies of 'Hey Schoolgirl'. Art has since referred it as 'a medium hit', but it was quite an achievement for two sixteen-year-olds just beginning in a tough business, facing strong competition from other young hopefuls and from experienced professionals.

Their next single didn't do so well, though. Then Big Records went out of business. Prosen immediately transferred the duo to another small label, Hunt, for the passionate ballad 'That's My Story'. That didn't sell either. Paul later described it in a characteristically concise if slightly inaccurate way: 'The next one was a flop, and the next one was a flop, and then the company went broke, and that was the end of it, so we went back to school.'

In fact they had never left school. They were disappointed about the singles but they had continued to study hard, nurturing plans of successful careers. Art at sixteen: 'I was the kid who was going to go to college and find some way to make a decent living.' And Paul: 'We loved to sing, but we were just kids at high school. We were hoping to go to college after that.'

Paul managed to buy a car with the money he earned from the record. He was very proud of his red Impala convertible. But one night at the corner of Artie's block the three carburettors caught fire. Paul leaped out as the car exploded. He had been within inches of losing his life. He stood in the street, watching helplessly, 'while my whole share of the record burned up'. There would be many other records and other cars but Paul didn't know that then.

They had tasted the thrill of show business and that would be hard to forget. For Paul it brought conflict: 'We didn't plan to go on with music as a career, but it wasn't for fun. We were deadly serious about everything we did. We loved making records.' Artie's dilemma was more complex. He definitely wanted an academic career rather than one in show business. 'I never thought I was seriously going to make my living this way. I thought sooner or later I would do something more reputable. But I sure did always want to be famous.' While the success of 'Hey Schoolgirl' was relatively modest, it was still Artie's first taste of a business he would be drawn into. For a sixteen-year-old with one hit behind him and blessed with a flawless voice, it created a tug-of-war between the academic life he was training for and the performing life he loved. This conflict would remain within him for the rest of his life.

Chapter Three

COLLEGE

Paul and Artie graduated in summer '58, both intending to go on to college. For a while their ways would divide, geographically at least. Art enrolled at Columbia College, a magnificent establishment on New York's West Side. In the winter of '58 he took an apartment in Manhattan and dedicated himself to serious study. He enrolled to do Architecture, though he would later admit that he chose it for all the wrong reasons. 'I was attracted to Architecture for the sound of the word "architect" . . . I liked the crispness of "tect" at the end. It sounded respectable . . . You could smoke a pipe, wear corduroy pants, gum-bottomed shoes.'

Paul opted for Queens College, just a few miles from his home. He decided to major in English Literature. He had been deeply impressed when the poet e.e.cummings had visited the school to read some of his own poems. Also: 'I think I had a girlfriend or a girl that I worshipped from afar, and she was an English major, so I decided to be one, too.'

Once embarked on the course, he realized he had found something he loved: a wealth of literature that would influence his own writing in the years to come. He became a passionate admirer of James Joyce, and nowadays one of his most prized possessions is a copy of *Ulysses* signed by Joyce himself. He read avidly: novelist Carson McCullers, poets such as T.S. Eliot, Robert Frost, Emily Dickinson. Paul would later regard this period as one that shaped his character. 'It was then that I started going on different paths from other people.'

One of these paths was still in pursuit of music though, for now, in a solo capacity. He earned extra cash making demo records. He discovered a talent for imitating the styles of established stars such as Frankie Avalon and The Fleetwoods. 'A publisher would get a song and they'd say, "This song would be great for Dion." So we'd get somebody in and I would be Dion, and then I'd sing all the background ooh-ooh-wah-ooh.' Paul would play all the instruments too, overdubbing them and his own voice several times so as to sound like a group. He was paid fifteen dollars for a song and he fitted in about two sessions a week, which meant he had 'enough money to go out, buy gas, or new guitar strings, just to support myself'. It was fairly enterprising. He was still only seventeen.

At Queens College he met a student called Carole Klein, later to become singer-songwriter Carole King. For a while they made demos together, overdubbing six or seven instruments. Paul played guitar and bass, Carole played piano and drums and they put four voices in the background. They would earn thirty dollars for each recording. One of their demos, 'Just to Be with You', was recorded in 1959 by the Passions and did well in the American charts. Encouraged by this success, Carole decided to give up her studies and pursue a full-time musical career. Paul advised her against it, telling her what his father had told him. 'I said, "Don't. You'll ruin your career." And she quit and she had ten hits that year.'

For Paul the most important thing about this work was that he was learning studio techniques: singing into a microphone, using his voice in different styles, overdubbing. All these skills would be invaluable later on.

In 1959, he recorded on MGM Records a ballad called 'Loneliness', performed under his duo name of Jerry Landis. A year later, he wrote and sang 'I'd Like to Be the Lipstick on Your Lips'. In later years he would refer to such songs as 'dumb teenage lyrics', which is a bit harsh because he was no more than a teenager himself.

That same year, 1960, he sang with the Mystics on 'All Through the Night' on Laurie Records. He saw an advertisement for a singer to front a band. 'I went along and they offered me either a percentage or seventy-five dollars' salary. I took the seventy-five dollars.' As it turned out, that was a shrewd move because the record flopped. Today, Paul has an autographed photo of the Mystics which reads, 'To Jerry. Hope all your records are hits.' If they had only known.

In 1960 Artie was also recording. He auditioned for Octavia, Jack Gold's record company. 'I wandered in one day as a soloist,' is how he later described it. He sang a song he had written himself, accompanying himself on the guitar. He would also record some singles for Warwick Records, discs that would now be precious collectors' items. Unlike Paul, Art abandoned the old Tom & Jerry name. He was now Artie Garr.

Those early college years were fruitful for Artie. As well as studying he was working hard at singing, and even a little writing. It isn't widely known that Art could (and can) play the guitar, much less that he ever wrote songs. He explained to *Rolling Stone* why he gave it up: 'My writing skill, I thought, didn't really keep pace with my growing up. I wrote some banal rock 'n' roll songs in the mid fifties, and then I wrote things of a more folky, sensitive nature later on, but I rated myself as weak. I never felt comfortable with it.'

All the same, he had a longing to write. 'In the case of poetry, I sometimes really feel this tremendous inspiration to say a certain idea or to examine one moment that I think everyone can relate to, and fashion it into a poem in this very rich, ten-hour period in which everything stops while I pace around until I polish it off.' (Art would return to this in later years and produce some very fine poetry.)

In his late teens, however, Artie didn't manage to sustain the feeling of creativity. Whatever had driven him to write seemed to disappear before he could finish the poem. 'I won't go back to it,' he thought then, 'I don't really feel like that's my thing.'

Music was Art's thing. From earliest childhood he had loved music and related to it in every sense. 'It came out of my ability to sing along to records and harmonize spontaneously. See, for me, the first singers were the Everly Brothers. I sang along with them. Finally, I heard notes held and harmonies and great articulation and diction, and a very interesting sound in two voices.'

This close study also taught him about chord structure. 'I could feel the chordal underpinning that makes up a song. If I knew the song from having heard it once, I could feel the next coming chord. I'd know where I was, as if I could graphically see the note. I was singing in relation to the melody whether it was a third higher or a fourth below. I'd feel the new chord coming up and know what my choices were and what would blend in. Then the next step was shaping the line, parallel movement, counter movement. By the time Paul and I were recording in the sixties, I could do all that.'

He spent much of his spare time in recording studios, singing for various labels. A lot of his effort, however, went into practising at home, using his old method of overdubbing his voice on two tape recorders. He tackled standards such as 'You'll Never Walk Alone' and 'I Believe', as well as some Everly Brothers hits. When I heard some of these early, primitive recordings, I was stunned by the purity of his voice. He reached for top notes and held them without a waver. He was dedicated to singing and those long hours went to perfect his craft.

By 1962, rock 'n' roll was in its last stages for Paul and Artie. In January, Paul sang the lead and produced for Tico and the Triumphs on 'Motorcycle', their single for Bell Records. It just nudged its way into the Hot 100 Chart, remaining at number 99 for one week in January. But Paul was becoming interested in the new style of folk music that was sweeping across America. 'Age made me change my style of music,' he said later. 'Age and the folk boom. Rock 'n' roll got very bad in the early sixties. Very mushy.'

By this time Joan Baez, a young folk singer, was attracting a lot of attention, her traditional, acoustic style coming as a revelation. Peter Seeger had become a mainstay of folk music, followed by a stream of singer-songwriters who performed in tiny New York clubs: Phil Ochs, Tom Paxton – and, of course, Bob Dylan. Dylan, who made his debut at the Newport Folk Festival in 1963, took audiences by storm. He was forceful, angry, rebellious, anti-racist, anti-establishment and above all young. Resembling the young, leather-clad James Dean and owing much in his music to his hero Woody Guthrie, Dylan strode through the folk world like a giant, sure of himself and his causes.

Paul started attending concerts given in Washington Square on Sundays, by musicians who would influence him – such revered people as Merle Travis picking on guitar in the style which took his name, and Earl Scruggs on banjo. Paul was captivated. 'I had to learn it. I didn't think – my gosh, music is changing and I have to shift now. I was just a kid, playing the guitar, writing and singing.'

He teamed up again with Artie and together they were able to sing the popular folk songs in this new style. Encouraged by the response of their peer group, Paul and Artie went on to get some bookings at coffee houses and small folk clubs in Greenwich Village in New York. They did concerts in Washington Square Park on Sunday mornings and they played at such famous places as Gerde's Folk City, the Gaslight Club, the Bitter End – venues that had recently seen the like of Joan Baez and Bob Dylan.

At the same time during this interim period Paul continued solo. At the start of '63 he released 'Lone Teen Ranger', his own composition, under the Jerry Landis name. It reached 97 in the Top 100.

On 1 February 1963, Paul graduated from Queens College with a BA in English. He started work at Edward B. Marks Music, a New York publishing company. He had to visit all the record companies, trying to interest them in the Marks catalogue, persuading them to have their artists record a particular song. He was learning about the music business from the inside and making connections with the major record labels.

In a sense, he was leading two separate lives. Each day he rode the subway to Manhattan, a middle-class young man, smartly dressed and inconspicuous. At night he was performing on the Greenwich Village circuit. He had also started writing songs under the pseudonym Paul Kane, a name inspired by the film *Citizen Kane* which Paul admired greatly. He chose a pseudonym because, being employed by Marks to sell songs, it was less compromising if he didn't appear as a songwriter as well.

He was feeling restless. A mood of unrest was sweeping across United States campuses. Young people were seeking new identities, challenging the old values, the barriers of class, colour and gender. They were shouting for radical changes, racial and social equality, civil liberty and sexual freedom. A new era had begun. Paul and Art, at twenty-one, were in the middle of it.

But although they were encouraged by the success they had enjoyed as a folk duo during the past months, they were also seeking careers separately. Paul was working in the music business, but Art's main direction was still towards an academic life, with performing as a sideline. In June '63, Art went across the country to Berkeley in California, where he lived and studied at the university and did some singing at local folk clubs and Student Union gatherings.

That same month Paul boarded a plane for Paris, for an extended holiday. He was looking for something he couldn't quite define – something he couldn't find at home. He travelled the well-trodden route of the wanderer, roughing it for most of the time, sleeping under the bridges of the Seine, his guitar strapped to his body. Later, he told a concert audience: 'When I was in Paris, we'd sit on the banks of the Seine, and when tourist boats would go by, I would yell out Capitalist Pig.'

Times were lean that summer. He earned money wherever he

could, busking in the streets and at underground stations. Later he recalled: 'I certainly don't miss it because it was embarrassing to just stand at a spot, start singing and hope some people would gather so you could pass the hat and make some money.' He rarely sang his own compositions. 'Just whatever was popular that had a loud, high ending. I was particularly good at loud, high endings. If you sang a note for a long time, you tended to get money for it.' You can hear evidence of Paul's talent for loud, high endings on 'He Was My Brother' and 'A Church Is Burning', which he would later record on his first solo album, *The Paul Simon Songbook*.

Paul's waking hours were filled with discovery in a city of crowds and excitement. He lived for each day, though at the back of his mind he was conscious of the secure career that had always been his goal. 'I always figured that, somewhere in the near future, I would have to stop this whole thing and think out a way I could earn a decent living. But at that age, well, I just happened to love what I was doing.' He had plenty of time. He was still not quite twenty-two.

One day, sitting on a park bench, he met a young man called Dave McCausland who was on holiday from Essex, where he ran a folk club in the Railway Hotel in Brentwood. They talked about the folk circuit that was emerging in England. Dave offered Paul a bed if he ever wanted to try his luck there.

In the autumn, Paul returned to New York with a handful of songs he had written. His first, 'He Was My Brother', was played to Artie, who was immediately excited by it. Later, he wrote: 'The ending is joyously optimistic . . . it was clearly the product of considerable talent.' The second, 'Sparrow', was also a new direction for Paul. They worked on arrangements for both songs and performed them that night at Folk City. The third song, 'Bleecker Street', was finished a month later. It describes a street in New York's East Side, filled with people trying, but failing, to communicate with each other, and living in an environment of sterility and despair. As Art noted, 'It touches poignantly on human conditions of our time' – the first in a line of Simon compositions to do that.

Then, on Friday 22 November President John Kennedy was assassinated in Dallas, Texas. In a horrifying, panic-filled few moments, he slumped down in the back of his car, from which he had been waving to thousands of overjoyed people. All over the world, viewers witnessed his death on television. America went a little crazy with grief and shock. In small towns all over the country, there were outbreaks of angry protest. Those cries were taken up on the college campuses. Nothing would ever be the same again. With the death of Kennedy, a dream had died.

It was in the context of this turbulence that Paul wrote his contribution to the sixties – a song called 'The Sound of Silence'. The song uses imagery of light and darkness to show how ignorance and apathy destroy people's ability to communicate on even a simple level. The light which should symbolize truth and enlightenment is a destructive, painful force with metaphors of stabbing, flashing – even worshipping the false Neon god. In such a violent context, the song was perfectly fitting. Paul had the theme and the melody in November but it took three frustrating months of writing and re-writing before it was finished. He played it to Artie in its completed form on 19 February 1964. Neither of them could know how drastically that song would alter their lives.

At the time of Kennedy's death, with the song as yet unfinished, Paul returned to Europe, this time to England. He still felt unfulfilled and seemed to be marking time. Later, he regarded it as a necessary phase. 'I should say there's nothing particularly exceptional about me. Everybody seems to get up at some time and roam around.'

Remembering the invitation of the young man he had met on a park bench in Paris, he made his way to Essex. There he soon settled in, living at the home of Dave McCausland's parents and performing regularly at the Railway Hotel.

Ron McCausland, Dave's father, liked Paul immensely. He

told me: 'We used to sit up until the early hours of the morning, discussing politics and putting the world right.' And he recalled Paul strumming an early version of 'The Sound of Silence'.

Paul played at most of the local folk clubs and acquired quite a following. But he didn't regard it as permanent. 'When I was going round, I figured, yeah I'd sing for a while until I got bored or people didn't want to hear it, and then I'd do something else.' As it happened, he never did get bored. And people went on listening.

It was around this time that Paul met a girl called Kathy. Pretty and slender with long brown hair, she worked as a secretary and lived in Essex with her family. She would become his constant companion, as well as the inspiration for some of his finest love songs. She was quietly spoken and shy, rarely speaking except among close friends with whom she felt most comfortable.

She and Paul were deeply in love. She played a very important part in those days in England, not only for Paul but also for Artie, who remained fond of her and recalled her with great affection many years later. She was a kind of muse for Paul, and complemented him in several ways: where he was restless and dynamic, she was quiet and passive; he was driven to write and perform and she was content to be with him in the background. She didn't want to be in show business and she avoided the limelight. But she was in love with him and that gave him a sense of stability.

Artie, meanwhile, was studying hard, but by the end of the autumn term of '63, he realized he was dissatisfied with the course he had chosen. He now felt that architecture required him to be, not an artist, but a hard-headed businessman. 'I had an unpleasant experience with architecture,' he said later. So he changed to mathematics, a subject for which he had always had a passion.

He also knew that he wanted to teach. He earned money to support himself and pay for his tuition by giving private lessons. It occurred to him that there was a strong link between teaching and performing, in the sense of being in control. 'Teaching was just like a little performance. You'd come into somebody's house and do your perfect fifty minutes. The game was never to look at your watch but to feel what the perfect fifty-minute thing was.' So in the spring of 1964, Art enrolled at Columbia University Teacher's College to study for a degree in mathematics and education. He felt he had decided on the shape his life was to take.

Also in spring '64, Paul went back to New York and resumed his work in the publishing business. He had made a few valuable contacts by now, including producer Tom Wilson at Columbia Records, the man who had recently produced Bob Dylan's album. Paul played 'He Was My Brother' for Wilson, who agreed to buy it for a group called the Pilgrims.

But Paul had other ideas. According to Artie, Paul said, 'Well, I have some songs of my own that I never showed you. Would you be interested in hearing them? My friend's uptown. He sings them with me.' Wilson let them audition and they made a demo of four songs, including the new song 'The Sound of Silence'.

Assigned as their engineer was Roy Halee, who would become their lifelong colleague and friend. Art recalls how Roy came out of the booth that day to adjust their microphones very carefully. Later, he told them, 'As soon as you guys started singing, I was very concerned that everything go right with this act.' Roy is a warm, generous man with a sense of humour and great timing. From the start, there was a rapport between him and the duo. As Art says, 'We sensed that he was very much on our side. We requested that this guy with the yellow, button-down Oxford shirt be the engineer again. And he's always been there.'

After the recording details were settled, the next problem was a name for the duo. Paul had already used two pseudonyms for performing and writing, Jerry Landis and Paul Kane. Art had used Tom Graph and Artie Garr and was now considering Art Garfield, that particular surname being a popular adaptation of the Jewish names Garfunkel and Garfinkel.

This was the real dilemma. Even in 1964, there was anti-Semitism in the US, and Simon and Garfunkel were fairly obvious

Jewish names. Bob Dylan had opted to conceal his Jewish origin along with his real name, Robert Zimmerman. (Dylan was reputedly chosen in honour of Welsh poet Dylan Thomas.) But Art and Paul didn't want to do this. While they realized that appearing as openly Jewish might work against them in some quarters, they felt it was important to present themselves as they really were.

As Paul said, 'Our name is honest. I always felt it was a big shock to people when Bob Dylan's name turned out to be Bobby Zimmerman. It was so important that he should be true.' On the other hand, Paul was concerned about how people would react to Simon & Garfunkel. 'Everybody thought we were a comedy act ... it was unheard of that anybody should use their real names. People would just laugh.'

Tom Wilson was supportive and brought the matter before the Columbia executives. They had a meeting to discuss the implications, and finally decided that in 1964 America ought to be ready for the names of Simon and Garfunkel. When examined in a historical context, that decision becomes a very important one in terms of Jewish identity. Since the Second World War, Jewish performers had tended to conceal their heritage by using Americanized names – as Paul and Artie had done in the early days. Simon & Garfunkel were one of the earliest groups to 'come out' with a heritage of which they had every reason to be proud. That is something of an achievement.

So Simon & Garfunkel were signed up to make the album which became *Wednesday Morning 3 am*. The cover shows them in the New York subway, dressed in conventional suits. Paul has his guitar and the train is just pulling in. Only five of the songs are Simon compositions, the rest being made up of folk standards. Presumably Columbia included these in order to ensure that the album sold since a brand new songwriter was always a risk. The album sold modestly, though it later won a Gold Disc when Simon & Garfunkel were famous.

The first side opens with 'You Can Tell the World', a stirring gospel by Gibson and Camp, followed by 'Last Night I Had the Strangest Dream', an Ed McCurdy composition with some effective banjo figures. In both songs, the Simon & Garfunkel harmony works well.

In 'Bleecker Street', this sweet harmony has an added dimension because it underlines the hopeless desolation of the people it describes. The street is a real place in New York, and this song was an early example of Paul depicting real locations. In 'Sparrow', the allegory is presented as a children's rhyme, rich in biblical imagery and fable; thus, the callousness of a society which rejects the poor and helpless in such polite language is brilliantly understated.

Then comes 'Benedictus', a Latin hymn taken from a sixteenth-century church mass originally performed by Orlando de Lasso. Art discovered the song while on a music course in his undergraduate curriculum and he researched it in the Columbia University Library. He then took it to Paul and they worked out an arrangement for it, writing a two-part harmony and guitar chords.

Side one closes with 'The Sound of Silence'. On the album sleeve Art describes it as portraying communication that takes place only on a superficial and commercial level: 'There is no serious understanding because there is no serious communication . . . no one dares take the risk of reaching out.' In many ways, this acoustic version with only Paul's guitar and two blended voices is the best and purest they ever recorded.

Side two opens with 'He Was My Brother', sung passionately. This is followed by two traditional folk songs, 'Peggy-O' and 'Go Tell It on the Mountain', both rendered in close harmony. They do a creditable version of Ian Campbell's classic, 'The Sun Is Burning'.

Then we have the obligatory Bob Dylan number, without which no sixties album was complete – 'The Times They Are A-Changing'. Obviously, the duo had to present a substantially different version from Dylan's, with the result that much of the cynicism is toned down. Paul and Art don't sound terribly comfortable with this one.

The album closes with the exquisite love song, 'Wednesday Morning 3am', written in April '64 according to Art. His sleeve notes read: 'The heightened intensity of "The Sound of Silence" has given way here to a gentle mood, and the melody is once again a soft, smooth vehicle. It is a painting that sets a scene, sketches some details and quietly concludes.' The song is both erotic and tender, touchingly innocent and overtly sexual. It sets a fine balance between the childlike quality of the sleeping woman and the intense and urgent fear of the man who watches her. The immaculate harmony serves to heighten the sense of poignancy.

It was a good album, and a very good first album. But after its completion there was a lull, and Paul began to feel unsettled in New York. The response to the duo was less than he had hoped for. 'Artie and I auditioned at a lot of clubs in the States, but nobody showed any interest in either me or my music ... we received absolutely no enouragement or acceptance whatsoever.' For Art, it was a different kind of feeling and a different situation. He faced it calmly. He had made a record and he had enjoyed doing it. The public weren't exactly rushing out to buy it, but the experience had been worthwhile. He had his studies to occupy him.

Paul still had the memory of those happy days in England. He had set his sights on the folk clubs: 'I could play music there. There was no place in New York City. They wouldn't have me.' In the late spring of '64 he packed up his guitar and a few clothes and set off, once again, for England – in search of his fortune, or perhaps just a place to play his songs.

Chapter Four

ENGLAND WHERE THE HEART LAY

Paul found himself a small bedsitter in a house near the underground station in Belsize Park, north London. Also living there was Martin Carthy, the well-known traditional English folk singer. Martin told me: 'My actual contact with Paul was very slight, considering we lived in the same house . . . We did a couple of gigs together. He was an amazing performer. He was very adept with a small repertoire, very good at spreading his capacities widely – and that's not a criticism. As a performer, he's still as good as he was then; he's adopted no tricks. He's now very much a songwriter in the old American tradition of Gershwin and Cole Porter, and that's where he was always destined to write, I think.'

Paul found work anywhere he could: smoky cellars, working men's clubs, noisy pubs, late-night transport cafés. He moved around on foot or he hitched rides from lorry drivers. 'I never thought of [singing] as a career,' he said later. 'It was just a great way to spend my time, roaming around in a strange country where everything was new and exciting.' He earned about three pounds a night, sometimes five. In a good week, he could earn twenty pounds, which he felt was more or less what he deserved. His needs were simple. 'All I ever did at that time was to play guitar, and in doing so, earn my keep and pay my rent, just from performing.' He regarded himself as a 'not-too-well-off professional musician'.

The most important thing was that he was being appreciated by the audiences. He told no one about his American records, or about his recent debut album with Artie. They accepted him as a folk singer from America. He was happy with that. 'Nobody had been listening in the States. In New York, I was a kid from Queens. That was bad. In England, I was an American. That was good.' He was deeply in love with Kathy, he had made friends on the folk circuit, he was financially independent and people were taking him seriously. He had a lot going for him.

In a tiny office at 5 Denmark Street in London's West End, three men were running a small music publishing company called Lorna Music. Alan Paramor was the managing director, Leslie Lowe was the professional manager and Peter Pavey was, in his own words, 'everything else', which included looking after royalties.

Early in 1964, Les Lowe came across a song called 'Carlos Domingues' in his catalogue. It was credited to a new writer, Paul Kane. He felt the song had potential, so he sent it to Val Doonican, who recorded it on his first album, which sold about 90,000 copies. A couple of months later, Paul Simon arrived at Lorna Music, wanting to thank whoever was responsible for selling his song. He said he'd been receiving royalties from Edward B. Marks Music in New York, the company which was sub-published by Lorna Music in London. Les asked him to sit down and they drank tea while Paul told him about himself and his songs. Years later, Les told me how much of an impact Paul made on him that day. 'This young American sat there, in our tiny, cramped office, took off his duffle coat and took out his guitar and started to play strange songs. I was very impressed and I had no doubt that Paul's work was unique. So I took him in to meet Alan Paramor.'

It was agreed that Lorna should take on Paul's songs. The next step was to organize some demo records. Les arranged for Paul to record a few songs at Regent Sound Studios in Denmark Street. Then he used the tapes to try to find some work for Paul. One of the people he approached was Jimmy Parsons, who was then an agent in an office downstairs from Lorna Music.

When I interviewed Jimmy in the eighties, he was running the famous Ronnie Scott's club in Soho. In his office there he told me about the Paul Simon of more than twenty years earlier: 'I listened to the tapes, about ten acoustic songs, which later formed the basis for Paul's solo album. I liked his sound. He wasn't an anti-social writer and his tunes were so melodic.

'When I met him, he was very polite and easy to talk to. I promised I'd try and find him some work. I made lots of phone calls, but he was totally unknown, so no one was interested. I did get him one appearance at a charity concert in support of one of the African countries at the Festival Hall. But most of the work he got for himself, just by turning up with his guitar and asking.'

Paul did gigs at Le Kilt and Les Cousins, folk clubs in Soho's Greek Street, and he played in many dark, cellar clubs. He was working hard, taking every offer that came his way. Gradually, he became a familiar face on the London scene.

One fellow musician who remembered Paul well from those days was the late Alexis Korner, one of the greatest British musicians and founder of many groups and many styles. He's respected, not only by fans, but also by the people in the music business. Previously he had been running a band called Blues Incorporated but by 1964 he was working on the folk circuit as a solo artist.

Alexis described Les Cousins in those days: 'It was a very small club. You could see everyone and everyone could see you, unless you happened to be one of the two people stuck behind a pillar. It attracted musicians who played in a variety of styles that were new and exciting.

'In a way, it was a training ground for lots of today's finest musicians. It tended to attract those players because its attitude was so much more flexible than that of the other folk clubs. It was the one club in London where you could use an amplifier and not be thrown out. Other clubs were very rigid, but the Cousins had all kinds of music – avant garde, jazz, early underground, all kinds.'

On a Friday and Saturday night, the club would be open from

seven in the evening until eleven, when it would be cleared of people. Then at midnight it would re-open for the all-night players who went on until about six-thirty in the morning, when the first trains started running.

According to Alexis, 'Usually, there would be two all-night players. Out of the six and a half hours, you were expected to play for four, so if two players shared an evening, they played for two hours each. It was hard work, but most of the musicians there had played in bands, so they were used to being on stage for long hours. But the money was good and it was useful practice. Occasionally, an all-nighter would get so carried away with his music that he would go on after six-thirty in the morning and the proprietor would have to throw him out.' It wasn't only the musicians who were so dedicated. Les Cousins attracted devoted audiences, too. As Alexis said, 'After all, if you were there from midnight until six-thirty, you either had to be able to sleep anywhere or you loved music.'

Alexis saw Paul fairly regularly during these months, when they shared all-night sessions. He remembered him as 'a pleasant-mannered young man who spoke nicely and liked playing bottle-neck guitar. He didn't talk much, really.' Himself a guitarist of much skill, Alexis said of Paul's ability: 'Well, I always thought other people played better than I did. But Paul was good. He was a very clean player. He wasn't at all sloppy.'

Meanwhile, back at Lorna Music, Les Lowe was far from idle. He took Paul's demo records to various A & R people at the record companies, hoping to interest them. It wasn't easy to persuade them to back a new, unknown singer, however talented he might be. Peter Pavey, Les's colleague, told me: 'Les had a lot of faith in Paul. When things are new in this business, people don't go for them until they're a bit successful. And then every-body starts leaping about as though they've all discovered him. When you're right at the start, they're not easily convinced.' Suddenly Les convinced someone. In May 1964 Paul cut a single for Oriole, a Bond Street record company, in a studio behind the most exclusive of London's West End shops. He sang under his Jerry Landis name, with composer credits to Paul Kane.

The A side was 'He Was My Brother', the second version of the song; the B side was 'Carlos Domingues', which Val Doonican had recorded months earlier. Paul never used it again. It's a pretty song, asking rhetorical questions about life, showing a man's confusion when he gets no answers. It has some Mexican-style guitar figures and a haunting quality. It marks the first appearance of the introspective loner who would later dominate Paul's songs.

After cutting the single Paul became a regular visitor at the Denmark Street offices, sometimes with Kathy, more often alone. Les recalled their lunches together at La Roma, a restaurant in nearby Frith Street – lunches full of laughter and the optimistic mood of the mid sixties among those who were young enough to enjoy it.

Sometimes, Paul dropped by the office in the late afternoon. Peter Pavey recalled: 'Les and I would go with Paul to this tiny café in Charing Cross Road, after we had closed up the office. And we'd have a cup of tea and a chat. Paul was very easy-going.'

Often they were joined by Jimmy Parsons. He told me: 'We used to have these frugal breakfasts of tea and toast. None of us had much money, but we used to swap stories and laugh a lot. Paul was a really nice guy. He would have been worth knowing even if he had no talent at all. As it was, he had an outstanding talent. But he was also a very sincere man.'

Around this time Paul met Wally Whyton, now a much-loved compère of BBC Radio 2's *Country Club*, undeniably an expert on music. Then he was a folk singer, working in clubs all over England. He had previously been the leader of the Vipers, a group that included Hank Marvin and became the nucleus of the Shadows, after Wally left them. He went on to do some busking in the South of France, returning to England to work on children's television programmes.

In 1964, he had been hearing a lot about an American folk singer called Paul Simon but he hadn't met him. The most usual way of getting to know another performer was being booked together in one of the bigger clubs that could afford more than one act on the same night. The Ballad and Blues Club in London, for instance, would book three acts on a Saturday night.

Wally was working as a duo with Redd Sullivan. The two of them were booked at the Railway Hotel in Brentwood, Essex, where Paul was still playing on a regular basis. When Wally and Redd arrived, they were amazed to see that the place was full. Wally told me: 'It was absolutely packed to the doors with people, something very unusual. And the audience was made up of people of all ages. Also unusual. At the time, the tendency was to find more youngsters there – college students who had come in as much to pick up a date as to listen to the music. On the whole, people were coming to folk clubs as a social event, rather than to hear the great traditional songs.

'On this particular night, there was an atmosphere of excite-ment in the audience. There were middle-aged men and women, and even children. And I was completely mystified until we found out that Paul Simon was booked there.'

It became clear a blunder had been made and they were double-booked. But Dave McCausland said they could all perform and all be paid. Paul arrived and went on stage first with a few songs. Wally recalled how young girls actually started screaming. 'It was a phenomenon that I had never seen anywhere. In the days of the Vipers, my group was screamed at, but we were new and we were frantic. We played hard, fast numbers. But here, Paul was singing "I Am a Rock" and girls were screaming and old ladies were jumping up and down. It was really quite staggering.'

After Paul's spot, Wally and Redd performed a few numbers. Then Paul suggested they all go on together and do some rock 'n' roll classics. Wally was astonished. 'If you knew the way folk clubs worked in those days, because it was new, it was fairly strict in approach. You went on and did half an hour and there was a break. It was all laid down and the guidelines were all there. And here was Simon, totally destroying all those guidelines. And not only destroying them by singing rock 'n' roll and doo-wap material, but getting screams from everybody as well.'

Quite undaunted, Paul began to sing. Wally and Redd did the background doo-wahs. From 'Teddy Bear', they went on to 'Peggy Sue', then a string of rock 'n' roll classics. It became an unforgettable evening for the audience and the artists.

Wally was impressed by the American. He told the journalist, Roy Carr: 'When Paul works on stage, he gives himself completely. Paul always believed he'd make it big. He always told us he would.'

Another artist who remembers Paul is Davi Graham, the British guitarist. He is perhaps best known for composing 'Anji', a piece he wrote in 1961 for the girlfriend with whom he was living on the French–Italian border, and who coined the nickname Davi. When I interviewed Davi, he recalled: 'I first met Paul Simon in the Troubadour, where I heard him play to a packed house in the basement. I was captivated by his "Sparrow", which was sung with great tenderness. The commonplace, which is the art of English poetry, wasn't lost on Paul. And it was so quiet in the Troubadour that night. Unusually quiet, considering it's a tiny stone basement with very good acoustics. One had the unmistakable impression that Paul would be a success.'

Soon after that, Paul visited Davi in his rooms in Wandsworth Bridge Road and told him how much he liked 'Anji'. 'We were sitting in the kitchen and he said, "Would you mind if I recorded 'Anji'?" I said I'd be delighted. His voice is with me still. He has such a gentle way of speaking.

'He was playing "Anji" by then, which, I should add, he didn't learn from my recording. I rather wish he had learned it from me. But he learned it from Bert [Jansch]. Of course, Bert learned it from a tape I made with him around 1962. Bert didn't play it quite accurately according to me, but that was largely my fault, because I hadn't learned to read music then, and the only available arrangement of the tune, which I played in A minor, was an arrangement in C minor for the piano. And so Bert only learned it from my tape recording of it. Paul played "Anji" as if he enjoyed it.'

Davi recalled a recording they made together a little later. 'We did "Richard Cory". That really sticks in my mind. And I remember, the record wasn't released because there was an irritating sound of a drill or something from an adjacent room. The studio wasn't good enough, wasn't soundproofed, so it was never released and Paul wasted money on that, because he paid me of course, and the other people on the session.'

Davi Graham summed up his feelings about Paul: 'I love Paul's music because he has such excellent taste. He won't tolerate the second-rate. He won't have it in the studio. I was very honoured to work with Paul. You were in the presence of a maestro of composing, and in my opinion, a very tender and beautiful voice as well. Paul was in love with the guitar. I rate him as one of the greatest musicians of his generation.'

Back in New York, college was finished for the summer. Art, needing a change of pace, set off in June for a tour of Europe. He fully intended to meet up with his old friend during the next few months.

In July, Paul went to Paris again on a busking holiday with Redd Sullivan. Paul had bought a white Sunbeam Alpine, a sports car which he intended to take back to the States with him. As Redd told me: 'There aren't many people who can say they've gone busking in Paris in a new Sunbeam Alpine.'

It was an amazing few weeks, very hot and crowded. The dollar was good against the franc, so Paris was filled with American tourists, swarming through the city with cameras and maps. During Bastille Week, Parisians celebrated joyously in the streets, and Paul was in high spirits.

Redd talked to me with great fondness of those weeks in Paris. 'We used to go and sing in the streets. We'd be standing, looking at everything that was going on. Somebody juggling, somebody singing. And one of the things I remember about Paul, when we were walking along and he was playing the guitar, he used to bend down near children and sing to them.'

Paul's dry sense of humour emerged when he and Redd visited a studio mogul with another folk singer. 'It was one of those places where they had nice windows that were fifty feet by eighty feet. It's an office, but they've tried to make it look like a cathedral. And the guy had a desk that was huge, and the guy's chair was two feet above yours. He had all the tricks, all the psychological advantages. And Paul, who, as you know, is not very tall, walked in with his guitar, looked round the place and said, "Well, it's simple, but it's home."

It was during this period in Paris that Paul learned of the death of his former classmate, Andrew Goodman one of three young civil rights workers who had been killed in Neshoba County, Mississippi. This famous case has since been dramatized (with names changed) in the film *Mississippi Burning*.

When he read the news, as he waited in the Paris American Express office, Paul felt suddenly sick. 'I had to walk outside. I was going to throw up. I felt dizzy. I was so panicked, so frightened. I couldn't believe that anybody I knew was dead.'

Journalists and biographers have since written that it was this incident that inspired Paul to write 'He Was My Brother', which describes the death of a freedom rider. This isn't true, because the song had already been written a year before – indeed, it had already been recorded twice, both as a single and on *Wednesday Morning 3AM*. Later on he did alter the lyric slightly, so that Mississippi was actually mentioned, whereas previously the place of death was simply given as 'this town'.

By early autumn, Artie had reached Paris and it was there that Paul contacted him, inviting him to come to London for a while before going back to New York. They could go home together, because Art was going back to Columbia and Paul had decided to do a degree at Brooklyn Law School.

It's not clear why he settled on law, though there is an

affectionate Jewish joke that the best career is to be a doctor, but if a young man can't stand the sight of blood, he becomes a lawyer. In Paul's case, it was almost certainly tied in with wanting to please his parents by choosing a stable and financially secure profession. He had as yet no clear plans for pursuing music in any serious, permanent way.

On their last night in London, Paul and Artie went to the Flamingo Club in Wardour Street to see the Ian Campbell Group. By the interval, promoter Curly Goss was worried because the group still hadn't arrived. He found himself with a very large audience and no act. He noticed Paul sitting with his guitar and asked him to play. Judith Piepe, a social worker in London's East End, was there that night. She would later become a close friend of Paul and Art and a great help in Paul's career. She recalls: 'This unknown kid from New York was dragged onto the stage.' Actually, this isn't quite accurate. Paul was far from unknown: he was a professional singer with a strong following in the clubs.

He sang 'A Church Is Burning', 'Leaves That Are Green' and 'The Sound of Silence'. Then he called Artie on stage and they did 'Benedictus' together. They were a great hit. Judith chatted to them afterwards, suggested they could stay in London with her, but they were going back to New York the next day.

Paul's time at Brooklyn Law School was short. He soon realized he would never be a lawyer. He withdrew from the college on 18 January 1965, packed up his things and boarded a plane for London. It was to be a ten-day visit, during which time BBC Radio, prompted by Judith, agreed to record some of his songs. Also, Curly Goss had arranged some club dates.

When he flew back to New York, he left the BBC with a tape of twelve of his songs. The BBC didn't really know what to do with the tape. Judith Piepe was bombarding them with daily phone calls and Les Lowe was contacting them from Lorna Music, urging them to give Paul a radio spot.

They finally decided to use the songs on the *Five to Ten* programme for two weeks. This was a five-minute religious spot which came on the air every morning. Les explained to me: 'This was a good plug for Paul's work, because it was after *Housewives' Choice* which had about twenty million listeners, and followed by *Music While You Work*, which was also very popular. Therefore, a lot of people would hear Paul Simon.'

Judith wrote the commentaries for the songs. She told me: 'Each morning, I introduced the song for that day. As it turned out, the actual time allowed was only four minutes and forty seconds, the rest of the the time being taken up by the announcer. I had to time each song and then write a commentary to fill in the remaining moments.'

The *Five to Ten* programmes went on the air in March '65. The response to Paul and the songs was overwhelming. The BBC offices were flooded with letters asking about him and where they could buy his records. In England the only record available was the Jerry Landis single on Oriole, 'He Was My Brother'. CBS in London, simply an outlet for selling American records, had just acquired Oriole and had many unsold copies of the record on their hands. They decided it would be too expensive to remove all the Jerry Landis labels and replace them with Paul Simon labels. As they wanted to cash in on Paul's sudden popularity, they agreed to let Paul make a solo album.

CBS brought in Tom Wilson, who had produced the American *Wednesday Morning 3am.* He arrived in London and discussed the business details with Lorna Music. Paul followed in May '65. He stayed at Judith's flat in the East End while he recorded '*The Paul Simon Songbook*' at a London studio. It took less than a week to complete. Nowadays it is a rare and valuable item because in the seventies it was deleted from the CBS catalogue at Paul's request.

Songbook is a very pure album, with only Paul's acoustic guitar for accompaniment. It's a fascinating record of how he actually sounded on the folk circuit. The cover shows Paul and his girlfriend Kathy, sitting in semi-darkness.

It opens with 'I Am a Rock' – a man withdrawing into the

safety of isolation because he fears being rejected again. American journalist Lon Goddard described it as 'a kind of defeatist heroism that said, "I won't confide in anyone, even though what I depend on can never see me through."' This original version is starker than the later one by Simon & Garfunkel. It's angrier and harder, and as a solo it makes us more aware of being alone.

'Leaves That Are Green' is a poignant song, with leaves symbolizing the passing of time – not an original image, but used effectively here. Then 'A Church Is Burning' cries passionately for justice with an inspiring chorus. Paul performed it a lot at folk clubs but never recorded it again. It's probably the nearest he got to a protest song in the Bob Dylan style.

Then 'April Come She Will', a song that would later be an Art Garfunkel solo. Paul sings it simply, accompanied only by delicate guitar plucking which would remain the same in all later versions. Lyrically, it's quite complex; the cycle of a love affair is compared to the cycle of seasons, with some sexually evocative images.

The second recorded version of 'The Sound of Silence' is another acoustic one. The diction is sharper than on later electrified versions. Similarly, Paul's solo version of 'A Most Peculiar Man' has more brutal impact than the later recording. Paul's voice sounds hollow, echoing in emptiness. He wrote the song in London, 'because I saw a newspaper article about a guy who committed suicide'.

'He Was My Brother' appeared for the third time on record, with the addition of 'Mississippi' as a nodding tribute to Andrew Goodman. Then came 'Kathy's Song', Paul's tribute to his English girlfriend. It was written in New York, just prior to his return to London in '65, and his lover is far away, filling his thoughts. The rain images which symbolize the weary futility of his life without her are enhanced by delicate guitar work which sounds like drops of rain. It blends a love of religious intensity with sexual imagery, a formula Paul would repeat in later songs. It's hard to imagine how a young man of twenty-three could produce a song as fine as this.

'The Side of a Hill' is another rare protest song, which Paul didn't use again, though some of the words became the basis for the 'Canticle' part of 'Scarborough Fair'. 'A Simple Desultory Philippic (or How I Was Lyndon Johnson'd into Submission)' is clearly a Bob Dylan parody, with some allusions to his songs. Literature gets a look-in too, in sly jokes which confuse Dylan with Dylan Thomas. Tom Wilson and Artie get a mention – and the reference to being left-handed alludes to Artie. Kathy is the friendly haiku: another joke for literature students, because a haiku is a very short oriental poem and Kathy rarely spoke.

'Flowers Never Bend with the Rainfall' takes on the gap between reality and illusion. The illusion is baffling, distorting the view of reality. Lyrically, it's an economical song – and musically very effective, especially in the raindrops guitar work. 'Patterns', which closes the album, is more disturbing. The sustained image, the pattern on his wall which represents his own puzzling life, is handled well. He feels trapped, like a caged rat – trapped in a tiny room, in darkness and shadow, in his own fears. These images pervade the whole song, and much of Paul's later work.

Paul returned to New York briefly after completing the album. He longed to be with Kathy, and back in London which he now thought of as home. By the time *Songbook* was on sale in England, he was living at Judith Piepe's flat, with Kathy and many aspiring performers. It was at this point that he met Roy Guest.

Roy is a man of diverse experience. A qualified psychologist, he decided to try something completely different – singing with his guitar on the folk circuit. He soon gave this up to work at the Harold Davison Agency, looking after folk singers.

In the USA, Roy encountered the young, unknown Bob Dylan, who offered him his entire European management – a gift indeed. But, according to Roy, his employer wasn't impressed by Dylan. After a bitter disagreement, Roy left and went to work at Cecil Sharp House, the London headquarters of the English Folk Dance and Song Society. There he looked after the careers of Martin Carthy, the Watersons, Cyril Tawney, Shirley Collins and others.

By 1964, he was becoming interested in the new breed of folk singer emerging in the USA – the singer-songwriter. Still regretting his lost opportunity with Dylan, Roy left Cecil Sharp House and set up his own agency in his flat in Gloucester Avenue, NW1. From there he arranged tours in Britain for American stars: Tom Paxton, Buffy Sainte-Marie and Judy Collins. His flat became a meeting place for folk singers who would drink coffee and discuss music while Roy tried to find them work in the two or three hundred folk clubs scattered across the country.

By '65, Roy had become very influential on the folk scene and was looking to find a new talent – a singer-songwriter in the same league as Dylan. I interviewed Roy at some length. He's a very careful talker, weighing up every comment, striving for accuracy and honesty, blending his knowledge of the music business with finely tuned instincts about people. He told me: 'I think it was Judith Piepe who brought Paul to my attention. She would phone me up regularly when somebody was talented. And I remember the first time I heard him. It was at the Troubadour in Earl's Court, one of the meccas of London's folk scene. I heard Paul's songs there, and I thought they were very good. I realized at once that he was enormously talented. I met him and he said, "Right – you can be my agent." So I started to get him some gigs. I don't think we ever had a written contract of any kind. Paul joined the circle of artists who were performing for the new company, Folk Directions.'

I asked Roy to tell me something about Paul. He considered it for some time, then he answered slowly and with great precision: 'He was totally consistent throughout. He was always disciplined and always totally professional. You always knew that if you got him a gig, he would go to it. You always knew he would arrive on time. He was no trouble at all. He wasn't one of those people who telephoned from Crewe, saying, "I'm supposed to be . . . some-

where else. I couldn't make it . . . how do I get there?" This was even more remarkable when you consider he was an American in

England. But he found his way round the country very well indeed and he seemed to enjoy it. He respected himself. He was a psychologically balanced person. He knew his work was good.'

Paul was happy living at Dellow House, in Judith's third floor flat in the gaunt, Victorian building in the East End. The building is still there, seeming crushed beneath the rattling, overhead railway viaduct and the imposing council flats which dominate the narrow streets. It was there that I went to see Judith Piepe in 1982. As I climbed the stairs to her flat, I was conscious of my own footsteps echoing through the building.

The flat itself was very small, filled with souvenirs from numerous countries. The walls of the living room were lined with exquisite hand-made guitars, the work of craftsman Stephen Delft. Judith, a social worker in the area since 1962, had experienced the horrors of her generation first hand. Born in Silesia, the daughter of a Jewish socialist politician, she fled with her family from Germany in 1933. She was well loved and respected in the community, with a reputation for collecting stray dogs and aspiring artists. She loved people; it was as simple as that.

Paul relished the East End. All his life, he would remember the sights and sounds of it, the delights of the food market in nearby Whitney Street, the friendliness of the local people and the sense of history which he felt all around him. Paul's enthusiasm for the place, the people and his beloved Kathy surely inspired him artistically in those days. Indeed, in the '80s he would refer back to them with longing in 'The Late Great Johnny Ace'. His days there were some of the best of his life. 'Everything was new and different to me, living off Cable Street. And I loved that market. I was just an American discovering Europe and those people with different faces and strange accents. It was a kind of mutual curiosity. I was different and they liked me, and they were different and I liked them.'

The days and nights at the flat were filled with laughter, companionship and inspiration. Living there at different times were folk singers Al Stewart, Jackson C. Frank, Sandy Denny (later of Fairport Convention) and Roy Harper, to name but a few. Then there was Kathy and sometimes Artie. There were also streams of visitors.

Jackson C. Frank had a small, devoted following, which included Paul Simon, who produced Jackson's only album in 1965. On it the second guitar was played by Al Stewart. Paul spent his advance royalties for *Songbook* on the production, which took only a few hours. Sadly, it wasn't successful, selling only a thousand copies, although over the years his cult following has survived.

Besides songwriting and performing, Paul was also trying his hand at writing short stories, one of which appears in the folio of the *Songbook* album. Entitled 'On Drums and Other Hollow Objects', it is a sensitive story about a young man's visit to his grandfather in a nursing home. It is carefully balanced, alternating between pathos and humour, clearly the work of someone who is learning to control his writing and our responses.

He wanted to do more writing. Later he told Tracey Thomas of *NME* that he had been working on a novel for some time. 'In between performances, I'm always writing, trying to develop characters so that I can do the Great American Novel,' he laughed. And he told *NME*'s Alan Smith: 'I'd like to finish a novel. It's the first one I've done. I'm attacking it by doing short stories. I'll incorporate [them] eventually into this novel.' He added: 'I think I would get more pleasure out of that than a string of hits. That wouldn't mean anything to me compared to the satisfaction of completing a novel.'

On 1 June 1965, at the close of another academic year at Columbia, Artie was awarded his BA. Paul invited him to stay in London at Judith's flat, so Artie boarded a plane and arrived there at the end of the month.

In the weeks that followed, they worked together as a duo quite a lot. When they weren't performing, they sat in the flat, writing or singing, talking about music or playing Monopoly. At times the small space was restrictive, so everyone would wander down to the all-night launderette in Commercial Road, where they would hold an impromptu concert while their washing rotated in the machines. Passers-by and lorry drivers would stop to listen. At 4 a.m. they would take their final bows and call in at an all-night shop to stock up on cigarettes and sweets, before going home to bed.

It was a time of very little money, but it was happy. Their needs, after all, were simple and few. In those golden days of the mid sixties, a spirit of optimism permeated the whole world – at any rate, the world in which young people existed. Like the Beatles, you could be a working-class lad and make good; like Bob Dylan, you could rebel against the establishment and have everyone listen to you and respect you. Sexual double standards had started to erode, and 'free love' was being advocated in all the media. There were mini-skirts and the pill, guitar music, education, travel, freedom – and above all, a wonderful sense that it would last for ever.

Art would later describe those days with great satisfaction. 'There were many highspots, but perhaps the English days were the best. Scuffing around London, not having – quote – "made it" yet, that was a charmed period that's still very sweet in the memory.' Artie paid tribute to those days in some of the poems he would later write, touching and sensitive verses written in his reflective moments. The poems recall Kathy, summer days in London, singing in the streets, friendly faces – and, above all, being young.

Paul also maintained a sense of great happiness in those days. He would later tell *Rolling Stone*: 'I was consciously aware that I was ecstatically happy. I'm sure that those will be the purest, happiest days of my life.'

Chapter Five

THE TOUR OF
ONE-NIGHT STANDS

After Artie's return to New York, Paul set off on a tour of northern England. This was the string of one-night stands later to be so graphically described in 'Homeward Bound'. This tour was a crucial one, because it was essentially the last Paul did as a solo artist before becoming half of a world-famous duo.

The tour began in Warrington, on a Wednesday early in September. The folk club, run by Jack and Norman Froggatt, was in the Lion, a popular local pub. These brothers had already founded their own folk group, the Minor Birds, a name borrowed from a Robert Frost poem. Since the first days of the group in the early sixties, members have come and gone, and Jack and Norman are the only two original ones left. They continue to be successful, performing all over Britain.

The Lion folk club generally had a full house of about two hundred and fifty people. Jack and Norman ploughed all their profits back into the club, especially into the hiring of top-drawer artists of the calibre of Paul Simon. It was Paul who had contacted Jack Froggatt, having found his name in *Folk Directory*. He telephoned, explaining that he was an American singer-songwriter, looking for work.

Jack Froggatt has a characteristic Northern directness and talked candidly to me, weighing his words, anxious not to mislead. He remembered Paul well. 'I was keen to try something new and we agreed to take him for a fee of twelve pounds.' Jack still has the receipt signed by Paul for this fee.

And Jack recalled the response to Paul: 'As a club, we weren't really into too much contemporary folk music. But he got a tremendous reception. His talent was obvious. He was an excellent guitar player and quite different, I think, from anyone else that we'd had. But he wasn't a flashy sort of guitarist. He was a very tasteful player. And all of his songs had a lot to say in them. I think he was an entirely new dimension for us as a folk audience, listening to him. He went down superbly well.'

After the show, Paul stayed with Jack and his wife, sleeping on their bed-settee as had so many visiting folk artists before him. Jack told me: 'The next morning, I was working, but I arranged for my wife to bring him into Warrington and we met in an Indian restaurant for lunch. Overall, Paul was very introverted, I think. He didn't have a great deal to say. He was very quiet. But then, we were a young married couple with a child, so it may be that we didn't have a lot in common with him.'

Paul's next stop was Chester. He went to the club directly for his Friday night show. The Tuning Fork was run by Chris and Robin Sherwen, a newly married couple who also enjoyed considerable success in a harmonious foursome, the Black Diamonds, singing a variety of traditional folk songs.

Chris, a woman gifted with an astonishing memory for details, vividly recalled her first sight of him that Friday night. 'We walked in and he was already there. He had an olive-green, polo-neck sweater, and I think it was an expensive one. And he was sort of olive skinned. His talk to the audience was funny. Very funny. I can't remember whether it was sarcasm – it was just witty. It was different, you see. We'd never had an American guest at the club before. We'd had a lot of traditional singers up to that point. But in any case, he was somebody so different. He didn't sing anybody else's songs but his own. His act was virtually *The Paul Simon Songbook*. His songs were super and the applause was outstanding.'

Robin also recalled that first night. 'Because he was American, I think we expected a lot from him. He was the first person who really played the guitar in our little folk world. I mean, the guitar wasn't an impediment to him. He was the first one to use the claw hammer style in our club. Everyone uses it now, of course. But he taught it to me. I remember him having difficulty in showing it to me because it was so automatic to him. He had to play it slowly and try to work out what he did. Of course, what he did then seems quite a simple style now, but to me when I was struggling, it was a revelation. He was a good guitarist. I wouldn't put him in the top ten of the world or anything like that, but what he did was perfect.'

After the show, Paul returned with Chris and Robin to their small flat in Osten, Birkenhead. The three of them sat up until the early hours, while Paul told them about himself. Chris recalled: 'He talked a lot about his father. I think he must have been quite proud of him. And he told us all about Artie, his friend from childhood. He seemed very fond of him. Obviously, he was a big part of his life . . . You know,' Chris mused, 'Paul must have impressed us, for us to be able to tell you all this, so many years later.'

Both Chris and Robin remembered Paul telling them of his career plans, giving details which reveal his determination and ambition. This business-like attitude to his career seems slightly at odds with the lifestyle he had, a carefree existence of bedsits and gigs, carrying his guitar around the country. Clearly, this life was not an end in itself – even at this stage, Paul had his sights set on stardom and wealth. Chris said, 'He told us he had a publishing company . . . And he did say that if he hadn't become a millionaire by the time he was thirty, he would consider himself a failure.'

This drive to succeed was something I would hear about again and again from different sources during this tour. Robin remembered it too: 'Yes, he did say that, about being a millionaire by the age of thirty. And we said, oh yeah. But thinking back, I realize he knew what he was aiming for. I think he had his life planned out. He knew exactly how he was going to get there. Obviously, he was a very deep person, but he didn't come across that way particularly. He wasn't moping about and worrying about his life, and he didn't appear to be moody. Okay, I suppose all songwriters have some personal experience in their songs, but to Paul, writing songs was also a living.

'He was a very interesting person to be with. He had done more with his life at that early age than most of us ever do. I got the impression that his life with Artie as Tom & Jerry was over, and it was Paul Simon on his own now. But obviously, that wasn't so. Perhaps it was part of his plan to go back and be Simon & Garfunkel. Or maybe it just happened.'

That particular comment takes on a greater significance when seen in the light of later events, when Paul Simon emerged once again as a solo artist.

The next day was Saturday. In the afternoon, Paul went with the Sherwens into Liverpool to go shopping. They made a beeline for Cranes, the guitar shop, where Robin showed Paul a Martin guitar which cost a hundred and fifty pounds. In those days, they weren't generally available in England; most were brought over by Americans. Paul told Robin, 'You should buy that. It's a good investment. You'll never lose money on that.' It was good advice, which Robin later followed.

After shopping, they ate dinner at the Sherwens' flat. Chris, not long married, didn't have the varied repertoire of meals that she now has. She was worried about what to give Paul to eat. 'One of my better meals was gammon with pineapple on top, and I thought, oh crumbs. Because you know, could I give a Jewish person gammon? But it was fine. I don't think he was Orthodox because he did eat it and he liked it.'

That evening Paul played at a club in Bebington, run by Bill Fogg and Artie Shaw. The Sherwens went along, taking him back to stay at their flat for a second night. Once again, they talked far into the night. On Sunday, after a traditional English roast beef dinner at Robin's mother's house, they took him to the Central Hotel in Birkenhead for his next gig. There they said goodbye.

Paul was met at the Central Hotel by the Sherwens' close

friend, Geoff Speed, in whose home Paul was to spend the next few days while he worked at a variety of local clubs. Nowadays, Geoff heads his own company in Widnes and lives with his wife Pam, their two children having grown up. He writes and presents Radio Merseyside's *Folk Scene* and maintains an extensive, well-informed interest in music. He is quietly spoken with a dry sense of humour.

In autumn '65, when he met Paul, Geoff was running the Howff, a large folk club with capacity for a hundred and fifty people. He was living with his parents in Widnes and dating Pam. Paul played at the Howff on the Monday night and was a sensation.

On Tuesday evening Geoff took Paul to the Peppermint Lounge in Samson Barlow's, a multi-storey restaurant complex in Liverpool. There they met a young reporter from *Merseybeat*. Geoff told me: 'This reporter was complaining bitterly that he'd lost ten shillings, which is fifty pence of course, but it was a lot of money then. He'd dropped it out of his pocket. And while I talked to this reporter for five or ten minutes, Paul said to me, "Geoff, can you lend me a pound?" Which I did. And he vanished upstairs to the roulette wheel for about ten minutes and then came back with the pound for me and ten shillings for this reporter. I asked him how he had done it and he very confidently said that he had a system.'

For the rest of Tuesday evening, Geoff gave Paul a tour of the famous sights of Liverpool. He recalls: 'I took him to the Cavern, which was my first and only visit there. I can't remember who was appearing, but it certainly wasn't the Beatles. They'd been and gone by 1965. We also went to the Blue Angel which is at the top of Seal Street in Liverpool; it's said to be one of the Beatle haunts. Paul was fascinated by the Beatles. I think *Help* was issued within days of his arrival and he spent a lot of time listening to it while he was at home, when I was at work.'

During the daytime, when Geoff was working, Paul spent many hours in the company of Arthur Speed, Geoff's father. Geoff laughingly recalled: 'My father talked to Paul more than I did about things that matter. I remember them having a long discussion about religion. My family have always been Methodists and, of course, Paul is Jewish. I remember them having one very loud discussion. I came in on it, and went out again very quickly.'

Arthur Speed remembered Paul with pleasure. He told me: 'We did have some discussions on religion, which we didn't quite see eye to eye on. But they were friendly discussions. There was a programme either on radio or television and it was Lord Soper, the great Methodist minister, who was very controversial. Paul disagreed violently with something on this programme. I can't remember what it was, but it led us to talk about religion. He obviously had his own beliefs and probably his own faith. He was a serious sort of lad.'

What kind of young man was Paul? Arthur recalled: 'He didn't watch television very much. He was writing most of the time. He seemed studious. Most of his stay with us he spent in our front lounge, and he was deep in thought and making notes continuously. He was obviously writing the words of a tune that he had in his mind. Now I can only guess that it was "Homeward Bound". He sat in front of the window a lot, looking out on to the garden. I think he enjoyed the relaxation. He was very nice to have in the home.'

Geoff's own discussions with Paul were less intense. He told me: 'I asked Paul about Dylan. I think he was impressed with Dylan's music, and I often wonder if he was coming to England in the steps of Bob Dylan, who had been over within the previous two years. He was missing his girlfriend, Kathy, in London. He spoke of Art in friendly terms. Art was obviously a good companion and they were close friends. And he talked about his father too.'

Again, Paul's sense of competitiveness emerged in the conversations. Geoff recalled: 'Paul was obviously a very intelligent person. He told Pam he had an IQ of 150. He also told her that if he hadn't made a million dollars by the time he was thirty, he would consider something had gone wrong. And one got the impression that this would be the case. Here was somebody who was a pleasant person, but obviously determined. He was a very easy person to talk to, and extremely relaxed. He had a lot of confidence.'

On Wednesday evening, Geoff and Pam had a date at the Liverpool Empire to see Victor Borge, so they drove Paul to the Central for his gig, then went on to their show. Geoff told me: 'Afterwards, we went back and collected Paul. He was playing to a full house. When we got there, he was still on stage and they had a closed circuit television relaying his performance into the bar. That was a new thing at the time. We actually couldn't get into the room where Paul was playing, such was the size of the audience.'

On Thursday morning, Geoff drove Paul to Widnes Station and put him on the train to Manchester to record a session for Granada Television. At that time, Granada would record sessions of three or four songs by an artist and these would be used as short fillers between programmes. On Thursday evening, Paul did a show at the Post Office Technicians Social Club (POTSO), which was held in a pub near the Liverpool Boxing Stadium.

On Friday, Geoff again drove Paul to the station: 'I think we got there just as the train was arriving and so I saw him get on to the train. He was going to Hull, I think to play at the Waterson's Club. Since then, it has been said that "Homeward Bound" was written at Widnes Station, but it's not really true. I think it's a bit of poetic licence.

'Paul was certainly working on a song at my house; it had been evolving and was going round in his head. I think he had already written some of the words, but the tune was giving him problems.'

The myth of 'Homeward Bound' and Widnes Station has grown in stature over the years; indeed, in the early '90s, Geoff was asked to unveil the plaque that now adorns the station, stating that the song was written there. Like most legends, its strength lies in the images it conjures up for people; so what does it matter if Paul actually ran for the train and didn't wait at the station, if the meaning of the song remains powerful?

Clearly, whenever it was written, 'Homeward Bound' grew out of this tour. Paul would later tell Roy Carr: 'If you know

Widnes, then you'll understand how I was desperately trying to get back to London as quickly as possible. "Homeward Bound" came out of that feeling.' But it wasn't the place itself he was describing, more the way of life. He told *Hit Parader*: 'I missed my girl and my friends. It was kind of depressing. I was living out of suitcases, getting on trains every day and going to the next place. It wasn't a pleasant ten days. I did like the north of England, the people. I got very homesick for London.' And in another interview: 'I used to think all the time when I was travelling on the road about how each town blends into the next town and how you went on each night as if you were sort of playing a game.'

Paul didn't know that this way of life was fast coming to an end for him. Back in New York, something was happening that would change his life irrevocably. Art called in by chance at Columbia Records and learned that Simon & Garfunkel were about to release a single, though neither of them knew it.

For the past few weeks, a disc jockey in Cocoa Beach, Florida, had been playing 'The Sound of Silence', one of the tracks on *Wednesday Morning 3 am*. People started writing to the station, requesting it. Soon the response was overwhelming. Columbia decided it was commercially viable to release it as a single. Tom Wilson lifted it from the album and overdubbed the original acoustic guitar with electric instruments, twelve-string guitar, drums and bass. Years later, while conceding that it was perhaps difficult to get in touch with them, Paul said: 'He never called to ask. You could do pretty much what you wanted with Paul and Artie in those days.' Artie was very surprised, too, but gave it a hearing. Later he said, 'I thought it was fair. And the record came out slowly, just as I expected.'

The disc hit the charts on 20 November 1965 and began to escalate. Paul, on a short holiday in Copenhagen, was astonished. The first he knew of it was when he saw that it was number 111 in *Billboard*'s Chart. He returned to London and watched its progress as it climbed into the Top 100. In a sense, he felt rather detached from it. After all, the song had been overdubbed without his permission, released without his knowledge, and was doing very well without his being there.

He was confused. During those weeks of waiting to see what would happen to his record and watching it climb, he told *NME*: 'I don't know how to react to it. The fact of the matter is, I don't even feel it at all. You see, here I am in London and this record is supposed to be selling well. I'm here in England and I'm going to folk clubs and I'm working like I was working always. It hasn't changed me at all. Oh, I'm happy, man. I've got to say I'm very pleased. It's a very nice gift.'

Nor did he relish the prospect of being in the limelight. He had moved on from a quiet life at college to a solitary, wandering pace as a solo performer. He found it impossible to imagine himself surrounded by agents and managers. Despite his very real ambition to be a millionaire, he felt the pop scene was too weird for him.

'I mean, this record industry,' he told a journalist, 'it encourages freaks. It's a pity they push people into doing more freakish things so that they'll be noticed and go to ridiculous extremes so that it obliterates what people are saying. I hope I never get to that scene where people will be looking rather than listening. Rather than that, I'd prefer not to be known. Not at all.'

But within weeks of saying this, he certainly was known. 'The Sound of Silence' reached number 1 in America, qualifying Simon & Garfunkel for their first Gold Disc. Paul realized it was time to go home: home to a public that was clamouring to see him, and to a partner who was studying at graduate school, quite bemused by the suddenness of all this fame. In some ways it was almost an accident – and Artie was not really prepared. It is interesting to speculate on whether Simon & Garfunkel would ever have come into being without this unexpected release of 'The Sound of Silence'. Would Paul have remained in England? Would he have remained a solo artist? We don't know.

For both of them their old life was over. For better or worse, a whole new era had opened up. They were on the brink of being a sensation.

Chapter Six

SIMON & GARFUNKEL

In December '65 Paul went back to the United States, where he was welcomed by Artie. Suddenly, they were in demand all over the country as the performers of a hit song. Paul would later describe this change in his life as 'slightly embarrassing. I had to make this transition from being relatively unknown in England to a sort of semi-famous type here. And I didn't adjust well.' Partly this was because he was closing a door on the days he had enjoyed in England, days of freedom and enormous satisfaction. This sudden success, though very exciting, brought with it some apprehension.

Simon & Garfunkel released 'The Sound of Silence' with 'We've Got a Groovy Thing Goin'', a rock 'n' roll number in which a departing lover ignores her man pleading for her to stay. They promoted the single with appearances and were received ecstatically everywhere.

Their business decisions were being guided by Mort Lewis, a veteran of the music world, who had already managed Stan Kenton and Dave Brubeck. On his advice, they refused many of the lucrative night-club offers they were receiving, and accepted weekend concerts on university campuses all over the States.

Paul didn't intend to stay in New York for long. He made a vow: 'I'll work at this for about six months and I'll get enough money to live in England for about another year.' He calculated that, during the next few months, he could earn $25,000 if he was lucky, and this would be enough to live comfortably in England for quite a while. As it happened, he would earn far more than that.

It was the money that daunted him most. The sums they earned were staggering to two young men who had recently been living quietly in average, middle-class homes. Paul told *NME*: 'I just can't grasp it; it means nothing to us.'

He would later recall the day 'The Sound of Silence' reached number 1, they were performing it at Madison Square Garden in Pittsburgh in a show with the Yardbirds, the Four Seasons and Chuck Berry. Paul and Art sang their hit and were paid $300. 'We came out there and we sang with this one little guitar . . . when that was over, we said, "We're not ever going to go on stage again. It's ridiculous." We felt like fools.'

They were astounded to realize that they had earned $1,300 in one weekend on the college circuit. A fee of this size made them uneasy. They decided that, from now on, they would just make records and save their money, ready for the day when they would quit.

But it wasn't so easy to quit. Simon & Garfunkel were in demand. And anyway, the problem was much more complex than money. Suddenly, they found themselves dislocated from everything they had known all their lives. They lost touch with old friends and old haunts. They became involved in business deals on a huge scale. Paul found it devastating at first: 'I became very insecure . . . the success was pushing me into money and places I wasn't prepared to deal with. I didn't know who to be friends with or where to live or where to go.'

He recalled sitting with Artie in his car one night, listening to the radio and chatting. 'The Sound of Silence' came on the air. Without thinking, Art turned to Paul and said, 'Number one record. I'll bet those guys are having a great time.' Ironically, the opposite was true. As Paul says, 'We were just sitting on 141st Street in Queens. We didn't know where to go.'

In January 1966, they released an EP which featured 'I Am a Rock', a faster treatment than Paul's solo version; there was also

'Flowers Never Bend with the Rainfall', with close and neat harmony, 'The Sound of Silence' and a new song called 'Blessed'.

'Blessed' was something of a departure from the sweet sound which the public had already begun to expect from Simon & Garfunkel. It struck a hard, discordant note conveying anger and despair, a modern, cynical version of the Sermon on the Mount. Paul wrote it in Soho, London, when he was caught in a sudden downpour of rain and stepped inside St Anne's Cathedral for shelter. A sermon was in progress. 'And what impressed me was that it didn't say anything. Nothing. When you walked out of there, it didn't make any difference whether you'd walked in, unless you dug stained glass. Because the meek are inheriting nothing. Nothing. And that's the basis of this song.'

He makes the point with a challenging lyric, underlined with angry guitar chords and hard, aggressive harmony. It ends on a puzzled and resigned note, adapting the closing line from Voltaire's *Candide* where the character decides he will spend his life cultivating his garden.

In March '66 they released 'Homeward Bound' with 'Leaves That Are Green'. Paul Simon proved, with the wistful 'Homeward Bound' that he is a writer who should never fear his words coming back to him in mediocrity.

The single did well in the charts, reaching number 5 in the USA and becoming their second hit. In Britain it reached number 9 in the Top 20. Paul came to London on a five-day visit in April and was delighted to find three of his compositions in the *NME* Top 20: the Bachelors with 'The Sound of Silence' at number 4, the Seekers with 'Someday One Day' at number 16 and Simon & Garfunkel with 'Homeward Bound' at number 15.

The duo couldn't perform in Britain now because of the Government ruling that prevented a foreigner from working for more than six months in one tax year. Paul had already exceeded that in the folk clubs. This meant they couldn't promote their records in Britain until July. It was disappointing, and probably affected the ratings of their singles.

Then rumours circulated in the press that Paul had criticized the Bachelors' version of 'The Sound of Silence'. In *NME* Paul denied them forcefully. 'I never said that I think their version of my song is disgusting, as one paper reported. I don't sit in judgement over them. They've pleased an awful lot of people with that disc. I think it strange that the Bachelors should choose to record a very hip song when their style is so conflicting. I feel some artists never get as much out of a song as I put into it.'

He was delighted that the Hollies were interested in doing a version of 'I Am a Rock' was hurt by the decision to cut out the word 'womb'. Today it seems odd that anyone would take exception to it. Paul was understandably indignant. 'Anyone would think there was something dirty about that word. I never wrote a dirty lyric in my life,' he said.

During this brief stay in London, Paul found time to call on his old colleague Davi Graham, composer of 'Anji' which was soon to appear on the new Simon & Garfunkel album. Davi spoke warmly of this meeting: 'He came down to The Cousins in Soho where I was playing and he said, "You can be expecting a lot of money." The royalties from "Anji". And I was delighted. It was just when I needed it. And in fact, I received fifteen hundred pounds from it.

'And then I went to see him at the hotel. I think it was the Hilton in Hyde Park, the twenty-second floor. I was broke and hungry and Paul said, "Would you like anything?" So I said, "Yes. I'd like a steak and salad and chips and a bottle of wine." And it was there within ten minutes.' For Paul, this stay in London at the luxurious Hilton was a sharp contrast to the last time he had been there, living at Judith's and doing a gig for twelve pounds a night.

With the success of their singles came the predictable pressure to make an album as a follow-up. They had to produce it within a month. Recording sessions were therefore slotted in at any vacant studios, in whichever city they happened to be working. They had performing commitments in New York and Los Angeles, so they recorded there. They put down 'I Am a Rock' in Nashville because they were performing there, but producer Bob Johnston suggested they should discard it. Artistic preferences were put aside in favour of speed. Paul and Artie, however dissatisfied they might be, had very little say about their album. As Paul said, 'It was a case of business trying to make the music conform to the situation.' In later years Simon & Garfunkel would not stand for such a thing – but this was 1966. Early days.

The album was somehow completed in only three weeks, thanks largely to the work of engineer Roy Halee who had been with them since their first album two years earlier. Now they knew him well, and they were conscious what an asset he was. To Art and Paul he was friendly and helpful but, in those days, their lack of confidence prevented them from approaching him directly with their problems and questions. 'We didn't pay much attention to him,' Paul said later. 'We looked to the producer for direction.'

Unfortunately, they had very little professional rapport with Bob Johnston. They felt detached from the whole process and that didn't help the album either. Their voices were overdubbed in order to get a separation between the singing and Paul's guitar. Although they already knew a lot about studio techniques – unlike many folk singers of the day – having made records in the fifties and worked on sessions, they had very little involvement in the production side of this album. They weren't even present for the mixing.

In April '66 the second album of Simon & Garfunkel was released. Entitled *Sounds of Silence*, it was immediately well received. The cover shows them walking along a country road, turning to the camera for one symbolic backward glance – at their old life, you might say.

Many of the songs on the album had already appeared on *Songbook*, the English album which no one in America knew about. It was fortunate that Paul had this collection of songs available so quickly to satisfy the demand for material, as he wasn't (and isn't) a prolific writer. The tracks recorded on

Songbook could be conveniently re-used and were, as far as most of the public were concerned, quite new.

The first few tracks on the album were re-issues of recent singles: 'The Sound of Silence', 'Leaves That Are Green', 'Blessed'. Then we have 'Kathy's Song', not very different from the original version on *Songbook*, but in another key. 'Somewhere They Can't Find Me' is really a reworking of *Wednesday Morning 3am*, lyrically at least. It has a different sort of melody, and the overall effect is harder, more urgent, with the addition of a chorus which emphasizes the escape theme. Also, the song is now addressed to the lover and is more overt in its sexuality.

Then comes 'Anji', the Davi Graham piece, followed by 'Homeward Bound' and 'Richard Cory', a song based on an Edwin Arlington Robinson poem of the same name. Paul uses the same basic story, in which the most envied and wealthiest man in town shoots himself, to the amazement of everyone. He modernizes the plot and gives a fuller picture of Cory – his charitable pursuits, his orgies, and the fine detail that he is the only child of a wealthy banker and therefore the focal point of the family's expectations. The political connections and over-zealous press, who even intrude into his suicide, are menacing. And Paul refines Robinson's climax by having the narrator, a factory worker, wish for his own death. Thus, factory owner and factory worker become linked as victims of the same society, albeit at opposite ends of the social scale.

'A Most Peculiar Man' follows, very fittingly as it's also about a suicide. It loses some of the starkness of the original *Songbook* version, but it works just as well because the harmony is used quite brilliantly. At the climax of the song, Paul and Art achieve a discordant effect which heightens progressively and intensifies the anger of the narrator.

Next is 'April Come She Will', which has switched from being a Paul solo to an Art solo. He sings it beautifully, holding the notes with stunning ease. The actual arrangement differs very little from *Songbook*, featuring the same guitar-plucking style.

Then the album closes with 'We've Got a Groovy Thing Goin''
and 'I Am a Rock', both previously released as singles.

Some critics said that the overall effect of the album was
depressing, that it was full of suicide and misery. Years later Paul
told Jon Landau: 'I tend to think of that period as a very late
adolescence. Those things have a big impact on the adolescent
mind.' It's worth noting that most of the songs were several years
old, so Paul had moved on emotionally since them.

Depressing or not, the album had phenomenal success. It
stayed in the bestseller charts for 125 weeks and it was awarded a
Gold Disc very soon after its release.

The alienation tag seemed to stay with Paul. Like most labels,
it was a gross over-simplificaition, but Paul later admitted that he
had unintentionally helped it along in the beginning. 'A kid comes
back from England with a big hit record and everybody says,
"You seem to write a lot about alienation." "Right," I said.
"Right, I do." "Alienation seems to be your big theme." "That's
my theme," I said. And I proceeded to write songs about alienation. Everybody had a tag . . . and it was a self-fulfilling prophecy,
so I wrote alienation songs.'

In June they released 'I Am a Rock' with 'Flowers Never Bend
with the Rainfall'. It reached number 23 in Britain but made the
Top 5 in the States, eventually climbing to number 3. Ironically,
'Red Rubber Ball', a song Paul wrote with Bruce Woodley of the
Seekers, was a hit in the States for a group called Cyrcle. The
Seekers had rejected it and, for some reason, Paul and Artie never
recorded it either, though they did sing it at concerts. It's a
pleasant, catchy number with an optimistic line. The red rubber
ball is the morning sun which brings a promise of new happiness
after a broken love affair. It's hard to imagine why the Seekers
didn't record it.

That summer, Paul and Art were rushed back into the studio
to make another album which was scheduled for Christmas
release. They were to go on the road in the autumn, something
they were both looking forward to.

Before the release of the album, they recorded a single which came out in September. 'Dangling Conversation', with 'The Big Bright Green Pleasure Machine' on side B, it had poor success commercially, not even reaching the Top 10. It reached only to number 25 in the States. Paul later described it as 'amazingly disappointing', and it was surely a surprise for the duo, with two major hits behind them, as well as a bestselling album.

'Dangling Conversation' was blamed for the fact that the single wasn't a hit. Paul later said: 'Why it wasn't is hard to know. It probably wasn't as good a song. It was too heavy.' In fact only the orchestration is a bit heavy. The song itself is a sensitive analysis of a relationship that's falling apart. Paul later told a US radio interviewer that it was a personal view of the kind of lack of communication described in 'The Sound of Silence', which is a societal view. According to Art, the song took Paul longer to write than any to date, and longer for them to record.

Over the years, reactions to it have altered. It has been attacked for its English Lit devices – the similes, metaphors, alliteration – and appallingly misinterpreted as a message song. It has also been praised as a desolate portrait of two people trapped within their apathy.

The song has been compared to T. S. Eliot's poem 'The Love Song of J. Alfred Prufrock', which centres on a thwarted and ineffectual hero who tries, but fails, to declare his feelings to the woman he cares for, while he is swamped by the trivia of social interaction and inaction. In Paul's song the silent coffee drinking, and the afternoon sunshine which is significantly kept out of the room by lace curtains, are allusions to the poem. When the suggestion was made to Paul, he replied on US radio: 'I know they've said it's like Eliot, but I think it compares unfavourably, if I might say so.' Well, maybe so – but the song is nevertheless the work of a craftsman.

The melody was Travis picked – the style made famous by Merle Travis, in which the strings are plucked with the thumb for accompaniment and one finger for melody. It was probably a mistake to add the full orchestration. A lyric like this would have been more effective with a simple arrangement, as in 'Kathy's Song'.

The other side, 'The Big Bright Green Pleasure Machine', is a satire on modern advertising, exploiting the slogans and clichés so familiar to us. It plays on our deepest fears – about social life, career, health and, of course, sex. We never find out what the product is. It's left to our imagination.

In the autumn Paul and Artie went on tour. Their relationship was generally good during these stressful times on the road, but the tedium of the routine often wearied them. After the initial thrill of seeing cities such as Paris, Los Angeles and Rome, they found the travelling very tiring. In any case, they didn't see much of the places in which they performed. They met very few people. They would arrive at the airport, drive straight to the hotel, then on to the hall, where they would check out the microphones and sound equipment, and Paul would change his guitar strings. After the show, they might seek out a good restaurant and try to unwind. Often it was just the two of them. Paul summed up his feelings on the road: 'I was in a state of semi-hypnosis. I went into a daze and I did things by rote.'

Like most successful performers of the sixties, Artie and Paul attracted a groupie following, though it wasn't something they particularly encouraged or enjoyed. They tended to attract what Paul calls 'the poetic groupies' – girls who wanted to read their own poetry, play their own songs and discuss English literature. That isn't the ideal way to relax after a show, so it was sometimes irritating.

On the other hand, Paul was often relieved when all they wanted was intellectual stimulation. 'I wasn't terribly involved with them as people, but on the other hand, I couldn't do something that I thought was insulting ... I wasn't into picking up girls on the road ... too embarrassing for me. I wasn't interested in their poetry either.'

Finally, he found the best way of coping was to opt out, going back to his room by himself and straight to bed – by himself. Consequently, his sense of isolation on the road increased. 'I always avoided any contact with people after the show. I never encouraged it.'

For Art, it was slightly different. He commented on Paul's recollection of poetic goupies. 'Not in my case. But I did sit up a lot of nights talking with kids about their families, aspirations . . .' When asked if most of the girls were attracted to him during those tours, he said: 'No, I wouldn't say that. I really had no idea what most of the women thought. That's a consensus kind of question. I always assumed there was a great deal to be interested in, in Paul Simon – certainly to anybody who was on to the idea that all these words we're singing are his words.'

In November their third album, *Parsley Sage Rosemary and Thyme*, was released. It cost a lot of money to produce, relatively speaking, and it took three or four months to complete. Paul would later comment: 'I remember that was the first time people started to say – boy, you really take a lot of time to make records.' Producer Bob Johnston didn't seem to mind, although Columbia executives wanted a quick turnover of profits, so there was some pressure on Art and Paul to release the album quickly. Nevertheless, the duo made certain that this time they had a free hand with most of the album decisions.

It was a landmark for them because it was the first time they had mixed an album themselves in the studio. Also it was the first eight-track session they had done. In fact they were the first artists to use eight-track recording at Columbia, though other singers soon followed. On this album they worked more closely, even exclusively, with engineer Roy Halee.

Artie would later say this album was produced 'the way we wanted to make it. From that point on, it became Roy and Paul and me. Truth is, we didn't really begin to make satisfying albums until *PSRT*, and I hope that people can listen to that album and tell that we made a positive effort. Defining a Simon & Garfunkel album concept.'

The cover is starker than anything previously, showing them shrouded in semi-darkness, like choirboys. Side one opens with 'Scarborough Fair/Canticle', now one of the Simon & Garfunkel classics. It was a team effort because Artie worked with Paul on the 'Canticle' and on the arrangement. The harmony is close and there is a subtle blending of the song with the counter movement; the two parts are lyrically unconnected but musically intertwined. It's based on a very old English folk song, originally set at Whittington Fair. Paul sustains the period feel with acoustic guitar.

Then there is a close harmony version of 'Patterns'. It is just as disturbing as the *Songbook* version, though the drums unfortunately detract from the lyric. The same is true of 'Flowers Never Bend with the Rainfall' on side two; it's more commercially pleasing, perhaps, but has less emphasis on theme. A song about isolation can never be ideal for two voices – solo versions are inevitably more fitting.

'Patterns' is followed by 'The Big Bright Green Pleasure Machine' and 'Dangling Conversation', both on the single. Next comes 'A Poem on the Underground Wall', one of Paul's lesser known compositions. The broad theme – the man's need to express his frustration in a permanent way – runs through other songs. At the Tufts University concert Art compared it to 'The Sound of Silence': 'The idea is that the people who do these things are in some sense writing a poem. What they are doing is expressing something that is very sincerely felt at the time – anger or whatever. But the point is, there's a reason.'

The song was based on a real event witnessed by Paul when returning home to Dellow Street on the last train, at Whitechapel tube station, 'where I had to change every time to get on that little Metropolitan Line to Shadwell. I never saw anything like that in New York, not where I lived.'

He creates marvellous suspense: the gloom of the station, the man lurking in the shadows like a criminal and the deed which he commits furtively, with wild excitement, almost sexual frenzy.

You could see it as a Freudian song, full of sexual imagery of crayons in pockets and trains in tunnels and doors which open to invite him but from which he withdraws. It's also a song with violent undertones, imagery of slashing and screaming. The man makes his statement in the most positive and public way he can, then escapes into a surrogate sexual refuge – the darkness which suckles him.

'A Simple Desultory Philippic' comes up again, with a few changes from the original. The subtitle this time, equally provocative, is a reference to Robert Macnamara. Musically it's different too, but it achieves the same jarring effect. The references have gone through some changes: Art still gets a mention but Tom Wilson makes way for Roy Halee, logically enough. The Bob Dylan flavour is retained and at the end of the song we hear Paul lamenting, 'I lost my harmonica, Albert,' a reference to Albert Grossman, Dylan's manager. Harmonica snatches come and go – Dylan is still there. The reference to Kathy has been taken out, which is interesting, because Kathy was still in Paul's thoughts and still his girlfriend, though they were often separated by the Atlantic Ocean.

'For Emily Whenever I May Find Her' is partly a tribute to the nineteenth-century American poet Emily Dickinson, who also got a mention in 'Dangling Conversation'. She lived an isolated, solitary life in New England and wrote poems of great sadness and beauty. The title of the song, with its stilted Victorian subtitle, sustains the period flavour. It's also a tribute to a real woman, asleep in bed beside him. The dream presents a woman who is idealized and enigmatic, but the lover beside him is real and comforting. As the dream merges into reality, the two views of woman, spiritual and sexual, merge into one. Perhaps this song does indicate that Paul was missing Kathy.

Paul would later describe how he wrote 'For Emily'. 'That was a strange song. I wrote it all one night. One of my fastest songs. I was playing around with a guitar melody and I sang the first line. It came quite easily.' He would come to regret not having made the song into an A-side single. 'I should have put some strings on it and it could have been another "Sound of Silence". It was Art singing on that one. His voice is really great.'

'Cloudy' follows, a melodious track which does evoke the nebulous quality of clouds, likened to a feeling of aimless wandering. Paul did a demo version of this as early as 1965, solo and with Seeker Bruce Woodley. He didn't intend using the song for himself and Artie. In April '66, he told the press: 'No, it's not Simon & Garfunkel's. They'd never do it.' But they did.

The album closes with '7 o'Clock News/Silent Night', in which the sweet harmony of the Christmas carol is gradually drowned out by the newsreader with a typical list of horrors – murder, demonstrations, and the death of comedian Lenny Bruce from an overdose of narcotics.

The album was well received, selling over a million copies, and soon winning a Gold Disc. The same month as its release, Columbia released 'A Hazy Shade of Winter', a new song, with 'For Emily' on side B. It wasn't a hit and they were disappointed, but with the huge success of the album they took it in their stride.

Paul wasn't really satisfied with the song anyway. He had written it in Manchester, on his northern England tour of '65. 'It didn't quite come off for me. It didn't exactly say what I wanted it to say. I finished it and did the best I could with it. If you're going to rewrite, you can rewrite endlessly. You have to reach a certain point and put it out. Then I'll go on to something else. Otherwise, I'd stay on a song for a year. You just put it out and live with it.'

The song has some good points, though the metaphor of age symbolized by the seasons doesn't work as well as in 'Leaves That Are Green'. Also, for such a bleak song, the punchy orchestration is rather inappropriate, though Paul would make this work in later songs to achieve an ironic contrast. But it's too fast, and the vocal struggles to keep up with the music. Although the song has some very succinct lines in it, mostly they're lost.

In 1966, Pickwick Records gathered some old Tom & Jerry

singles and released them on an album, along with two instrumental pieces. Almost immediately, in January '67, a legal battle began. Art and Paul claimed misrepresentation, on the grounds that Pickwick had used a recent photograph of them on the cover and billed them under the names of Simon & Garfunkel, which implied that the material was recent. Paul told the press he was angry. 'If they had released it saying this is Simon & Garfunkel at fifteen, it might have been interesting. And I would have said, "Okay, that's me at fifteen and I'm not ashamed of it."' Paul and Artie won the suit and the album was withdrawn from the shops. Now, as often happens, the album is a collector's piece.

In itself the album is interesting in showing where Simon & Garfunkel came from. They followed the styles of popular singers, a Johnny Ray sob in 'Teenage Fool', the Everly Brothers' harmony in 'Dancin' Wild', the Buddy Holly break in the voice in 'Don't Say Goodbye', and a mixture of Holly and Gene Vincent in 'True or False'. The talent is already there, and that makes the album fascinating. It gives us a glimpse of how Paul and Artie must have sounded in the basement of the Simon home, overdubbing their voices, bursting with enthusiasm – a rough sketch of what would later be a masterpiece. It is sad that the release of this album should have caused a legal battle, for it provides rare testimony of the duo before they became the highly successful Simon & Garfunkel.

Chapter Seven

SUCCESS

In March '67, Simon & Garfunkel released a new single, 'At the Zoo', with 'The 59th Street Bridge Song' on side B. Paul later regretted not following his own instincts and putting 'Bridge Song' on the A side. 'I knew that record was a hit as soon as I wrote it,' he said.

They had recorded it quickly, comparatively speaking, but Paul wasn't satisfied with it. Moreover, he altered the original title. 'I mean,' he explained drily, 'us recording a song called "Feelin' Groovy"? So I thought – well, give it a more intellectual title. I thought of "59th Street Bridge Song".'

He began the song on the bridge itself, the Queensboro Bridge that crosses the East River from Manhattan to Queens. According to Paul, the lyric came into his head while he was going home in the early hours of a June morning, after having been out all night. As he was crossing the bridge, he suddenly felt gloriously happy. 'What a groovy day it was. A real good one. One of those times when you know you're not going to be tired for about an hour.' The song carries that spirit of optimism, a sense of *joie de vivre*. In the last verse, he echoes a line from Robert Frost: 'For I have promises to keep . . .'

It's certainly true that 'Bridge Song' is more typically hit material than the A side, although in many ways 'At the Zoo' is more rewarding. With sharp satire it presents society as a group of animals, significantly in cages, looked after by a zoo keeper with a fancy for rum. There's something touching about the kindly but dumb elephants, something ludicrous about reactionary zebras.

As it's about a zoo it reminds us of Tom Paxton's little song, 'going to the zoo, zoo, zoo'. Paul might have had this in mind, because he knew it well and performed it, tongue in cheek, at university concerts. What Paul's song projects is a concrete zoo, with animals which remind us of ourselves. It's as firmly based in New York as 'The 59th Street Bridge Song', tracing the route on a cross-town bus from Queens to the zoo in Central Park – which reminds us that both Paul and Artie spent their childhood in the city.

By 1967 Roy Guest, the man who had been Paul's agent during his London days, had teamed up with Jim Lloyd, something of an expert on folk music, who became presenter of the very popular *Folk on Two* on BBC Radio. In the sixties, Jim and Roy were established in an office in Parkway, London NW1, as concert promoters. In that capacity Roy wrote to Mort Lewis, suggesting a three-concert visit to England for Simon & Garfunkel.

The duo arrived in England in March, not just for the concerts but also for some TV appearances: Jim Lloyd arranged them a spot on Manchester TV to promote their new single. The tour was to cover three major cities: London at the Royal Albert Hall, Birmingham at the Hippodrome and Manchester at the Free Trade Hall.

The audiences were mixed in their response to Simon & Garfunkel. Roy Guest explained: 'In Birmingham, I think only three hundred people turned up; and in Manchester, perhaps five hundred. This was at the height of their success in America. They were well known, but they hadn't quite clicked here yet. In concert promotion, London is a year or two ahead of the rest of the country. They didn't mind that there was a small audience in Birmingham. London was a great success and they were pleased with that. And Manchester was pleasant.'

Fittingly, the London concert was fully booked and

enormously encouraging. Jim described to me what it was like the night they appeared at the Albert Hall, the magical moment when Artie and Paul walked out on stage. 'It was just like that scene in *Close Encounters of the Third Kind*, when the spaceship lands and you have all the lights coming on in the darkness. That's how it was when Simon & Garfunkel stepped on that stage. The hall was in total darkness, and then the spotlight landed on these two tiny figures in this huge place. It was wonderful.'

Roy accompanied them on the tour. He told me what it was like during the off-stage hours. 'I remember we had great fun on the road. I particularly remember sitting up with Paul and Artie in the hotel in Birmingham, and getting to know them well. I'd never met Artie before, but he was very nice. It was a good atmosphere on that tour. They're good with agents and managers, as far as business decisions are concerned. They were very professional. Because they respected themselves, they also respected other people.' Jim recalled: 'They were always very polite and very business-like. Paul knew a lot about London and knew his way around, and he seemed to enjoy being here again.'

After the three concerts, they flew back directly to New York. Art had lectures at Columbia the next day and couldn't miss them. He was still pursuing an academic life, though it was becoming harder to keep both careers going. Similarly, with the success of Simon & Garfunkel, Paul's original plan to stay in America for just six months and earn enough money to live well in England had disappeared.

In April the duo returned to London and attended a press reception held for Jimi Hendrix, the Who and Track Records. In an interview with Norman Jopling, Paul said that he was finding it hard to write songs and was obviously under pressure to come up with some for a new album.

'I haven't written anything recently: four songs in six months. I can't seem to write anything. Sometimes I think I should write especially for Britain, for the kids, but I can't. It's a pity because I want to make the charts in Britain, to have some hits.'

At the same reception, Art expressed his irritation with journalists who were giving the impression that the music business was influenced solely by drugs, particularly in America. 'If you read them, you get the idea that everything concerned with pop music in the States is drug dominated. It's just not true. There is a percentage, a small percentage.'

Visiting California soon after that comment, Paul and Art encountered that percentage of people. There in the opulence and glamour of Hollywood, Simon & Garfunkel, very much New Yorkers, felt like outsiders. 'Artie and I thought it was unbelievable that anybody could actually take their money and live there,' Paul said later.

They were startled by the attitudes of many of the celebrities. Paul visited a folk festival held by Joan Baez and was astonished to see that everyone was naked, lounging near the hot springs and chatting as though they weren't naked at all. Paul's reaction was one of shock. 'This is really odd. Everyone's pretending there's not men and women here with their clothes off.' He found he couldn't adjust to that degree of physical abandon; it created 'a disorienting feeling'. He was, after all, a middle-class kid from Queens.

During his time in California, he noticed that there was something weird about everyone he met. They smiled at him mysteriously, which made him uncomfortable, more so because they didn't talk about it. A whole culture was happening around him and it seemed to be a well-kept secret. 'I'm a very verbal person. I felt hopelessly out of touch.'

In San Francisco someone offered him some acid. Although he'd never tried it, he didn't admit that. 'I pretended it was fortunate I had bumped into him because I always take acid after breakfast and I didn't have any for tomorrow.' He saved the tablets and eventually took them in New York, on the night the Arab–Israeli war began, the same night that Muhammed Ali lost his title. Paul was alone and it was very late, three or four in the morning. 'I thought, well, I'll try this now.' The trip was weird and not at all pleasant, starting in the early hours and going right through till nine the following night. Some of it was good, but most of it was bad. 'I had a stretch of about four or five hours that was very paranoid.'

He ended up phoning Columbia Records and persuading a few engineers to come to his apartment and record all the sounds he made for the whole day. They didn't refuse. After all, Simon & Garfunkel were top stars. They did the recordings. 'Those tapes are still at CBS somewhere, I'm sure,' Paul says. The engineers went away, and eventually Paul came out of his trip and began to feel much better. All the same, following the falling-off-a-horse theory, he tried acid again. 'I wasn't going to let any acid trip throw me just because it was bad.'

In later years, he would come to regard the whole scene with regret. 'I would say it was stupid behaviour on my part . . . I did it because a lot of people were doing it, and I was curious to know what would happen.' And what happened was that he suffered all the typical hallucinations: his hand seemed to curl backwards when he looked at it; music seemed more heart-breaking and poignant than ever before – a characteristic of the drug that has been an inspiration, according to quite a few songwriters.

But for Paul it wasn't inspiring. The rational part of his brain went on working, assuring him that it was just an illusion. 'It made me a little schizophrenic, I guess,' he said. At times he found it very frightening. Even as he told himself that nothing was really wrong, he felt the terror of being under such a powerful drug. 'At the depth of the thing, I said . . . I'm afraid because I've got a chemical in my head. But that didn't stop my heart from pounding and being afraid.'

In the end, he felt it had been a waste of time. Several months later, he came out of it and felt normal again, but he was drained and exhausted. 'And I didn't get anything from it. I think it was like taking a beating . . . I took it because I thought I was going to get some big chunk of information for free. I was going to learn something about myself chemically rather than learning something through my life.' Whatever he was looking for – insight, self-knowledge, that San Francisco feeling – he didn't find it.

Art also tried acid simply for the experience, but his trips weren't horrific. He recalled: 'Funny, shadowy things, clouds passing.' Like Paul, he felt he'd gained nothing from it. Acid hadn't helped him creatively as a performer. 'I almost feel they're a little contradictory. For me, acid was a very humbling experience, but the drive to succeed in show business is achievement-oriented. It's anti-humility, in a way.'

Then, in April '67, a group of businessmen conceived an idea for a pop festival that was to be of great significance in music history, setting a precedent for future music events. Alan Pariser, concert promoter, thought of a non-profit-making festival, featuring rock artists both established and new to the business. He took the idea to Ben Shapiro, a Los Angeles booking agent, who had been handling top stars since the fifties.

Shapiro liked the idea, but strictly as a business deal and, at his suggestion, Pariser reluctantly let go of the charity idea. They found the site, the County Fairgrounds in Monterey, home of the Jazz Festival, and they leased it for one weekend, 16–18 June.

After hiring Derek Taylor, famous for being press officer to the Beatles, as their chief publicist, they approached John Phillips, leader and spokesman of the Mamas and the Papas, who were by this time one of the top groups in America. They asked him if the group would be headliners for $5,000, considerably less than their usual fee. Paul happened to be at Phillips's house that night, so Simon & Garfunkel were offered a place on the bill.

Phillips and Paul listened to the plans and eventually agreed to do the festival, but only if the non-profit concept were re-established. After all, the fee involved wasn't enough to influence the Mamas and the Papas, or Simon & Garufunkel. But both groups would contribute to a festival that would widen the boundaries of pop music and support worthwhile charities. Phillips called in his manager/producer, Lou Adler, who also wanted to keep the charity idea. Together they bought out Shapiro.

Within days, Phillips, Adler, Simon & Garfunkel, Terry Melcher (record producer and son of actress Doris Day) and singer Johnny Rivers, all loaned ten thousand dollars each to the festival, to be repaid from the profits. They set up a committee. Pariser and Taylor continued in their original capacity; Phillips and Adler became co-directors, appointed by the board which included Andrew Oldham (manager of the Rolling Stones), Johnny Rivers, Abe Somer (booking agent), Smokey Robinson, Terry Melcher, Paul Simon and Alan Pariser.

The planning hours were long, but the festival promised to be huge and generated interest all over the country. They decided it must be international in its choice of acts, selecting from many music fields. In that spirit, Paul invited Beverly Martin, a folk-singer friend from his London days.

In view of this international flavour, it's ironic that there was some friction between the Los Angeles groups such as the Mamas and the Papas, and the San Francisco groups like Jefferson Airplane and the Grateful Dead. Paul, as a New Yorker, was often called in as mediator. Inevitably, he spent a lot of his time in California during those spring months, helping to organize the event.

The Monterey International Pop Festival lasted for a whole glorious weekend. It had a showcase of stars – Janis Joplin, the Who, Jimi Hendrix, Eric Burdon, Otis Redding – performing for over seventy thousand people. Paul and Art went on stage on the Friday evening, to round off the night. Accompanied only by Paul's acoustic guitar, they sang 'Homeward Bound', 'The Sound of Silence', a new song called 'Punky's Dilemna' and 'The 59th Street Bridge Song'. With the sheer perfection of their perform-ance, they moved the massive audience to utter silence, followed by joyous applause.

The weekend was a great success. People slept in the open air, got high and sang songs. The atmosphere was idyllic, blissfully peaceful and almost pure. There wasn't a single outbreak of violence, only flowers and idealism and love. In one sense, it was the climax of the hippie ideology, and the dream inspired everyone who was there, and many who were not there.

There would never be another Monterey. No concert afterwards succeeded in capturing that special atmosphere, that indefinable something. The three days came to an end. Everyone went home, and the dream went with them.

It had also been worthwhile financially. It had cost three hundred thousand dollars to produce, but with the profits from tickets and film rights, they ended up with nearly two hundred thousand dollars' clear profit after all the expenses were paid. The board of directors sat down to think how to use the money.

Some of it was given to the Sam Cooke Memorial Scholarship, to the Monterey Symphony Orchestra, to scholarships for music lessons for youngsters from inner city ghettos in New York, to the Los Angeles Free Medical Clinic, and the rest was shared out in smaller amounts to various other charities. Unfortunately, quite a large sum was skilfully embezzled, but the Bank of America agreed to pay back most of the money.

Early in August '67, Simon & Garfunkel gave two concerts at the Forest Hills Stadium for packed houses of thirteen thousand. They were climbing higher and leaving the days of local fame, even regional fame, far behind.

The same month, they released a single, 'Fakin' It', with 'You Don't Know Where Your Interest Lies' on side B. 'Fakin' It' is an interesting song, exploring the sense of inadequacy and failure which haunts most of us throughout life. Paul told Jon Landau that he wasn't happy with the single, though it was much improved a year later when it appeared on *Bookends*. He felt the single version was too jumbled and sloppy, it was in mono and it was too slow. They used strings, two drummers and handclapping, but 'it didn't hold together'.

The lyric shows how Paul had been thinking about his life and what a strange situation he was in, earning money by writing and performing songs. He realized this couldn't have been his career if he'd lived a century ago. He wouldn't have been an American;

he'd be living in Austria, where his ancestors originated. He wondered what profession he'd have followed, and the line went round in his brain: 'I surely was a sailor'. Then it struck him: 'Well, what would a Jewish guy be? A tailor. I would have been a tailor.' Some time afterwards, he was talking to his father about his grandfather, also named Paul Simon. He had been a tailor in Vienna. The coincidence made him suddenly and profoundly aware of his heritage.

One odd thing in the song is that mysterious, almost psychedelic part – the ringing of a shop bell and the Englishwoman addressing Mr Leitch. The woman was Beverly Martin, the singer who had come over for the Monterey Festival, who was also friendly with Donovan. 'So we decided to make up this little vignette about the shop; we wanted to come up with a name.' Beverly suggested Donovan's real name, Leitch.

The B side, 'You Don't Know Where Your Interest Lies', is disappointingly uncharacteristic of Paul's attitude to man–woman relationships, in that it accuses the woman of not knowing how lucky she is to have him. It is a weak composition, sounding more like a pop song than anything else Paul wrote. However, it did well in Britain, so maybe it was the hit song he had wanted to write for the British charts.

In every sense now, Simon & Garfunkel were doing well. All the same, they still regarded themselves as outsiders in show business. Paul says: 'We didn't think there was any room for the kind of work we did, the kind of lives we lived.' But in a very short time, the world would stand aside dramatically and make room for them – at the very top.

Chapter Eight

THE GRADUATE AND BOOKENDS

In 1967, Mike Nichols was looking for a musician to write the score for his second film. In the early sixties he had teamed up with Elaine May in the popular comedy duo Nichols and May, making TV appearances both in the USA and in Britain. Their style of monologue and dialogue established a genre of comedy that would remain influential for the next twenty years.

Subsequently, Nichols had become an equally successful Broadway director, then made his film debut in 1966 with Edward Albee's play *Who's Afraid of Virginia Woolf* in which he directed Elizabeth Taylor and Richard Burton.

Now he had *The Graduate*, a Buck Henry screenplay of the novel by Charles Webb. He needed a soundtrack, something that would underline the theme of the film, which depicts Benjamin Braddock's progress from being an uneasy, sexually inexperienced youth to a confident man, as he struggles to gain his identity and find direction in middle-class society. Nichols heard *Parsley Sage Rosemary and Thyme* and decided this was the sound he was looking for. He contacted Paul, sending him a copy of the novel and inviting him to write some songs for it.

At first, Paul wasn't that excited. He didn't like the novel and Dustin Hoffman, who was to star in the film, was still an unknown actor. But out of respect for Mike Nichols he agreed, thinking he would neither lose nor gain by doing it.

Paul and Art watched the first rushes of the film and decided to put in 'Scarborough Fair' until Paul could write something to replace it; later, it seemed to work well in the context, so they left it there. This was a first for a movie soundtrack; until now, no one had used previously released songs, always new material written for the film.

'Mrs Robinson', later to be a monster hit, was actually an accident. Originally Paul had written the music, intending it to be an instrumental piece, but it didn't quite work. Artie said to him, 'Sing the words "Mrs Robinson" to that thing you were writing.' Then, according to Artie, when they were working with Mike Nichols and discussing ideas for another song, Art said casually, 'What about "Mrs Robinson"?' Nichols shot to his feet excitedly. 'You have a song called "Mrs Robinson" and you haven't even shown it to me?' As it turned out, it was the only new piece for the film. In fact, it was just a fragment, different from the full version which became a hit. Other songs were used effectively as a backdrop to the action. They were 'The Sound of Silence', 'Scarborough Fair', 'April Come She Will' and 'The Big Bright Green Pleasure Machine'.

Overall, they were pleased with the film. Paul commented: 'In that particular context, the songs were good and they worked well. Looking back, I feel that they helped the picture a great deal. To be honest, it was the first time that anyone took any time to make sure the sound was good. They didn't let the picture interfere with the music.' And Art's comment: 'The Graduate was a terrific time for us. In those days we thought we were so lucky to get that movie, but now Paul and I have come to realize just how lucky the movie was to get us. There's no denying it, our songs helped that movie more than people realize.'

The film was a box office smash. While it might be slightly dated now, it is nevertheless a valid comment on the world it depicts. It shows the acting talent of Hoffman and Anne Bancroft and, incidentally, gives a fleeting glimpse of Richard Dreyfuss and Ben Murphy making their debuts.

Suddenly, Simon & Garfunkel were rocketed to international fame. Until now, they had enjoyed wide recognition in the USA and Britain, especially on college campuses. Now they were the proverbial household names receiving worldwide acclamation.

After such success with his first score, Paul had many offers to do others. He rejected them all. 'After *The Graduate* I stopped because I thought, where do I go from here? I was inundated with requests to supply movie scores – write the title song for this, or write the music for some real inane, bullshit, youth movie. I'm sure you know the thing – unrest on the campus.'

He was asked to score *Midnight Cowboy* and was even approached by its star, Dustin Hoffman. It seems a pity that he declined because the themes of loneliness and lack of communication pervade the film, and Paul's insight into New York City life would have been an artistic asset. But Paul had his reasons. 'I think I figured, at that particular time, that I didn't want to look like Dustin Hoffman's songwriter.'

The soundtrack of *The Graduate* was to be released in the summer of 1968, simultaneously with their new album, *Bookends*, which they had been working on for a long time. In March, Artie and Paul were to do a concert at London's Albert Hall and it was fully sold out far in advance. But when he arrived in London, Art collapsed and was too ill to appear, so was flown back to New York. Meanwhile, Paul remained for a week and gave some interviews from his suite at the Hilton Hotel.

All in all, this was a lonely period in Paul's life. He had broken up with Kathy, no doubt partly a consequence of their prolonged separations. But also, Kathy was a quiet girl and Paul's life now was anything but quiet and, more importantly, anything but private. Somewhere in the fast lane, Paul and Kathy had lost each other; there was no going back to the simpler, more intimate days of England and the folk circuit. Paul was a part of show business and Kathy didn't want that life.

Now, Paul felt cut off from people, trapped by the very success he had worked hard for. He told Penny Valentine: 'Money is a neutral thing to me. People say I'm a dollar millionaire. I don't really know. I could be. All I know is that I'm a lonelier person than I ever was at the beginning. It's a lonely life being a part of this business – people watching you, looking at things you do.'

Later, looking back on this period, he would say: 'I was just by myself. I was crazy most of the time, high and relatively depressed throughout those years. Quite alone. I lived on the East Side, by the river, uptown. So even where I lived was not connected to anything. It was largely unaffected by the youth culture.'

In April 1968, 'Mrs Robinson' hit the singles charts. It had phenomenal success, remaining at number 1 for four weeks in America and holding its place for thirteen weeks in the bestsellers' charts. In Britain it reached number 4 and stayed there for a week, and in the bestsellers' charts for twelve weeks. It won a Gold Disc; later it would win a Grammy Award.

This version was extended from the film, hit material in every sense. It has a powerful, compelling rhythm, sung with energy, and a lyric that sounds like fun. But there are disturbing overtones – the reassuring, clinical language of the psychiatrists, taking information for their files and urging her to feel at home in their institution. This stifling restrictiveness pervades her whole life and respectability traps her within a routine of trivial domesticity. Her problems, hidden beneath suburban social activities, must be hidden from the children, the neighbours, herself.

The refrain that Jesus loves her, undercut ironically by the irreverent 'wo-wo-wo', raised some objections in '68. Paul recalls: ' "Mrs Robinson" was the first time that Jesus was mentioned in a popular song. Nobody had said Jesus before. People thought it was a word you couldn't say in pop music. On the radio they wouldn't play it; they'd find it blasphemous.' Moreover, in his cover version of the song, Frank Sinatra changed Jesus to Jilly. 'Jilly loves you more than you will know' makes no sense at all.

Some critics have said that the woman in the song has no connection to Anne Bancroft's portrayal in the film, but that's not true. They haven't listened to the song. Paul captures her – angry, frustrated, neurotic, trapped in suburban emptiness, precisely the woman who pursues Benjamin in a last pathetic bid for excitement.

The song ends on a universal note: the loneliness of a nation searching for lost idols who personify the American Dream. Paul used Joe Di Maggio, although his own baseball hero was always Mickey Mantle, the only 300 hitter in the Yankees, holding the league in homers. Years later, when they met on the *Dick Cavett Show*, Mantle asked him, 'How come you didn't sing about me instead of Joe Di Maggio in that "Mrs Robinson" song?' With characteristic dry humour, Paul replied, 'Nothing personal. You were always good too, but I needed the syllables.' Moreover, 'Mrs Robinson' prompted comment from Joe Di Maggio himself. Years later Paul described, on the US TV series *Sixty Minutes*, how the baseball hero confronted him. 'At first, he was going to sue me. He didn't really know whether it was making fun of him or not. His point was: "Why are you saying – where have you gone, Joe Di Maggio? What do you mean, where have I gone? I'm very much here." He obviously hadn't begun to think of himself as a metaphor.'

While they were working on the soundtrack to *The Graduate*, Paul and Art were also recording their new album, *Bookends*. This was an idea they had conceived right after *Parsley Sage Rosemary and Thyme*, to make an album with a common theme running through it, presenting the lives of people at different ages.

It took longer than any of their previous albums and, for the first time, they saw it through personally to the very last stage. They were given sleeve credit as co-producers along with Roy Halee. According to Paul, they had never needed a producer in the strictest sense of the word. 'I don't need a producer to say – here's a good piece of material to do. And I didn't need someone to say – that's the take, or it's in the wrong tempo.' Roy Halee, of course, wasn't just technically skilled, he was sympathetic to their way of doing things, and he listened to their ideas. All decisions were made jointly, the three of them voting and having equal weight.

They worked hard on this album, as Paul later told the press.

'It took us a long time to get it together because you change your mind about so many things.' They made extensive use of the studio, and spent a lot of time on singing and punching in – a method of recording in tiny, separate fragments, sometimes as little as one note, then piecing it all together. They hadn't done that in previous albums. 'We might have repaired a line or something like that,' Paul said. 'But the concept in *Parsley Sage* wasn't to get each line perfect, and it was in *Bookends*.'

The album was eagerly awaited by press and public, since there had been a gap of twenty months since the release of *PSRT*, an eternity in the pop world. Paul had been finding it difficult to write songs. Unable to force his ideas or settle for less, he had remained silent. He told the press: 'It's been bad lately. That's why there was such a gap ... I couldn't write anything for over six months.' Now the album was finished and he was pleased. 'Lyrically, I think it's far better than anything we've done.'

Bookends is a strange album, falling into two distinct parts: the first side is all new material, following the stages of development from youth to old age; the second side consists of songs already released as singles. Paul later said he was pleased with 'Mrs Robinson', recorded at the same time as the new songs, but was dissatisfied with the re-issues: 'Hazy Shade of Winter', 'At the Zoo' and 'Fakin' It', what he calls 'the dry patch of Simon & Garfunkel'.

The album opens with the haunting 'Bookends Theme', a comment on the passing of time and innocence, the keynote of the album. 'Save the Life of My Child' follows, a chaotic song with a biting, ironic lyric. Paul captures the irrelevant and detached chatter of the crowd who watch, fascinated, as a youth leaps to his death from a New York skyscraper. The demented cry of the mother is haunting as it weaves in and out of the crowd's comments – and it's a cry that ironically makes a good headline for a newspaper story which isn't important enough to be in the *New York Times*.

'America' is a masterpiece of natural dialogue, written in

blank verse, which Paul rarely uses. It describes a bus journey taken by himself and Kathy. The dialogue, the jokes about the other passengers, the intimate and realistic style, come across brilliantly within the restrictions of musical phrasing. His desolate cry of despair, escaping while she is asleep, becomes a universal search for peace and self-knowledge – a search Paul comes back to later in 'American Tune'. Both literally and symbolically, the streams of cars on the highway are searching for a lost America, all empty and aching without really knowing why.

'Overs' must be one of the finest songs written about a relationship between a man and woman. Simon & Garfunkel first performed it on the *Smothers Brothers* TV show in America on 15 October 1967, a week after Paul had completed it. He described it as being 'about two people in a relationship that's over, but every time they're about to leave, they realize that there's really no place else to go'.

Their relationship, once passionate and loving, has disintegrated into a polite and distant tolerance of each other; they exchange civil smiles as they pass in the hall, like hotel guests; they don't sleep together any more and they don't laugh together because all that is over. It is time, and the waste of time, that urges the man to make a positive decision. In the wistful interlude, sung by Artie, time is pressing him to leave her. But he waits and thinks it over – over, the word he started with. It's a neat piece of wordplay.

'Voices of Old People' is a track Art conceived and worked on, in keeping with the overall theme. He spent weeks recording the talk of various old people in the United Home for Aged Hebrews and the California Home for the Aged. The track is disturbing, a montage of voices, fragments of their sad, bleak conversations. They talk about physical pain, relatives, loneliness. When a cheerful woman asks, 'Are you happy?', there's no answer. Paul commented on the track. 'It was very interesting. We're a long, long way from old people. They have a world of their own.'

'Old Friends' follows, linked in theme. It's a moving portrait of two men, discarded by society, merely waiting to die. They live in a world of silence, paradoxically within a bustling, noisy city, in which they have no place. They are held together by the past and by the future – especially by their fears of what the future might bring. This has remained a popular song, partly because it seems to remind us of Paul and Artie, looking ahead to when they are seventy.

'Punky's Dilemna' first made its appearance at the Monterey Festival. It's a pleasant little song, with some funny touches of cliché. I suppose you'd call it a happy song, though there is a reference to draft dodging.

In June 1968, *Bookends* and *The Graduate* were released. Both albums had phenomenal success. By the week ending 15 June, Simon & Garfunkel had no fewer than five albums in the charts, dominating the top three places. *The Graduate* was number 1; *Bookends* was number 2 (these two albums constantly alternated for first place); *Parsley Sage* was at number 3, all the way from November 1966; *Sounds of Silence* was still going strong at number 27, after nearly two and a half years; *Wednesday Morning 3am*, now a massive seller, was still there at 163, which was pretty good after four years.

The new releases soon earned Gold Discs. *The Graduate* wasn't solely a Simon & Garfunkel venture, some of the incidental music was composed by Dave Grusin, a successful musician in his own right. Nevertheless, there was a feeling that summer that anything connected to the duo was automatically a winner.

After the release of the albums, Artie went to stay with Paul at his rented summer house in Stockbridge, Massachusetts. By autumn '68, he was back in his one-roomed apartment in a greystone building on New York's East Side. A fairly modest dwelling, it gave him the privacy he needed. It was clearly the home of an ex-architecture student, tastefully and expertly decorated.

The apartment consisted of a multi-level floor of vivid and

dramatic colours; the rich blue carpet of the upper level descended into the grey of the lower level, which contained two black sofas. Behind a cork-lined panel was the third level, the bedroom area. One wall was stripped to bare brick; there was a floor-to-ceiling window, from which hung rich drapes. Off the main foyer, a small, bright kitchenette housed a breakfast table behind a balustrade.

Art's evenings were spent mostly with friends, ending with a dawn breakfast. Sometimes he would go back to Paul's apartment, also on the East Side, and listen to the new songs in progress. Or he would go home to read.

He was leading a very quiet life, as he'd always done. His fame hadn't really changed that. He was thinking seriously about his future. He told the *New York Times*: 'I want to have a married life and a family life.' This is something Artie often longed for – years later he reiterated his wish to be a father, and it was some years before he achieved it. In that sense, this period was also quite lonely for him.

In October '68, the duo appeared at the Forest Hills Stadium before a packed house. At the climax of the show, the audience rose to its feet to applaud. Paul and Artie left the stage, returning to do three encores, one more than the usual.

In spite of this ovation, however, Artie didn't feel satisfied. Back in the trailer they used as a dressing room, he sat quietly shaking his head. 'This was one of our worst shows.' Paul looked at him and shrugged. 'It wasn't so bad. It wasn't so good, but it wasn't so bad.' Clearly, Simon & Garfunkel set their own standards for success and failure, irrespective of the adulation of the crowds. Perhaps, also, the joys of performing together were growing a little stale. They had been together as a duo for three crowded, hectic years now. They both needed something else.

Near the end of '68, Simon & Garfunkel made an appearance at Shea Stadium in New York, a fund-raising concert for Peace candidates. As far as Paul was concerned, it was a total flop. First of all, it was set up at very short notice, with insufficient promotion. Consequently, only 20,000 people came, instead of the 50,000 expected – and justifiably expected with a bill that included Janis Joplin, Creedence Clearwater Revival, John Sebastian, the Rascals and Johnny Winter. From the start, Paul had doubts about it. He saw it was badly organized, but he believed in the cause so he hoped for the best. 'I said, "Well, okay, right. I'll do my thing. I don't think this concert is well planned, but I'll do it."'

They did their thing, certainly. But even Simon & Garfunkel couldn't save the show. It was, as Paul said, 'a relative stiff' and there were no profits at all. They took in a hundred thousand dollars at the door, and that was more or less how much it cost to put on.

Paul was very angry. 'If you do a concert and it comes out lousy, when you come off stage, you're mad. It doesn't matter who you do it for.' The money issue puzzled him, too. 'Where was it spent? I certainly didn't make any money out of it. Nobody I knew made any money.' As a matter of fact, Creedence Clearwater Revival lost money because they had to pay all their own expenses – the air fare and cost of moving their stage equipment from California. Paul tried to find out who had controlled the money and where it had gone, but without success.

As time went by, he began to feel disillusioned about the whole concert. 'Naturally, you're left with a feeling of having been taken. Nobody benefits. The peace candidates, whoever they are, didn't benefit.' He vowed he would never play at Shea again; the noise of the aircraft continually flying overhead had often drowned out their singing.

Paul remained furious about the failure and the way everyone had been abused. 'Everything's bad, and so I'm slugging through it because it's a worthwhile cause. And it's all over. It's all for nothing.' In November 1968, Richard Nixon was elected President of the United States of America. This proved to be the end of an era. The love and peace ethic of the sixties was in its last days;

the seventies would be more cynical and more troubled. In time, Nixon would be brought down by Watergate, one of the most scandalous events of American political history. The concert had indeed been for nothing.

Chapter Nine

A FILM, A BOXER
AND MARRIAGE

As Simon & Garfunkel moved into 1969, Paul's writing pace was again slow. He hadn't written anything since *Bookends*, so now he felt there was considerable pressure on him. He had never been an artist who could write to order; his standards were very high. He was throwing away most of what he put on paper. He told Lon Goddard: 'There are a lot of artists today who write a lot, but don't take much time to say it well ... I take time to write what I feel is a genuine contribution and try not to repeat myself. Once you've said it, you shouldn't repeat it.'

Practical problems were restricting his writing. With heavy performing, producing and business commitments, there were many demands on his time these days. 'Having to be in a thousand other places at once is keeping me from writing as much as I'd like to.'

Paul was facing the paradox of being a successful writer. By its very nature, writing is a solitary pursuit, done best by people who are introverted and analytical. It's also a very time-consuming activity. When a writer is also a performer, by nature an extrovert, public way of life, the two things must inevitably clash. The singer-songwriter embodies a private and internal paradox: how to fulfil the demands of two essentially diverse ways of life. For Paul these days, it was proving difficult and painful.

Paul was also falling in love, and with complications. The woman was Peggy Harper, the daughter of a housepainter whose family had lived in the foothills of the Smoky Mountains for hundreds of years. Unfortunately she was married to their business manager, Mort Lewis. This obviously wasn't an easy situation, and Paul later described it in 'Train in the Distance' – his own determination to win her, her hesitation, the passionate nature of their feelings for each other.

Meanwhile, Art had struck a workable relationship with Mike Nichols, both personally and professionally. When Nichols was casting for his new project, a film of Joseph Heller's bestselling novel, *Catch-22*, he offered Art the role of Nately.

Art's initial reason for accepting was: 'I like the idea of having another string to my bow.' Originally Paul was to have a part as Dunbar but Buck Henry, who was writing the screenplay, felt there were too many characters to include in the movie, and Dunbar was one of those he cut. Art described Paul's feelings in a tongue-in-cheek way: 'Like there wasn't enough candy to go around and he was left out.'

It's easy enough to see Art's move into films as the thin end of the wedge, the first break between Simon & Garfunkel. But things are never that simple. When I talked to Artie in the mid eighties, he spoke at great length of his reasons for this move. 'I thought it would be a great thing for the duo – notice, the duo,' he told me emphatically. He wanted to enrich their creative output, bring something new to their repertoire, open up a new horizon. It was never his intention to take anything away from them; in fact, he was striving to do just the opposite.

And, it must be said, he did. His venture into films was not only successful, it also brought another dimension to the work of the duo. Paul would later appear in films himself, even write and star in one. Perhaps it's fair to say that Artie began all that with his acceptance of a part in *Catch-22*. It's too easy to blame this one act for the dissolving of a partnership, when clearly the reasons behind that were far more complex, far more deeply rooted.

Art started filming in January 1969. The movie had a large budget and locations all over the world. Later, this would prove to be a problem, as the pressures of his singing career became more intense and the film career more demanding.

The setting of the novel is a United States Army air base on the Sardinian coast, but nowadays it bears little resemblance to the barren desert of Second World War days. It took over a year for Mike Nichols, producer John Calley and designer Richard Sylbert to find the right spot to build their island of Pianosa and its air base. Finally, a hundred thousand acres was found near Guaymas in Mexico: desolate scrub and cactus land, which was soon covered with tents, makeshift huts and sets of all kinds.

There was also a 6,000-foot landing strip which was actually used by the fleet of Second World War B-25 bombers selected from the few planes that could still fly. Eighteen B-25s were bought and repaired to a safe flying condition at an average cost of ten thousand dollars. One of them, a wedding present from heiress Barbara Hutton to playboy Porfirio, arrived complete with reclining seats and leather-panelled toilet. A group of authentic fighter pilots was rounded up to fly the planes, with the actors sitting in for the close-up interior shots.

Mike Nichols and his team worked hard to ensure that every detail was accurate. Every building was an interior set as well as an exterior one; the base was an exact reconstruction in every sense; there were even scattered copies of movie magazines with Alice Faye and Betty Grable on the covers.

Today *Catch-22* is one of the best known works in modern American literature. It is the story of a group of flyers in a little island community in the Mediterranean in 1944. They are scared and courageous, blasphemous and touching, sad and funny. The title of the novel has entered our everyday vocabulary. What is catch-22? The only way a pilot can stop flying is to be certified as crazy; but then, he must be crazy anyway to have become a pilot; so if he asks to be grounded, then he isn't crazy, so he has to keep on flying. That is catch-22 – the inescapable reality, the irony of life.

Into this madness comes nineteen-year-old Captain Nately, a

rich American boy who has lived most of his life without ever knowing tension or hatred or conflict of any kind. The film gives us all too few details about him, but the novel tells us that his mother is descended from the aristocratic New England family of Thornton and is a Daughter of the American Revolution. His parents never let him forget that he is an aristocrat in the true sense, unlike so many other millionaires who are soiled by commerce and industry. He is a Nately, and the Natelys have never done anything for their money. But this Nately does something. He goes to war. With the blindness of youth, he naively falls in love with an Italian prostitute who remains indifferent to him until the last stages of their incongruous relationship.

Nately's role is important to the structure of the work. In the scene where he confronts the old pimp in the brothel, the filmed narrative takes on the symbolic interpretation of the novel: a weary, worldly Italy versus a virile but tragically innocent America. Nately defends his country loyally – speaking for his generation, without understanding that he is a blind victim, not a glorious victor. He accuses the old man of being a heartless, unpatriotic opportunist, and the pimp comes back at him with the ultimate weapon – his superior age. Nately retaliates proudly: 'I'll be twenty in January.' The old man's parting shot is swift and, as it turns out, prophetic: 'If you live.'

Nately does not live. With all his ideals and courage, he is shot down. Artie told me that while he was filming the part, he was conscious that Nately has to be missed by the audience. We have to feel his death as a tragedy, even as it is ironically underplayed in both novel and film. And it works – Nately's death becomes the symbol for the futile and senseless waste of many lives. Moreover, the grief felt by Yossarian, Nately's friend and protector, is his turning point in rejecting the system that has sent them to war.

In March 1969, Simon & Garfunkel walked away with two Grammy Awards. Paul received one for the score of *The*

Graduate, and the duo received one for Best Contemporary Pop Performance, 'Mrs Robinson'. Paul was particularly surprised at that one: 'I didn't expect it. I thought "Hey Jude" was the record of the year.' It was a great honour and, at the time, they couldn't have guessed that it would be just the beginning of their large collection of awards. Paul didn't attend the presentation, but watched on television while his partner went to receive them.

Meanwhile, Paul had come up with a song he had begun writing the previous summer, finishing it in December '68. Destined to be one of his greatest compositions, perhaps one of the greatest songs ever written, it was simply called 'The Boxer'.

The words and melody came to him simultaneously, something quite rare for him. 'The words to the first verse . . . came with the melody line; they had a flow to them that made them easy to sing. Consequently, I found I had started a song about a poor boy who had squandered his resistance for a pocketful of mumbles. I just tried to make the rest of the lyrics follow as naturally as possible.'

It's a narrative ballad, possibly the most popular and enduring genre in American folk songs. The story tells of a young boy who leaves home to seek his fortune, something Paul would return to in the years to come. The boy is vulnerable and encounters hardship and loneliness. He discovers the lives of the ragged people of New York City, and finds unexpected kindness and comfort from the prostitutes of Seventh Avenue.

He has courage, facing up to his mistakes and coming to terms with reality. In the final verse, he looks at the boxer (and some critics assume that he *is* the boxer, which isn't right at all) and admires him for the classic qualities of manhood: strength and endurance. While the boxer clearly symbolizes these qualities, he also represents the way out of the ghetto. The boy, like the boxer, is hurt but not beaten. Ultimately it's an optimistic song. Though tinged with desolation and pain, it has no trace of self-pity. There's a lot of Paul Simon in it.

Rumours suggested that it was written about Bob Dylan's life and, admittedly, there could be some parallels. But then, when viewed on a superficial level, it could be about anyone. Clearly it is in fact a very personal song, written from the inside.

Paul commented: 'I would say it's autobiographical, although it sure surprised me. When we recorded it, someone said to me, "Hey, that's a song about you." And I said, "No, it's not about me; it's about this guy who . . ." and as I'm saying it, I thought, "Hey, what am I saying? This song is about me and I'm not even admitting it." One thing is certain, I've never written anything about Dylan; and I don't know of his personal life.'

The track took a long time to record; it was said to have used up over a hundred hours of studio time. It was recorded in many different places. The basic track was put down in Nashville, the end voices and horns in St Paul's Church, New York, and the strings and main voices in New York's Columbia Studios.

It involved innovations in their recording technique. Simon & Garfunkel were the first artists to persuade Columbia to use sixteen-track recording for the song. Paul recalled the problems they encountered: 'It wasn't a sixteen-track machine; it was two eight-track machines synchronized. And it was a bitch to get them to work together. In other words, you had to press the button at the same time to record that way. Halee rigged it out. It was hard.'

Later on, with these difficulties in mind, Columbia invested in sixteen-track machines. As Paul said: 'We were the group that was recording all this weird stuff, and we were multi-tracking, doing voices and recording by layers. At Columbia at that time, nobody else was doing that.'

Musically, it's a very weighty production, and some critics complained that they couldn't hear all the words, which is a fair comment. This is partly because one word merges into the next – or, as Paul put it: 'The end of one sound went into the beginning of another sound.' The difficulty is probably the orchestration, which tends to outweigh the vocals. If you listen to later versions – Paul's solo on *Live Rhymin'* or the duo version on the *Central*

Park album, both very different and both superb – the diction is much clearer. With a song that's lyrically so powerful, it's vital to hear every word.

Then there is the fade-out, the 'lie-la-lie' on this original version, which is simply too long, so we lose the sense of desolation created by the song itself. It reminds us too much of 'Hey Jude'; since 'The Boxer' is a superior song, that comparison isn't really desirable.

Paul had some misgivings about the fade-out, and later used the song as an example of how the relationship between Art, Roy Halee and himself operated: 'Each person had a relatively equal say. If Roy and Artie said, "Let's do a long ending on 'The Boxer'," I said, "Two out of three" and did it their way. I didn't say, "Hey, this is my song and I don't want it to be like that." Never did it occur to me to say that. "Fine," I'd say.' But apart from doubts about the fade-out, Paul was happy with the version they did. 'It's one of my favourites of all the Simon & Garfunkel records.' He also told the press: 'I think that's one of the best things we ever did . . . I like the song and I like our record of it.'

There were many cover versions, notably one from Bob Dylan, which he put on *Self Portrait*, his album containing the songs of other writers, and produced by Bob Johnston. Paul had reservations about it: 'I don't know. It's hard to say. You see, I identify very strongly with that song. Yes, I suppose it's okay, but I like the Simon & Garfunkel version. [Dylan's] was fine . . . it was original. Like anything Dylan does, it has its own thing. He did it differently and I didn't think anyone could do that. Dylan's version makes me smile.' However, Paul was excited by the cover versions from Aretha Franklin and Stevie Wonder. 'They both did it in a way that was very natural for the song, and they made it for me. I love it.'

In April 1969, Paul and Art launched 'The Boxer'. It climbed the charts rapidly. As Lon Goddard put it: 'It spent at least ten seconds shooting to number one in America. It might have been ten or fifteen seconds before it reached number one in Britain, but it did, and the world was at their feet.'

The flip side was 'Baby Driver', in one sense a light-hearted contrast to 'The Boxer', also about a youth encountering his first, tentative sexual experiences. But this boy is secure, financially and emotionally, living with his parents and looking for adventures. The song sustains the connection between cars and sex, both of which the boy pursues with energy. His unsubtle advance to the girl is made in the naive language of a childhood he has barely left behind him.

The spring of 1969 brought great personal changes for Artie, for then he met the woman he would later marry. She was Linda Grossman, four years younger than him, a native of Nashville who had graduated as an architect then moved up north some five years earlier to work as a graphic designer.

It was a very romantic meeting. Art was taking a two-week break from *Catch-22*, in order to record 'The Boxer' with Paul. He was walking along 55th Street and Park Avenue with Mort Lewis, on their way to lunch in a restaurant. Linda was visiting New York from Boston, and happened to be passing in a cab going downtown on Park Avenue. She recognized Art and jumped out of the cab at the next block. Later she would tell him he had a nice smile and seemed 'reachable'. On impulse, she spoke to him. Art recalls: 'I spotted her halfway up the block coming toward me and I thought – there's the girl I could get serious about.' He was delighted when she approached.

Later, he analysed the instant attraction he felt. 'At that point in my life, I was looking to stop running around and playing around. I was ready, my rhythm was already going.'

Linda was immediately attracted to him. She had seen him years before in a concert at her college. That night, he invited her to the studio to watch them recording 'The Boxer' and, for four hours, she watched them intently over the engineering console.

'She was going to know everything,' Art said later. 'I was

impressed and flattered. And we went out afterwards and I was very charmed, and we dated a lot. It took us about three years, though, before I had the courage to ask her to marry me.'

In the summer of '69, Paul married Peggy Harper. Like Linda Grossman, she was a native of Tennessee. Peggy wasn't directly involved in show business but as she had been married to Mort Lewis, she was already a close friend, and someone Paul felt he could trust. She was slightly older than he, a vivacious and attractive woman. They were deeply in love. In the years that followed, she would inspire his love songs and enrich his life.

Paul and Artie had reached a new stage in their careers and private lives. They were hugely successful now, though even greater success lay just around the next corner. Both men were ready to settle down and were looking for something permanent, someone of their own. In 1969, both men found the woman they would marry. Amid all the professional turmoil that was in store, for the present at least they had found a private sanctuary.

Just ahead of them was the greatest album they would ever produce and, ironically, the end of Simon & Garfunkel.

Chapter Ten

'BRIDGE'

In the summer of '69, Paul and Art rented a house in Blue Jay Way in Los Angeles, made famous by George Harrison's song. At the time, the local residents were nervous because of the recent horrific Charles Manson murders, which had taken place in the nearby hills and which had cost the life of the young and beautiful actress Sharon Tate.

Besides Paul and Peggy, Artie was there when he wasn't filming *Catch-22*, together with session musicians and technicians. It was a working holiday. The making of *Bridge over Troubled Water* was a very troubled time for the duo. Both of them were working hard, tackling problems both practical and emotional.

Paul found Art's absences difficult to cope with. *Catch-22* was running late and taking up a lot of Artie's time and energy. 'For me it was frustrating,' Paul said later, 'because I'd be ready and raring to work and he'd be in Rome shooting scenes. My interest and loyalty lay with the LP; I was only secondarily interested in *Catch-22*.'

The practical organizing of the recording was making him very tense; he told one interviewer how Art might be away for anything up to three months, while Paul continued by himself. Art doesn't sing at all on 'Baby Driver', and is only in the background in 'The Only Living Boy in New York'. He wasn't in the studio for the mixing of 'The Boxer', so Paul did it with Roy Halee.

Paul was very torn. Deep down, he supported Art, as 'The

Only Living Boy in New York' indicates. In the opening of that song, he addresses Tom, Art's name in the old Tom & Jerry days; he urges him to catch his plane on time, reassuring him that his part will go well. It's clear that 'Tom' is filming in Mexico, the location for much of the shooting of Catch-22, so in spite of the frustration Paul must have been rooting for his friend.

Art was equally in conflict. He was torn between two projects that he wanted very much to complete. He had a large part in the film and it was his first venture into acting, so he naturally wanted it to be a success. He couldn't have predicted that the delays would keep him from the album. Equally, he had a large stake in Simon & Garfunkel.

When he was in the studio with Paul, Artie gave the album his very best. When asked if Art had lost interest in the album, Paul replied: 'No, I can't say that. He had other interests that were very strong. But he certainly was interested in making the record. From the point of view of creativity, I didn't have any other interests than the music. I had no other distractions.'

A fair comment – the voice of a man who is trying to be reasonable. They were both trying to be reasonable. It was just getting more and more difficult. They began to work separately, each recording his own part of the song by himself, when it could be slotted into his schedule. As Paul described it: 'It's a Simon & Garfunkel record, but not really. And it became easier to work by separating. There are many songs where you don't hear Simon & Garfunkel singing together.' The overall musical quality of the album remained the same but the new working method almost certainly helped pave the way for their solo careers.

There was one particularly happy session in the living room at the Blue Jay Way house, recording the track that became 'Cecilia'. In separate interviews both Paul and Art have since described it with pleasure.

Art had a TC-124 sound-on-sound Sony recorder with a re-verb effect on it, so that it gave a kick-back on every sound. Paul started to get into the rhythm created by the time delay, and everyone spontaneously joined in. Paul was on guitar, his brother Eddie on piano bench and a friend, Stewey Scharf, on choked guitar which had no tonal quality. With Artie banging things to keep the beat, they were experimenting with the sounds they could make. Paul liked the rhythm they had created, so he kept the recording. 'Every day, I'd come back from the studio, working on whatever I was working on, and I'd play this pounding thing.' He thought of turning it into a record.

They took the basic track to Roy Halee, and the three of them started overdubbing. What Art called 'a lot of fooling around sound' included dropping a batch of fifteen drumsticks on the parquet studio floor – dropping them in rhythm because they liked the effect. Then they found a xylophone. Paul suggested they use it for percussion, not for tonal quality. But, according to Art, 'None of us could play xylophone, so Paul went out and did a great job. One of my favourite overdubs is this one. Roy limited the sound, which is compressing it and taking just the electric ticky-tacky of it, so that it didn't matter that Paul was going to play the wrong notes; all that mattered was the feel of it. I rode the dial in the mix.'

They copied it over and extended the length to double, so as Paul said, 'We have three minutes of track and the track is great. So now I pick up my guitar and I start to go.' The words came immediately. Art loved the track, describing it as 'a very earthy, home-made record'.

Paul decided to write a ballad for the album, and what he came up with was very much more than that. 'Bridge Over Troubled Water' is a tribute to Peggy, to friendship and to love itself. It's possibly the greatest song he ever wrote.

At the time, Paul was listening to a lot of gospel music, particularly to a guitar gospel group, the Swan Silvertones. In their song 'Oh Mary Don't You Weep', there was a line that stuck in his mind: 'I'll be your bridge over deep water, if you'll trust in my name.' Then there was a totally diverse source of inspiration – two bars from a Bach chorale. Another part was borrowed from a country song, 'Long Time Gone'. The merging of these sources gave us 'Bridge over Troubled Water'.

Everyone recognizes that it's a wonderful song. Part of its secret lies in the subtle blending of a childlike faith – I'm on your side – with an adult love that is steadfast and unquestioning.

At this stage, Paul had only the first two verses, and he felt that was enough. He showed it to Art, saying: 'Here's a song I just wrote. I think you should sing it.' According to Paul, Artie didn't really want to sing it. 'He couldn't hear it for himself. He felt I should have done it.'

Art's recollection comes to much the same thing. 'Paul showed me "Bridge over Troubled Water", and he felt it was his best song. I felt it was something less than his best song, but a great song. I knew the way he was singing it was terrific; he had a lot of feeling for it. He sang it in a high range and he got into falsetto and I thought it was a very interesting sound for him. And my first instinct was that Paul could do a bitch on that vocal. I knew I could too.'

And according to Art, when he suggested that Paul should sing it himself, Paul protested: 'No, you should do it. I wrote it so that you would do it.' So Artie finally agreed: 'I said, "Crazy – I'll do it."'

The next hurdle was the arrangement. Paul had composed it on guitar in the key of G, so it had to be transposed into E flat for Art's voice. An arranger who had worked with them before came over. As a favour, he transposed it into E flat while Paul read it out in G. Later, he won a Grammy Award for his arranging work on that day.

Then they handed the song to Larry Knechtel, the highly respected LA session musician, a member of Bread. They told him they needed a gospel piano sound, and that took about four days to achieve. Paul recalled: 'Each night, we'd work on the piano part until Larry really honed it into a good part.'

As Larry was playing the two-verse song, Paul realized that it wasn't long enough. 'I think it was Artie's idea to add another verse, because Larry was sort of elongating the piano part. So I said, "Play the piano part for a third verse again, even though I don't have it, and I'll write it." Which I eventually did after the fact.'

Art's memory of it captures the sense of panic. 'We said, "Well, we need a third verse – quick." ' And he was impressed by how efficiently Paul delivered that third verse. 'We began to hear the record you could make, and all that was missing was some more song, and because we were driven by the concept of the record, everything fell into place in a very natural way. It took Paul just a couple of hours to write that last verse in the studio. That's when it goes good. It sort of makes itself.'

Paul was less satisfied with it. He hadn't wanted to add the verse because he had no words. 'The metaphor got ruined. I didn't have time to fix up a lot of things.' He wasn't happy with 'all your dreams are on their way'. But on the whole, Paul came to accept the last verse – apart from a few quibbles. 'I always felt you could clearly see that it was written afterwards,' he said. 'It just doesn't sound like the first two verses.' One can see what he means, but he's being hyper-critical here. The break is *not* obvious – and it's a superb lyric. In 1972, in an introduction to a book of his songs, he conceded: 'Apart from this weakness, I think "Bridge" is my strongest melody to date, even if not my best lyric.'

The piano accompaniment was finished and they added two bass guitars, and some vibes in the second verse. They recorded the drum in an echo chamber with a tape-reverb to create an afterbeat effect. Finally, they sent it to have the string arrangement written.

Unfortunately – and unbelievably – the arrangers wrote down the title as 'Like a Pitcher of Water', claiming that this was how they heard it on the demo tape. It's hard to see how anyone could make such a huge mistake: the syllables don't fit and it's a ludicrous title anyway. To add insult to injury, they also mis-spelled Garfunkel.

Later, Paul framed their efforts for posterity. He recalled: 'We did the string part, and I couldn't stand it. I thought they were terrible. I was very disappointed. It had to be completely rewritten.'

He responded to the final string arrangement with a cautious approbation: 'I would say I was happy. It was changed around quite a lot and there was a lot of engineering added to it. I think it served its purpose. I don't think it bears a lot of scrutiny. If you listen to just the string part, it's not really great.' He agreed that it expanded the record, turning it into a huge production, but he felt the final note of the song was too long.

Art and Paul left Los Angeles and returned to New York to do the vocals. It was to be a Garfunkel solo, even though Paul could easily have done the harmony in the third verse. Artie worked hard for days to get everything perfect.

The vocal style was inspired by a Phil Spector production of 'Old Man River', sung by the Righteous Brothers. Their technique was to use very light production until the climax when, as Art puts it, 'They threw in everything.'

Personally, Artie loved the sound. 'Saving all the production for the last line of a song seemed like all of that potential energy running through the whole record until it exploded. It was a lovely production idea.' And there's no denying that Artie really does throw in everything in that last verse, in that beautiful final note.

All told, the song took somewhere between ten days and two weeks to record, and then it had to be mixed. They recorded it meticulously, using the punching-in technique, so that each line was perfect. No matter how many times we hear it, it remains quite stunning in its perfection: the merging of a brilliant composer and a flawless singer.

Chapter Eleven

TROUBLED WATER

The successful recording of 'Bridge' was followed by a period of frustration. September '69 was packed with hard work and very little satisfaction. The pace hadn't let up at all. Now they were making a TV special. It turned out to be a long and complicated business, fraught with angry clashes with media people, only increasing the tension that had been growing all year.

Originally, Simon & Garfunkel were to make a guest appearance on the *Bell Telephone Hour*, to coincide with the start of their concert tour planned for the following month. Basically, the special was to promote the tour. As Paul said: 'To say to people, here we are again. We're back, even though it's a year later.' But the concept of the show continually expanded in the planning stages, until finally Bell Telephone asked them to do a complete show, their first special for television. They agreed. Bell Telephone were delighted, because they were running a recruiting campaign, and the support of Simon & Garfunkel could help them to gain the interest of young people.

Meanwhile, Art and Paul thought a lot about the show's content. They asked Charles Grodin, who had starred with Artie in *Catch-22*, to help them. Grodin, an enormously talented and versatile actor, writer and director, said to them: 'If you're going to get an hour on television, instead of doing an ordinary show, let's think up something that would be different.'

They settled on a show all about America, highlighting contemporary, controversial issues. Bell, on the other hand, believed they were doing a typical light entertainment programme. As Paul said: 'They didn't know that we were planning on doing a show that had anything to do with real life.'

A week before the show was due on the air, they showed the film to Bell, who rejected it completely. It was out of the question. They strongly objected to a sequence with Robert and John Kennedy and Martin Luther King, using 'Bridge over Troubled Water' as background. According to Paul, their objection was on the grounds that: 'They were all Democrats. There's no Republicans in there. And we said, "Is that what you get? How about that they were all assassinated?"' They also rejected a film clip of Jesse Jackson, Ralph Abernathy and Robert Kennedy, because there would be trouble if they showed it in Alabama. Bell accused the duo of using their company funds to make propaganda and spread their own political views. Bell wanted no part in the footage of Woodstock or Vietnam. But according to Paul: 'They said they could live with *The Lone Ranger*. If we wanted to keep that in, it was all right.'

Paul was passionately angry. 'So we said, "You mean to say that there are people who will object if we say you must feed everyone in this country?" And they said, "You're goddam right someone would object." They said, "You'll have to change this; it's not going on." And we said, "Well, too bad then. It's not going on, because we're not changing anything."'

Paul and Artie remained firm. Bell Telephone remained just as firm. Paul later said: 'It was a terrible experience. Really awful. One of the most frustrating things I ever did in my life was to work for hours and hours on that show and to hear somebody just put it down in the worst terms possible.'

Angry and exhausted, Paul and Artie gave the company executives an ultimatum: 'This is the show we made. This is what we believe in. Don't put it on, then.'

They didn't put it on. Paul and Art went to CBS and met with their censor executives. For the most part, CBS sympathized with the concept of the show. They finally forced it on to the air, in spite of Bell. It was scheduled to be screened on 30 November.

By October, they had finished work on the show and immediately began their tour, which was sold out well in advance. The strain was beginning to tell. Paul remembers: 'We had just finished working on this television special, which really wiped us out because of all the fighting that went on. We were very tired.' Because of this crammed schedule, they were forced to postpone working on their album until they returned from the tour. A sense of dread was hanging over them: more work had to be finished before they could take a break.

The tour itself was a great success, right across America. But Paul was becoming increasingly aware that things were strained between them. Ironically, some resentment had set in around his composing triumph, 'Bridge over Troubled Water'.

As the tour went on, he began to wish he hadn't insisted on Artie singing it. It wasn't simply because it was so incredibly successful; there was something else. Night after night, he sat off stage, listening to the pianist and Artie singing alone, and he regretted his decision more and more. The song became exclusively associated with Artie.

'People would stomp and cheer when it was over, and I would think, "That's my song, man. Thank you very much. I wrote that song." It's not a very generous thing to think, but I did think that. I resented it and I was aware of the fact that I resented it. And I knew that this wouldn't have been the case two years earlier.'

One of the concerts on this tour was at Ames, Iowa. It was significant because when they performed the Everly Brothers hit 'Bye Bye Love', they were fascinated by the audience's handclapping and asked everyone to try to keep in beat so that it could be recorded. It worked well, though they had to do it twice because it was too ragged the first time. The album later included this vibrant track with the sound of eighty thousand people clapping along.

When the television special was shown at the end of November, the duo were inundated with letters urging them not to present their political opinions on the air, just to sing. Paul was irritated. 'I used to say to Artie, it's like if you decided to go to the bathroom and somebody said, "Don't go to the bathroom. Just sing. That's what you do. Don't do anything else. Don't make bacon in the morning. You're not a bacon maker. You sing." As if you had to have some qualifications to say, I'm alive today.'

As soon as the tour ended, they rushed back into the studio to finish the album which had been postponed for so long. Frustrated by the delays and physically drained, the strain on them was now very noticeable.

Paul recalled: 'Yes, there was tension building up. And as is typical when you're tired, you get short tempered. And we fought. I wouldn't say it was a big fight. It was one of those things where you've had it, you're tired and you just want the album out of the way.'

Before they knew it, it was December and they had to postpone work for Christmas. Early in January, they got back on the treadmill and the pressure increased. In Paul's words: 'We were really exhausted. Well, at that point, I just wanted out. I wanted to take a vacation. So did he, I guess. So we stopped at eleven songs.'

Originally, they had planned for twelve songs. Paul had written a number called 'Cuba Si Nixon No', for which they had cut the basic track. Artie didn't want to do it. Paul would later admit to the press that he didn't think it was a very good song, either.

However, it developed into a sore point between them. Artie suggested they should do a Bach chorale instead. Paul said no. Both men were adamant. Paul told Jon Landau: 'We were fighting over which was going to be the twelfth song, and then I said, "Put it out with eleven songs if that's the way it is." We were at the end of our energies over that.'

The album was finished in the last weeks of January. They

were greatly relieved. Paul had no more songs left and had used up all his ideas. Both men had come to the end of their creative juice. As Paul later said: 'In my mind, I said, that's the end. It's good because we had all our strength for this album and we did a hard amount of work on it, and now we've finished it. And we'd just about cleaned ourselves out.'

The close of January saw the release of the single 'Bridge over Troubled Water'. Predicting that it would be a huge success, CBS executive Clive Davis urged them to issue this song as the album's first single, backed by 'Keep the Customer Satisfied'. He was right. It shot up the charts alongside the album, which was released on 6 February 1970. Its impact was staggering. The single and the album topped the charts simultaneously in Britain and the USA. Until now, no artist had managed to hold first place in both charts at once, not to mention in two countries.

After the title track, we have 'If I Could', an English version of 'El Condor Pasa', which Paul first heard in Paris in 1965 when it was performed by Los Incas, a South American group who greatly impressed him. He played their Philips recording of it from time to time, because he loved the melody. Then he wrote some English words to it and obtained their permission to sing his words over their original track, hence the authentic South American feel. It's a simple, nursery rhyme lyric, contrasting being tied down with the joys of freedom.

Then there's 'Cecilia', the fast track describing a young man's woes because his girlfriend isn't faithful to him. Paul referred to the famous opening lines as 'not lines at all, but it was right for the song. It was like a little piece of magical fluff, but it works.' It's traditional rock 'n' roll, with a breaking-my-heart, down-on-my-knees situation, and good fun.

'Keep the Customer Satisfied' is another of Paul's on-the-road songs. A young man is relieved to be at home, lamenting the hostility he finds in the wide world. There are some gems in the song, humorous and lyrically economical – and there's a strong element of Paul's sense of showmanship and determination. As he wails, 'I'm so tired,' we're aware that, at the time, Paul Simon was indeed tired.

The first side ends with 'So Long, Frank Lloyd Wright', which many critics have mistakenly regarded as no more than a tribute to the great New York architect. But the song is much more than that, when we remember that Art Garfunkel was a would-be architect in his college days. The song is a tribute to Artie and to their long-standing friendship. Otherwise, why is Paul remembering nights of harmonizing till dawn, laughter shared? The song also focuses on a writer's greatest fear – running out of ideas, running dry. This 'Frank Lloyd Wright' is special because he gives inspiration, whereas real architects, however great, just come and go and never change one's point of view. It's a poignant song, tenderly humorous and sung by Artie himself. Sadly, in hindsight, we can see that their song was, indeed, gone so soon.

For Art, the best part of the song was the ending, the fade-out in which he repeats 'so long'. In the background, you can just hear Paul and Roy Halee saying, 'So long, already, Artie.' When they recorded it, they were actually shouting the words, but it was then mixed down so that we hear it very softly. Art later regretted this. 'I realized that we mixed down one of the things I really enjoyed, because nobody ever told me they heard it. I loved it.'

Art had, in fact, wanted the line to be louder, but Paul and Roy had been very dubious about it. Art commented: 'We were always cautious about jokes, even though we were always fooling around. We'd almost never keep anything that was light-hearted in our records. Who knows why?'

'The Boxer' and 'Baby Driver' open the other side. Then we have 'The Only Living Boy in New York', which features Paul singing the main vocals, with Art on harmony and background. At this point, Art was experimenting with open-mouth harmony: in other words, singing very loudly, then mixing it down softly. On this track, he and Paul were actually screaming at the top of their lungs in an echo chamber, and this was overdubbed about eight times. Art would later recall how Bob Dylan happened to call in at the studio while they were recording it. 'We came out of the booth after all this screaming and there he was.'

'Why Don't You Write Me?' isn't a profound song, but it has a sad irony. It was significant in Paul's musical development because the dissatisfaction he felt with the sound he got was one factor which later made him decide to go to Jamaica to record reggae with authentic musicians. 'I got that by making a mistake, because "Why Don't You Write Me?" was supposed to sound like that but it came out a bad imitation.'

'Bye Bye Love' comes across with a lot of warmth, a tribute to the idols of their adolescence. In one sense, Paul and Artie had come full circle with this song, returning to their roots with their final album.

It closes with the haunting 'Song for the Asking', a tiny fragment, a declaration of love written for Peggy. It's lovely in its simplicity, a few lines packed with hesitation, doubts and honest knowledge of what he can offer. It presents an adult view of the compromise needed in relationships. Its final note is plaintive and poignant – a quiet man offering everything he has, hoping it will be enough.

So this was the album that swept across the world, becoming the bestselling album of 1970, 1971 and 1972. At that time, it was the bestselling album ever made. In the USA, it stayed at number 1 for ten weeks, and in the bestseller charts for eighty-five weeks. In Britain, its success was even more staggering: at number 1 for an unbelievable thirty-five weeks (almost nine months), and in the bestseller charts for 285 weeks – sprawling across the years from 1970 to 1975.

In March 1970, a mere two months after its release, it was awarded a Gold Disc. And that was only the start. It was to win an embarrassment of riches in Grammy Awards. By the end of 1970, the US sales were already 2½ million. By 1975, global sales were estimated at well over 10 million.

Obviously, it was a financial boost for both of them. 'It made us a pretty penny, as they say,' Paul commented with a smile. 'But then, I was not in bad shape before *Bridge* came out, so the success didn't affect my financial life.'

Financially, perhaps not. But it was an incredible thing to come to terms with. Art said: 'You know, it's a bit mind-boggling to conceive a million of anything, let alone a million people buying your record. So how can you possibly imagine ten million? You can't.'

The single did just as well. It was the top disc of 1970, remaining at number 1 in the USA for six weeks. In Britain, it was number 1 for four weeks, and twenty weeks in the bestseller charts. By March, it had already earned a Gold Disc like the album. By April, sales were well over 2 million. All told, it sold over 6 million copies. Simon & Garfunkel had the rare achievement of a single and an album simultaneously at number 1 for five weeks, dominating both charts, both selling 2 million in just two months.

Some critics noted a similarity between 'Bridge' and The Beatles hit 'Let It Be'. Paul commented: 'They're sort of both hopeful songs and resting, peaceful songs. The first time I heard "Let It Be", I couldn't believe that he did that. He must have written it about the same time as I wrote mine, and he gave it to Aretha Franklin, which is funny, because when I first wrote "Bridge", I said, "Boy, I bet Aretha could do a good job on this song." It's one of those weird things and it happened simultaneously.'

Indeed, Aretha did a good job on one of the many cover versions that appeared. Paul liked her rendition: 'Aretha's version is tremendous, the best I've heard except Artie's.' It was said that, at the end of 1970, Paul had earned seven million dollars, just in royalties from the cover versions of this song.

Meanwhile, Art's acting career was flourishing. He had accepted a starring role in Mike Nichols's next film, *Carnal Knowledge*, and would begin filming in May. Paul was delighted for him, but had misgivings: 'Psychologically, I wasn't able to play second fiddle to the movie career. I felt that he was going to take a shot at becoming a movie star, and that if he succeeded, the records would be secondary. I don't know if he seriously thought of the consequences of his movie role as regards his career with me.'

Art has consistently denied that he gave up one career in favour of another. 'It was no more than a diversion for me, an opportunity that came along. To call it a change in career or a conscious new direction on my behalf is completely false and incorrect. I was simply offered a script and asked if I would read it and see if I could identify with the character. I read it, liked it and agreed to do it.' Mike Nichols also asked Art to select the music for the film.

But that was to start in May. Beforehand, there was the much-needed vacation. After the release of the album in February, Art went to Britain for a long break, taking Linda Grossman with him. She was now very much the woman in his life, and they retreated to a remote Scottish cottage for a couple of months.

Paul decided to study, relax, catch up with his reading and see old friends. His sudden decision to study again wasn't really that sudden. On finishing 'The Boxer', he'd discovered he had a writer's block. A friend of his, a musician, urged him to stop playing folk music all the time, using the same G to C chord. He added, as a challenge: 'You could be a really good musician, but you don't know enough, you don't have enough tools. Forget about having hits; go learn your ax.'

Paul did just that, taking lessons in classical guitar and advanced music theory. He widened his scope enormously with other kinds of music: Jamaican ska, gospel – and this he felt very comfortable with because it has a lot in common with rock 'n' roll, sounds he had grown up with. He was fired with energy and enthusiasm, with all the things he wanted to learn. 'It's very frustrating to me that if I want to write a horn part, I have to call in a guy and sing a horn part to him and he writes it down and goes outside to the men. I want to learn how to do it, and I want

to learn all the instruments and about all other kinds of music.'
No small task.

In April, 'Cecilia' was released as a single, with 'The Only Living Boy in New York' on the B side. It was a huge seller, number one for a week and selling a million copies by June, earning them another Gold Disc.

In the spring, Paul and Artie went back on the road for a short tour of Europe that included Moscow, Amsterdam and London. Paul told the press that, unlike other tours in which the travelling was monotonous, the atmosphere on this tour was relaxed: 'I would go with Peggy, and everyone would bring whoever they wanted, and it was more like festivals because we didn't go out too much. We went to places we wanted to play.'

At the end of April, they appeared before 6,500 people at London's Albert Hall, returning there after an absence of two years. In an *NME* review of the concert, Andy Gray wrote: 'They seemed to be so alone in such a vast hall and they seemed so friendly towards each other in that initial lonely fear.' After all, it wasn't for the first time.

They were dressed informally: Paul in a sleeveless pullover with a pink shirt and blue jeans; Art all in black, a sweater and trousers. They were appearing casually and unpretentiously.

The concert opened with 'The Boxer' and fervent applause broke out. Immediately they followed with 'Homeward Bound' and 'Fakin' It'. Other hits that night included 'The 59th Street Bridge Song', 'So Long, Frank Lloyd Wright', 'I Am a Rock' and 'Mrs Robinson'. Paul's parents had made the trip from America and were in the audience, so Paul included 'Dear Old Daddy' as a tribute to his father.

Art sang 'Bridge', accompanied by Larry Knechtel on piano, while Paul sat at the side of the stage, no doubt nursing those feelings of resentment, however involuntarily. Art told the audience that he'd been living on a remote Scottish farm for two months, where one photographer had doggedly tracked him down, asking him to pose on a hump-back bridge to illustrate the song. 'The idea was so funny, I nearly did it,' Art concluded.

The show ended with 'A Most Peculiar Man', followed by tumultuous applause. People stood and cheered, while Art and Paul joined in the clapping, acknowledging their gratitude for such a warm response. Applause continued after they left the stage, and they returned for their customary two encores, but no more, even though the audience continued to stand and applaud for another seven minutes. Tito Burns, the presenter, finally came on stage and said that the show was truly over.

Simon & Garfunkel made their final appearance as a duo back in their own home town, at Forest Hills Stadium. It was fitting; they'd travelled a full circle, back to the neighbourhood that had witnessed their first, tentative appearances at school functions. All in all, it had been a very good tour, fully sold out everywhere, rapturously received by audiences, appreciatively reviewed by critics. Nonetheless, Paul was having reservations about performing. 'It gets very hard singing "The Sound of Silence",' he told the press. 'This time we went out and sang mostly new songs, and people don't want to hear that. They want to hear the songs that you're famous for. I was talking to Dylan, and I said, "That's my problem with going on the road. It gets boring for me because of this." He said, "Well, I'd like to see you, and if I came to see you, I'd want to see you sing 'The Sound of Silence' and 'Scarborough Fair'."'

Paul himself admitted that, when he was in the audience recently at a Rolling Stones concert, he had wanted to see them do 'Satisfaction'. 'I think it's very hard to ever escape from that.'

Paul and Art had no particular plans to tour again in the near future, though they weren't ruling it out. 'It's possible. We could easily do it,' Paul said in May 1970. He confessed to the pull of a live audience, the thrill of performing. 'Probably I'll come to miss it. It's very emotional. On really good nights, I can get very emotional on stage – what's going on between the audience and us.' But he also talked about how he suffered before shows, despite having done somewhere between 330 and 400 concert performances with Artie, as well as solo work as a folk singer. 'We always come on late, because we're always saying – ten more minutes, have another cup of coffee, have a smoke and then go out.'

Paul also commented on their recording plans. 'Probably we will make another record. We've always waited a long time between records, so we don't feel compelled to put out another one in six months or a year from now.' Anyway, Paul had no more songs ready.

What they were both longing for was some way of channelling their creative energies – a way that was fresh and new. Paul said: 'I don't say that we will never perform again; there are several things that we want to do before we think about that.'

Art had found some fulfilment in making films. He had a witty, interesting script by cartoonist Jules Feiffer and was co-starring with Jack Nicholson and Candice Bergen in a film that traces the friendship of two men, Jonathan and Sandy, from college to middle class, middle age.

Art played Sandy, the idealistic and sensitive young man who marries the girl he loves (Candice Bergen) without knowing that she has been unfaithful to him with his best friend Jonathan (Jack Nicholson). He becomes a successful doctor, a respected member of the community, a loving father and a stable man. But something is missing.

As the years go by, he goes through a bewildering process of disillusionment. Finally, he arrives at some sad, bleak conclusions: that maybe sex isn't meant to be fun with a woman you love; that life is more than a series of games; that his wife, after all, didn't really love him; that even a best friend is capable of betrayal. Ultimately, though, he is more balanced and mature, certainly more content, than his friend. He faces up to life and finds he can cope with it, by taking love wherever he encounters it, and by being honest.

From the start of the film, we can see what Sandy wants from a relationship; he rejects Jonathan's sexism with 'I want more of a companion'. And this is eventually what he finds in Jennifer – a peace of mind that will always elude Jonathan, who is doomed to a soul-destroying and degrading tour of prostitutes. Art felt he could relate easily to the part. He was able to portray Sandy as a gauche, sexually inexperienced college student, desperately trying to impress a girl and keep up with his sophisticated friend. We're convinced by the role.

While Art was working on the film, Paul went on with his music study, pursuing it with characteristic intensity. He found it worthwhile. 'I improved my technique in that I learned more about harmony and orchestration, and now I find it easier. I can change keys when I want to, and I know more musical options than I did in the past. I don't just have to Travis pick in the key of G.'

Though they hardly realized it, they were drifting apart. In late spring 1970, while Art worked on *Carnal Knowledge*, Paul began teaching a once-weekly class in songwriting at the workshop of the New York University School of the Arts. He was, in a sense, following his family tradition; his mother was a teacher and his father, after years of being a musician, went into the profession he loved as a Professor of English. He was able to do this because it was no longer necessary to support the family – so difficult on a teacher's pay. Paul's brother Eddie also became a teacher of music.

Paul saw the role as one of guiding rather than instructing. 'You can't teach anyone how to write a song. But I am dealing with people who already write songs, so what I can do mainly is to tell them what I've learned.' The course was designed to be practical, much of the time being spent in a studio, cutting the songs the students had written.

Paul had very personal reasons for taking on this role. 'I like talking about songwriting. I like to hear what people are writing and I'd like to spare people some of the grief that I went through by learning by trial and error. Some of the errors can be very costly. I'd go on a course if the Beatles would talk about how they made records, because I'm sure I could learn something.'

In his own early days, he had wanted to talk to Dylan, to find out how he wrote a song. On their first meeting at Dylan's house, he had found everything in a mess, scraps of paper littering the floor. While Dylan was pacing up and down, talking and thinking aloud, Paul followed him, picking up every scrap of paper, anything with words on it, and stuffing them into his pockets. 'I wanted to know if he was doing it like I was doing it. But I couldn't find out what he did.'

One of his students in this small group was Melissa Manchester, a New Yorker from a musical family who had graduated from the High School of the Performing Arts in Manhattan. She went on to cut a debut album for Bell Records in 1973. She was eighteen when the course ran, her heart set on being a songwriter. 'It was one of the most remarkable experiences of my life. To have Paul Simon advise me on something so all-important was a gift beyond description.'

It's through Melissa's memories of the course that we can visualize Paul Simon as a teacher. It was 'a very loose situation'. Paul entered the room on the first day and said to them, 'Listen, I've never done this before, and I'm not sure I know how. But we'll keep at it until it ends itself.'

He got them to play their songs, sometimes the same piece over and over again, taking apart the lyrics and analysing them. He told them about the paranoia that's part of being a successful songwriter, and anecdotes from his early career.

Melissa described Paul as 'an explorer. A little sad, maybe, the way most artists are, but available for a laugh on life and the dumbness of an industry that sells art. I think he was one of the most decent, sincere human beings I ever met.'

She recalled how one student asked him, on the first day, 'Paul, how does one write a song?' And Paul simply said, 'Oh, what makes you want to write a song?'

Paul later assessed his teaching. 'I had a good time and so did everybody else, and that was the end of the class.' He didn't resume after the summer vacation because he had started work in the studio, sketching out an album of his own.

Chapter Twelve

SO LONG, SO LONG

In June 1970, *Catch-22* was released with very mixed reviews. Mostly, they concentrated on the direction and screenplay. As always with a brilliant novel, it was no easy task to convert it to the screen and please everyone. Much of Heller's sharpest irony lies in the narrative, anyway.

Paul went to see the film with Artie. '*Catch-22* was a big disappointment for me,' he told the press, 'but he was fine in the role.' By and large, the critics shared that view. Though it was Art's acting debut, and mainly a supporting role, he attracted a lot of attention and many favourable reviews.

Judith Crist wrote that Art's major scene with the Italian pimp 'is one of the unforgettable moments of *Catch-22*'. And Gary Arnold in the *Washington Post* wrote: 'He embodies a kind of youthful sweetness and idealism that the material desperately needs in the face of so many manic and inhuman characters.'

Time was passing and Paul and Art were pursuing different paths. There was no definite split between them. They had no plans to do another album, and it was really the absence of plans that marked the break-up.

Later, Paul described it as 'A combination of the *Bridge* album, *Catch-22*, *Carnal Knowledge* – just a lot of things that were going in different directions. We both had different interests.'

Well, obviously they were developing in individual ways, and drifting far apart creatively. They no longer had to work for money, and were less consumed with the desire to perform and make records. Art was very interested in films; Paul was engrossed in his musical studies. Paul was married to Peggy; Art was deeply involved in a relationship with Linda. It seemed natural to diverge for a while.

In any case, Paul had no clear idea which direction the duo should take now. After *Bridge*, where could Simon & Garfunkel go? They could put out an album from time to time, and they could do tours. Only 'That was over. I didn't want to go on tour. I didn't want to sing "Scarborough Fair" again. I didn't want to sing all of those Simon and Garfunkel songs every night.'

Besides, touring isn't the ideal life for two men who have recently settled down to a close relationship with a woman. They were leaving behind their twenties, getting ready for a more stable kind of existence. Tours are for people with no ties – or they're an occasional thing. Not a way of life.

And making albums? Well, the difficulty in doing that lay, ironically, in the very success of *Bridge*. Years later, Paul would describe the strange conflict it presented. 'Paradoxically, it was the end of Simon & Garfunkel, but it was our most intense success. As our relationship was disintegrating, the album was selling ten million copies.'

Well, how on earth do you follow an album like that? As Artie put it: 'You start looking for other planets to conquer. It's like you've transcended the globe. That's it for this globe, we've done it here, so where's the new territory? Where's the new game to play? Where are the new competitors?'

They had unknowingly set themselves a phenomenally high precedent. Inevitably that put enormous pressure on both of them, but impossible demands on Paul as the writer. 'I'm delighted that I didn't have to write a follow-up, which I think would have been an inevitable let-down for people. It would have been hard on both of us, but harder on the writer because he takes the responsibility. If an album stiffs, I think to myself it stiffed because I didn't come up with the big songs.'

One way of relieving that pressure was to start again as a solo artist. Then whatever he did wouldn't be compared unfavourably to the previous album – simply because there was no previous album.

Of course, it was no easy thing to announce to Columbia that there would be no more Simon & Garfunkel albums. How do you say, there will be no follow-up to a property that sold ten million copies?

Paul dreaded it, but he saw it as preferable to attempting to produce another *Bridge*. 'For me, it really saved my ass, because I don't think we could have followed it up. And it allowed me to just naturally drop down a couple of rungs on the ladder because there was less attention. I could go and learn what I had to learn again about writing and singing and making records. It was like stepping back into the shadows for a while. It was good; it gave me a chance to think.'

Columbia – of course – didn't see it that way. In his autobiography, president Clive Davis described his personal shock and disappointment at Paul's decision. That feeling was quite widespread among the executives.

Paul found their response 'terribly discouraging'. He realized that they regarded his decision as temporary, imagining that he'd soon get the notion out of his system and go back into the studio with Artie.

After so many years, it was painful not to be taken more seriously. When executives at Columbia continued to ask him about the next Simon & Garfunkel album, he became angry. He was, by now, intensely committed to doing a solo album. 'It was important to me. And they would want to know when I was going to put aside this little toy.'

In time, it became apparent just how determined he was. They realized he wouldn't give way. So then they began to ask him why he was doing it. What had gone wrong? This was also very frustrating for Paul. 'Everybody said, "Gee, I always liked Simon

& Garfunkel. Boy, that's too bad." It was too bad, but that was it. It was over.'

Clive Davis told Paul that, after all, Simon & Garfunkel were household names; that no matter how successful he became as a solo artist, he would never outdo his duo success. Paul responded angrily to Davis: 'Don't tell me that,' he said. 'How do you know what I'll do? I don't even know what I'm going to do in the next decade. It could be my greatest time of work. Maybe I'm finished, maybe I'm not going to do my thing until I'm fifty. People will say then, "Funny thing was, in his youth he sang in a group. He sang popular songs in the sixties. Fans of rock 'n' roll may remember the duo Simon & Garfunkel." That's how I figure it.'

Everyone was shocked when Simon & Garfunkel split up. It seemed to be the end of an era, the end of something fine and lasting. Art described how he felt: 'I was very disappointed at first, but then I too became part of the dismantling process. I felt disappointed because, when people came up to me in the street and said, "What, no more albums?", I knew exactly what they meant and how they felt. I could immediately see that they felt the loss of something that was very personal, something which had given them a lot of satisfaction.'

The loss wasn't just musical either. Their split was like the end of a dream, because the unity of the duo was shattered – and their unity had always seemed durable. As Art put it, 'Beyond the words of the songs, I felt that Simon & Garfunkel projected the hopefulness of an ongoing friendship as a sort of public message. I liked that about Simon & Garfunkel.'

One could endlessly analyse the reasons for their parting, but it would be ultimately fruitless. As Art said: 'It's the kind of thing I don't want to get into, really. Things work in a relationship and things don't work.' And when a relationship is very close, the parts that don't work hurt more and more.

One of the difficulties they'd always had to cope with was the unevenness of their creative contributions. It would be impossible to divide what each artist gave to an album, because there are too many factors to consider. Creativity is often born from the combining of talents, ideas and effort. Even Paul and Art would find it impossible to assess exact contributions.

Nevertheless, creatively there was a discrepancy because Paul wrote and performed, while Art only performed. At times, that presented problems for both of them. For Paul: 'Artie and I shared responsibility but not creativity.' In 1982 he added: 'Musically, it was hard to keep the balance because I wrote the music and he only sang it. It fell out of balance as a team; it was always falling out of balance. We were always trying to prop it up.'

But this situation was equally frustrating for Art. 'Looking back, I know, too, that I felt envious of Paul's writing and playing, especially on stage where I had nothing to do with my hands.' And in an ironical mood, he described his contribution in a characteristically mathematical way: 'Ninety-eight per cent to two, in favour of Paul. That would be more or less correct. Maybe I tuned the strings a little bit. Once, I put oil on the guitar.' Witty, certainly, but revealing some deep-rooted concerns.

Paul was aware of Art's dilemma. Later, Paul said: 'He felt, even more than I did, the frustration of having people ask, "Did you write the words or the music?" At least I could say, "I wrote both." Arthur had to say, "I wrote neither." And that's a drag if people keep asking you.'

Another factor was the difference in their musical tastes. This is unmistakable when we listen to their later solo albums, but it was detectable even then. Often, Paul and Artie had argued about how to do certain tracks. Of course, it's certainly true that, out of these disagreements, they were able to achieve the sound that made them great. All the same, it had become an emotional strain over the years.

Paul later said: 'I wouldn't say that my ideas were bigger than Simon & Garfunkel, but I would say that my ideas were different from Simon & Garfunkel. And I didn't want to go in that direction of a duo.'

Artie also realized this: 'On occasions, Paul's ideas were not the same as mine. OK, Paul might relent and do things my way, but I knew that, deep down, he felt, "The record is not exactly the way I want it to be."'

Perhaps the greatest factor of all, the most urgent, was that Paul wanted to do something on his own and of his own – something that reflected his own style. 'I always felt restricted as a singer,' he said. 'Partly because there always had to be harmony and it had to be sung in the same phrasing and then you had to double it. You couldn't get free and loose with your singing.'

Art didn't feel that: 'Quite honestly, I really don't know what Paul means by that. Did he feel he had other kinds of music that he wanted to do? 'Cause I didn't feel that we'd gone as far as we could. Personally, I would have gone on to make an album that was much better than *Bridge over Troubled Water*, simply because I don't think there was anything restrictive about our format. You can do virtually anything and everything within that format. I didn't feel that we had to fit into any set pattern.'

But it was evident that Paul felt he had to build up another, separate identity. Perhaps he missed the old solo days that had given him so much pleasure in the folk clubs in England. Perhaps he had just grown tired of being in a duo. He was, after all, in the enviable position of being financially secure and very famous. 'I knew I could never top the success of *Bridge*, so it's kind of a nice place to be. So you start again, but actually you have nothing to lose.' Clearly, he had everything to gain: the excitement of experimenting with the new sounds and skills he was acquiring, the thrill of being a solo artist again, the uncertainty about whether he would be accepted on his own terms. 'I had no idea where I wanted to go. It was a chance to back out and gamble a little bit; it's been a long time since it was a gamble.'

And so, finally, the partnership was easier to let go than to maintain. In separate interviews, Paul and Art described the situation during those last months in a strikingly similar way. Art's view was: 'We both felt that the amount of fun we got out of being Simon & Garfunkel was getting to the crucial point where it was not really worth the effort. Granted, it was terrifically exciting to have made the *Bridge over Troubled Water* album. Much of it was ecstatic, but there were also many difficulties.' And Paul said: 'During the making of *Bridge over Troubled Water*, there were lots of times when it just wasn't fun to work together.'

Surely, to a large extent, it was inevitable. As Art said: 'Relationships often wear themselves down over the years. Also, you come to want to be more specific about your taste. You want to express the thing that is uniquely you.' And he added, philosophically: 'I guess a certain amount of the juice that comes with any partnership is bound to dry up a little with time.'

They parted amicably. The partnership was over, but the friendship would always be there. They both gave strong indications that, though their careers had diverged, they shared happy memories of the duo days, which would hold them together as friends.

Paul still regarded Artie's singing with the same awe he'd felt when he first heard him sing in the school auditorium. 'To sing with Art Garfunkel is a very intimidating experience because his voice is a wonderful gift and I always considered that my job was just to surround it with some harmony and let it shine.'

Art recalled the 'highs in the control room. It was a thrill to make music.' When he looked back on his career with Paul, it was with much affection: 'I have such good feelings about all those songs and records we made together and the fact that, in my twenties, I was fortunate enough to make my living in such a nice way.'

In the late summer of 1970, Art and Paul were working on separate projects. Art was making *Carnal Knowledge* and Paul was working on a solo album. The break had been gradual until Paul settled the matter. As Paul later described it: 'We didn't say, that's the end. We didn't know if it was the end or not. But it became apparent by the time the movie was out and my album was out, that it was over.'

Chapter Thirteen

ON MY WAY

In his hit 'Me and Julio down by the Schoolyard', Paul would describe a character who is excitedly on his way, but not knowing where he's going. This describes that period in his life very well. He knew he was embarking on something quite new, something challenging. But he didn't know where it would lead. And that was the thrill.

Early in October 1970, he made a donation of $25,000 to set up a new scholarship fund at New York's City College. The fund was established by the Education School to provide $625 yearly to worthy students who were enrolled in the experimental pilot programme in teacher education. Over half the students in the programme were black and Puerto Rican.

On 10 October, the *New York Times* reported the names of the ten students chosen for the current academic year. They also revealed the name of the scholarship. Named in honour of its benefactor though not directly after Paul himself, it was known as the Mrs Robinson Scholarship.

For the next few months, Paul and Artie went on working – each pursuing a separate career. They were entwined again momentarily when, in March 1971, *Bridge over Troubled Water* won a clutch of Grammy Awards. The title song was Best Song of the Year, Best Arrangement Accompanying Vocalists and Best Record of the Year. The album won the award for Best Album of the Year. At the Grammy Ceremony on 17 March, Paul requested that Aretha Franklin sing the song.

In a sense, it was an ironic victory. The world's best loved and most successful duo arrived to receive an unprecedented number of the industry's highest awards, while everyone was painfully aware that there would probably be no more albums from them. Simon & Garfunkel were now just a memory, a piece of history.

Carnal Knowledge was released in 1971 and the critics were heated in their reactions. It was a controversial script, after all, so it was inevitable that critics and audiences would disagree. Some would appreciate the hard-hitting cynicism of it, some would find it offensive. Some would regard it as a satire on greed and sexism, and others would see it as a celebration of those things.

However, Art's performance won praise. In the *Scotsman*, Allen Wright commented: 'Arthur Garfunkel gives a very sensitive performance as his [Jonathan's] shy companion, seeking some tenderness in his relationship with women.' And *Time* wrote: 'Folk singer Arthur Garfunkel has become an authentic screen presence, one of the few American actors who can portray naïvité.'

After the release of the film, Art retired into an isolated existence, becoming almost reclusive with his music and Linda. He was looking for a positive direction in his life. 'It was a hard time for me,' he said later. 'I didn't understand why certain things weren't working. I immediately found that there's a tremendous value in verbalizing the issue. There are things I was in conflict over for years. But when I had to state the bottom line, I suddenly understood.'

Paul's lifestyle was also undergoing changes. Having given up dope a year earlier, he now gave up cigarettes. He found it improved his singing. His range went up and he could phrase and sustain a note with more ease.

In another of those striking parallels, Paul was also verbalizing the issues. He still went to analysis, the same analyst who saw Elliot Gould, but he had cut down his visits from four to three times a week. 'It was helpful,' he commented later, 'but it doesn't cure you. I'm verbal, given to introspection, so it's natural for me to lie down and talk about things.'

He moved cautiously into his solo album. He knew he wanted to do it, but 'I procrastinated because I had to initiate it myself. I was lazy and a little insecure about doing something on my own.' He felt he now wrote better songs than in the Simon & Garfunkel days, and he was determined to do an album that reflected this. Most of the people around him were doubtful, but ultimately Paul held on to his own belief in himself. The doubters would realize he was right when the new album came out – 'That was my fantasy.'

At first he found it strange to be working without his partner. But there were compensations. 'You have the disadvantage of not having someone's ideas which are very bright and creative, and then you have the advantage of never having any conflicts, so that whatever you want to do, you can go ahead and do it.'

Until now, he had relied a lot on Artie. He'd also relied on Roy Halee to a great extent. 'I just suspended my judgement. I let him do it. On my own album, I learned that every aspect has to be your own judgement. You have to say, "Now, wait a minute. Is that the right tempo? Is that the right take?" It's your decision. Nobody else can do it.'

One thing Paul found easier was singing alone. Phrasing was far easier now. In the S & G songs: 'If you found yourself in a tricky phrasing thing, you had to remember when singing one voice of two, that somebody's got to follow. Therefore, things had to be simplified as far as phrasing went. Otherwise, it was like riding a bronco.'

He was able to work at his own pace. It was like being reborn, so he savoured it. The album took a leisurely ten months to complete. 'I'd record for a while, then I'd stop. I'd stop and start.'

Shrewdly, he surrounded himself with gifted and experienced people to work with him and, even more shrewdly, he listened to them. 'There are still plenty of people around for me to bounce ideas off,' he told the press. He gathered some of the world's finest musicians, different ones for each track, all playing in their own distinctive styles. Therefore each song had a very different sound from the last. This would become a trademark in later albums, a marvellous eclectic quality.

Paul spared no expense to achieve this. 'I'd write a song and think, "Wouldn't it be great if so-and-so would play on this?" I'd really just fantasize. Like saying, "Wouldn't it be great if Eric Clapton would take a solo here?" If I'd been comfortable enough to do it, I would have called Clapton. But I wasn't. I don't know him.'

Even without Eric Clapton, the musicians on the album were an impressive crowd. Paul gathered guitarists Stefan Grossman and Jerry Hahn, violinist Stephane Grappelli, pianist Larry Knechtel and Los Incas, the South American group who had played the musical track of 'If I Could'. Thus the album became a cosmopolitan collection of jazz, reggae, blues and rock. There was an international flavour throughout, and no wonder, because it was recorded in studios in New York, Los Angeles, Paris and Kingston.

Paul took great pleasure in using music from different cultures, just as he had enjoyed learning about it. He saw no reason why, as a white New York musician, he shouldn't experiment with blues, light jazz or reggae. 'I know it's not mine, but then you know, what's mine? Anything's up for grabs. I don't believe in all this stuff – hey, that's black music and only so-and-so can do this, and you can't sing rock.' These comments are interesting when considered with the benefit of hindsight. Paul would confirm them in later years with the enormous success of *Graceland* and *Rhythm of the Saints*.

He learned all about Brazilian music when he went with Peggy to judge at the Brazilian Song Festival. He started buying records there and took them home with him to study. He also went to Paris, where Los Incas were based, to do a session with them. 'Their version of "El Condor Pasa" had a real magic for me. I have a lot of affection for that tune.' Hence there is a South American flavour on the album, in the song that became 'Duncan'.

'The amazing thing is that this country is so provincial,' he told Jon Landau. 'Americans know American music, but Americans never get into South American music. I fell into Los Incas. I loved it. It's got nothing to do with our music, but I liked it anyway.'

And he liked reggae: Jimmy Cliff, Desmond Dekker, Byron Lee. He sent to England for the Chartbuster albums that weren't available in the USA. 'I like them. I get off on it. So I say to myself, I love it so much, I'm going to Kingston, Jamaica.' He spent a long time in Kingston, working on the song that would become 'Mother and Child Reunion'. He wanted to get an authentic sound, remembering how dissatisfied he'd been with 'Why Don't You Write Me?'.

'So I said, "I'm not going to get it out of the regular guys. I've got to get it out of the guys who know it. And I've got to go down there, willing to change for them."' This was no reflection on New York session musicians. He was working on the principle that specialization is the basis of true craftsmanship. 'Certain musicians will be perfect for certain things. But they could still be fine musicians and not be able to play something else. I mean, I can sing a certain kind of song very well, but if you booked me to sing "In the Midnight Hour", I wouldn't be the right guy.'

So he went to Jamaica, willing to change. And sure enough, he found he had to change. When he started playing with them – at this stage just music, no words – to show them how the song should go, he found he couldn't fit in with their musical sound. He played the track again, just rhythm guitar, then wrote down the chords so that they could learn it. 'So I sat down and said, "You play it. Play what you want." That's the key thing. Let them play whatever they want and then you change. You go their way. That's how you get that.'

He learned a lot from them. They told him the difference between the various kinds of Jamaican music. 'There's a difference in rhythm. But they said ska's old; they're always doing reggae.

So I said, "Well, what's the difference between reggae and ska? I thought it was the same thing." So they started to play: this is reggae; this is ska; this is bluebeat. Each has a different style.'

Paul built up a rapport with the Jamaican musicians. At first, he felt slightly awkward because he was the only white person there, and an American, famous and wealthy. He feared they might resent him.

Also, he hit a practical problem: they had a system of being paid for each song, not by the hour like American session musicians. With Paul's slow, craftsmanlike approach, they were losing out financially. He would work on one song for several days. After two days on the same track, he realized that paying them ten dollars a song wasn't fair. He said to them: 'Look, just assume I'm doing three tunes a day, okay? So I'll pay you like three tunes a day.' It worked.

Paul returned to New York, aware that he was leaving new friends behind, and with the sound he wanted. He now had the completed musical track for 'Mother and Child Reunion', with no words. These, as well as the voices and background, would be added later. For now, he was very pleased.

He'd read and heard a bit about Stefan Grossman. Curious to meet him, he made up his mind to write a song that would include some bottleneck guitar. He contacted Grossman in Europe and asked him to come over. 'I played him a song or two. We fooled around a bit and eventually settled on the song he'd play on. It was a bitch. He really played fine. He's a very fine musician.'

Rumours floated around in the press that Grossman might be Artie's replacement. Paul categorically denied them. 'I never contemplated becoming an act with Stefan Grossman. I was strictly interested in his talent as a guitarist.'

The months passed and Paul worked hard on the album. He soon developed a reputation for being very meticulous, striving constantly for nothing less than perfection. Duck Dunn, the bass player from Stax, played bass guitar on some of the sessions in Columbia's new San Francisco studios. They were working on a song that was never actually finished: Duck, Jim Keltner on drums and Paul on guitar.

In interview, Duck said that Paul would lay down a take which everyone would like, but he'd insist on redoing it over and over until he was satisfied he'd succeeded in capturing the mood he wanted. In a separate interview, when he was reminded of this, Paul smiled. 'I was looking for something,' he explained. 'But I wasn't quite sure what I was looking for. They're both really fine musicians and I probably drove them crazy. I didn't really say anything. I kind of wanted to see what would come and it didn't upset me in the least, because I was used to working that way. I had plenty of time and I was just sort of formulating my ideas.'

Paul also explained how the final songs all took some time to evolve. While he was working with Duck, the sound they came up with just didn't make it as far as he was concerned. 'It's not so much that I'm meticulous about these things. It's just that I'm waiting for something to happen. It can happen one way and I just don't want to do it that way, because that's not the way I hear the song.'

Duck also said that Paul doesn't really need any other musicians for back-up, only his own guitar. This opinion is held by many a veteran Paul Simon fan. Paul's own comment was simply: 'That's a very nice thing for him to say.'

In August 1971, Paul did a solo performance at Shea Stadium in New York, not a particularly lucky place for him. His last concert there had been by his own estimation, a failure. And this time was no better.

He opened with 'Me and Julio down by the Schoolyard', one of his new songs. The crowd was restless and noisy. He persevered with 'Congratulations', another new song. Several times he appealed to the crowd for silence, without success. After a few more attempts at songs, he stopped in the middle of 'Scarborough Fair' and angrily left the stage.

In December '71, Paul came on a short visit to London, bringing with him the acetates for his new album. He had come on business to buy back Pattern Music, his publishing company in England, from Granada, which had taken over Lorna Music.

When Pattern was formed, named after Paul's song, it came under the umbrella of Lorna Music. Now that Lorna had been bought out, it meant that the publishing rights of Paul's complete catalogue in England, from his first songs right up to 'Bridge', belonged to Granada. They agreed to sell the songs back to him. 'There's nothing wrong,' he said. 'Just that they're my songs and I have a personal attachment for them.'

While in London, en route for Paris, he stayed at the Grosvenor House Hotel and gave some interviews. In such opulent and stately surroundings, he saw a party of people that included Columbia Records executive Clive Davis, singer-songwriter Nilsson, and producer Richard Perry.

He was asked repeatedly about his present relationship with Art Garfunkel. In response, he made an official statement: 'Simon & Garfunkel are no longer a working relationship.' He told Lon Goddard: 'There was never any legal binding between us. We were free to do exactly what we wanted.' Asked about plans to work together again, he said: 'We may well do it. I don't think Artie wants a full time career in acting. I think he'll take parts that come along if they're good, but he'll keep on singing.' He stressed that there was no bad feeling between them. 'We're still friends.' He told reporters that they had had dinner together only a week earlier, and that he'd been to see both *Catch-22* and *Carnal Knowledge* with Artie.

Paul also talked about performing live again, but with some misgivings. 'I'm thinking of starting again. I don't think I could just get up and do one now. I'd have to work on it awhile. But I think I'll go back on the road again.' There were problems. He definitely didn't want to return to the stage simply to perform all the old S & G numbers. That sense of staleness had, after all, been one of the reasons for the split. 'It's almost like instant nostalgia. Entertainers get to a certain stage and it almost becomes necessary for them to become caricatures of themselves. The audience demands that they be what they loved in the past.' Years later, Paul would reiterate this fear in 'You Can Call Me Al', using the same kind of metaphor, ending up as a cartoon in a graveyard of cartoons.

Would he ever, he was asked, perform on his own, as Paul Simon? 'Certainly I'll do something solo,' he told the press. 'But I wouldn't rule out that I'd go and sing with Artie again. There's really no animosity there.'

Repeatedly, during those interviews, Paul was asked if he would ever team up with another singer or musician. He stressed that would never happen. 'I didn't feel I needed to work with a replacement; I just wanted to do something myself. I suppose we both did.' He told Roy Carr: 'As I stand right now, I have no partnership with Artie. He's my friend, but I don't have a partner.'

Clearly, there was still a strong bond between them. When asked if there was any particular performer he wanted to write songs for now, Paul replied without hesitation that he'd like to write for Artie, if he could succeed in rousing him from his country home in Connecticut. 'He could make a good album,' he said, adding loyally: 'He needn't if he didn't want to. He hasn't got anything to prove to anybody. All I know is that Artie likes to sing and record.'

Meanwhile, in December '71, while Paul was in London, Art rented a villa in Yugoslavia for the next two months. He was going to learn the harpsichord, having discovered a passion for the music of Bach. After that, he wanted to travel. He had been taking a rest from being in the limelight, from show business itself. It was a chance to stand back and assess his position and his options. Also, he had returned for a while to another great passion in his life, and had spent much of 1971 teaching mathematics in a private school in Connecticut. He had enjoyed it greatly, but now the other side of his personality was needing attention. He wanted to sing for a while. Perhaps now it was almost time to step back into the studio once again.

Chapter Fourteen

SOLO ALBUM

In February 1972, the solo album *Paul Simon* was released. The title itself established the performer's single identity, and the cover made a similar statement – pictures of Paul alone.

The album opens with 'Mother and Child Reunion', a rousing and energetic track, which later became a very successful single. The title was inspired by a meal in one of New York's downtown Chinese restaurants: a dish of fried chicken and boiled eggs. Paul made up his mind that this title was too good to waste.

But the song has more serious overtones. The summer before, Paul's dog was run over and killed. His sense of loss was keen. He thought about Peggy and the rest of his family, and how he'd feel if they died. And the words came to him. Somehow, in his mind, there was a connection between the dog's death and Peggy. 'Some emotional connection. It didn't matter to me what it was. I just knew it was there.'

But the song confused some critics. As Paul explained to the *New Yorker*: 'It has nothing to do with my mother. What I'm talking about here is the unbelievable, shattering experience of encountering death.' It seems incongruous to combine such profoundly painful words with a Jamaican syncopated beat, but it's something Paul does very often, and effectively. It creates, by the very conflict of style and content, an irony.

The second track, 'Duncan', is, as Paul said, 'a ballad about a young boy, growing up and discovering sex'. It's a narrative ballad, like 'The Boxer', treating the boy's transition into manhood honestly, one might say cynically. The balance is maintained between poignancy and irony. His sexual encounter in the woods with the religious girl who befriends him is furtive and spontaneous, also touchingly innocent. He evokes Eden in the memory of it: the garden of delight is literally a translation of Eden.

Los Incas accompanied Paul on the track, and the purity of their sound heightens our sense of Duncan's youth. Their main instrument is the charango, a double-stringed mandolin made out of an armadillo shell. They recorded the track in only one studio session, and Paul wrote the words a few weeks afterwards. It seems amazing that this lyric, which flows very naturally, should have been fitted to an existing melody.

'Everything Put Together Falls Apart' is, Paul says, 'a simple, self-evident statement'. It's a bleak, desolate comment on life, offering a warning about drugs, and presenting a starkly realistic and unsentimental picture of overdosing. It's horrifying and accurate, shown through the eyes of the people who deal with it clinically. The song's effectiveness lies in its understatement. The ultimate message is low key. The narrator resigns himself to coping with life, walking that borderline between sanity and its opposites. Jon Landau has suggested that the song embodies the theme of the album. I would add that, as it appears on the first solo album, we inevitably think of the partnership that had recently fallen apart.

It's fitting that 'Run That Body Down' follows, as it's a piece of advice to look after your health, first given to Paul by his doctor, then passed on to Peggy, then offered to young people in general. Although it has serious implications, it is essentially light-hearted. Paul deliberately avoided 'a preachy song' because he felt it would sound too much like a Nichols and May routine. '"My God, your mother and I are sick with worry." You can't do it in a song.' He was thinking about health a lot, having recently given up dope and cigarettes. He was also reading Adelle Davis, and liked the idea of writing a song about health.

The track features a solo by guitarist Jerry Hahn. What's also interesting musically is the compelling, almost metronome beat which dominates the song. The melody derived from a Bach prelude Paul was playing at the time.

Side one closes with 'Armistice Day', which Paul had begun in 1968 in a D tuning he no longer used. He considered it to be the weakest song on the album. It refers to no particular war; in fact he chose the title because Veterans' Day has replaced it in common use. He told Jon Landau about the theme of the song: 'Let's have a truce. I just meant that I'm worn out from all this fighting, from all the abuse that people are giving each other and creating for each other.' And in the *New Yorker*, he insisted: 'Armistice Day is not a protest song. Protest songs are a little trite at the moment.' The song ends on a negative point: the narrator desperate to see his Congressman, but being put off.

'Me and Julio down by the Schoolyard' opens the second side, and again, it's a song with a lively, syncopated beat. And again, there are serious implications in the lyric. The whole narrative is told by the boy – and Paul captures the rhythm of his speech in a wonderfully realistic way. The story is confused, but packed with details: even Corona, an area in Queens, gets a mention.

Fascinatingly, the song says more about second- and third-generation immigrant youths than many a sociological study, because it's convincing and vivid. The boy brags about his sudden notoriety but we feel he is somehow doomed. Even the title has a childlike, grammatically incorrect structure, something that appealed to Paul. 'I think it's funny, to sing me and Julio. And when I started to sing me and Julio, I started to laugh.'

Everyone wondered what the two boys were actually doing, to cause the stir. Paul admitted that he didn't really know. 'Something sexual is what I imagine, but I never bothered to figure out what it was. Didn't make any difference to me.' He was amused by a magazine which quoted Truman Capote, author of the famous *Breakfast at Tiffany's*, as saying that he thought the song was about homosexuality. 'I can understand how people would read that into it,' Paul admitted. 'But as a matter of fact, it is not about a homosexual encounter.' Actually, the prank itself isn't important.

'Peace like a River' follows, what Paul called a 'serious song, although it's not as down as you think.' It's about turbulence and unrest, but also idealism. The middle section of the song has a surrealistic feel, partly created by a sound effect that's not really audible on the track. Paul explained that it was achieved by hitting the bottom notes of the piano with his hand, playing it at half speed, backwards, and taking out the middle part. It produces a low-level rumbling noise, which is effective although not obvious. 'It's a dark colour. It creates tension.'

The song ends on a deliberate anti-climax, as the narrator wakes at four in the morning (the way so many Paul Simon narrators do), troubled and unable to go back to sleep. The political theme of the song then becomes acutely personal, narrowed down to one person and a dilemma. Paul returned to this negative kind of ending again and again.

'Papa Hobo' combines a relaxed melody with a lyric that depicts the ugliness of the big city, in terms that are ugly: carbon monoxide, evocatively described as perfume. The boy grows up there, longs to escape in search of adventure. He has a lot in common with Duncan.

The city itself is important here. Paul describes it sardonically as a 'basketball town', a put-down line which he explained: 'It's got a little bit of bitterness, but in its own way, an element of humour.' He uses the city landscape to underline an ironic situation; he is writing about Detroit, the car capital of the country, and: 'What I'm really talking about there is the fact that cars give us our freedom at the same time that they're killing us with carbon monoxide.'

'Hobo Blues', a short instrumental piece, is a collaboration with the great violinist Stephane Grappelli. Coming where it does on the album, it leads us from Detroit to the New York City of 'Paranoia Blues'. This is a disturbing song, another of Paul's street songs, portraying the violence and hostility of modern life. It was written from his own experience: 'Every time I fly into JFK from Europe, they take me into this little room, lean me up against a wall and search me for drugs, presumably because I have long hair and I'm carrying a guitar. The first time it happened, I was scared stiff.'

He captures fear in the song: being stabbed in the street, but also metaphorically stabbed by his 'friends'. The seriousness of it is undercut by a wry humour: even his Chinese meal is stolen when he glances away. But the worrying part of the song is the hard repetition of the dominant question, which builds up, more and more urgently – the question of whose side we're on.

The album closes with 'Congratulations', a sardonic reversal of our expectation of the word, for it's about the break-up of marriages. Paul backs a desolate, painful lyric with a slow, wandering melody. The crucial question ends the song – can a man and woman really live in peace together ?

There were some critics who didn't like the album, and some who completely let rip in their criticism, saying it was hostile, depressing, unbearably pessimistic, bleak, unforgiving – and the adjectives went on. But others saw it as a totally new concept, a new Paul Simon, more liberated, more imaginative and more versatile than before. Paul even won the praise of a few critics who had never liked his work within the duo; they now felt his writing was more direct and less pretentious.

Paul Simon was released soon after John Lennon's *Plastic Ono Band*, so it was compared to it by some critics. But Jon Landau, in his *Rolling Stone* review, saw them as contrasts, since Paul's album was less obviously and crudely confessional. 'Simon's music,' he wrote, 'rather than abounding in blatant and obvious attempts at expressing the soul, serves as a continually ironic counterpoint to the emotions, ideas, images and feelings expressed by the lyrics.' Landau also paid tribute to Paul's work, assessing the album as his 'least detached, most personal and painful piece of work thus far. This from a lyricist who has never shied away from pain as a subject or theme.'

It was only natural that Paul should have a few misgivings about the album. Only two months before its release, he said: 'It's inevitable that people have got to compare it to when I sang with Artie. It doesn't matter. It's their prerogative as an audience to stand up and boo when they don't like it, and scream when they love it. People love to criticize. Take away people's right of criticism and you'll take a lot of joy out of the world. People love to speculate. That's all right. That's fine.'

While musically and lyrically Paul's compositions had always been a reflection of him, the final product of the album had always been a mixture of himself and Artie. That was, after all, what created the unique Simon & Garfunkel sound. Paul now felt that the solo album was closer to his own personality. 'The vocal style is looser and more characteristic of me.' He compared the album to *Bridge*, realistically and honestly: 'I can't follow that, I know. And I don't want to have to follow it. We didn't think it was going to be the biggest seller ever. You don't. And I'm not even thinking of my new LP in terms of commercial success. I just hope that artistically, people will say, "Oh, he's still writing interesting songs." I hope I won't get a feeling of disappointment and failure, simply because I don't match *Bridge*. For inevitably, whatever I do is going to be compared against it. Personally, I feel I'm writing better now, but that doesn't mean I'll sell more. I'm sure I won't.'

And he didn't. Nevertheless, many critics did remark on his writing, that it was more interesting, less commercially pleasing but more profound. Also, he'd been much more ambitious musically. But the pervading mood of despondency and introversion didn't have the same commercial appeal that the S & G albums had always had. The sales of *Paul Simon* were about a million, wonderful for most artists. For example, it outsold all of the Rolling Stones albums except *Sticky Fingers*. It was five weeks at number 1 in the British charts and also did well in the States. It was awarded a Gold Disc.

All the same, even if Paul's 'failure' did equal or top the

success of other artists, he was disappointed. He found the lower sales 'unsettling'. He had prepared himself for it, perhaps for even worse. 'At first I said, "Look, when it breaks up, you're going to have to start all over again. It may take you a couple of albums before people will even listen." But actually, emotionally, I was ready to be welcomed into the public's arms as I had been in the past.'

The lasting significance of his album is that it opened up new areas of expression in rock music. It set a precedent because it was an exploration of desolation and confusion, presenting stark emotions and analysing them with relentless, penetrating honesty. It wasn't the sort of album you'd escape into, dance to, or enjoy on any casual, superficial level. Until now, the emphasis of pop music had been to entertain, not to analyse or explore.

Landau's review asked how much patience audiences would have with such an album, which took such risks. He concluded that the album and the response to it would be a test of the audience as well as the artist. 'For by any objective criteria, this artist has done his work: to reveal the truth.'

Paul took a breathing space after the album, while he thought what to do next. He was in a unique, enviable position. 'I never felt trapped by my own success,' he said. 'I always knew that I could stop performing. It's just that you're trying to find something interesting and something that engages you, and which, in turn, gives you a feeling of purpose. The more successful you get, the less feeling of purpose you have.'

He had found more success at thirty than most people find in a lifetime. He had fulfilled his early ambition to be a millionaire, but he was also an acclaimed songwriter and performer. Now he had a different kind of problem: the need for a new goal, something to rekindle his energy. He was, after all, a person who thrived on challenge. 'Well, I suppose you're always happy struggling,' he mused. 'You're working hard at something you feel that you're going to succeed at. Everyone is encouraging you and wishing you well. Once you succeed, then people quite rightly feel that they have the right to judge what you did because you're holding yourself out as an artist.'

To some extent, the solo album had provided him with a fresh incentive, letting him start again. As a solo artist, he was striving to meet his own standards, which were always high, irrespective of what other people thought. 'What I feel is that you generate your own pressures and your own standards,' he said. 'I have my own standards for when I think I've done something well.'

He had a busy schedule for the next few months. He wanted to produce an album for his friends, Los Incas. And he thought about going on tour, perhaps accompanied by Los Incas and Stephane Grappelli, though he hadn't ironed out the difficulties yet. The main problem was that when he tried to write a list of songs, he felt he couldn't stretch it to an entire show. He was reluctant to sing the S & G standards without Artie there to harmonize. Then there was 'Bridge': he couldn't really leave it out of a programme, yet he felt sure he couldn't sing it. 'I would feel extremely anxious about it because I don't have the same vocal instrument Artie has, and it's a song so associated with his rendition,' he said. Of course, he did perform it, but that was much later.

Meanwhile things seemed to be falling into place for him personally. He and Peggy divided their time between a farm in Bucks County, Pennsylvania and a brownstone triplex apartment on New York's Upper East Side, once the home of guitarist Andre Segovia. And they were expecting their first baby in September. In those early months of 1972, Paul was thrilled. He was giving a lot of thought to it. 'When you have a child, that's the main part of your life. It requires constant attention.' He started reading books about babies. He was getting ready for a new and exciting phase in his life.

Chapter Fifteen

GREATEST HITS

The early months of 1972, which brought Paul happiness, brought for Artie a period of painful but crucial evaluation. He had travelled abroad, he had studied classical music. 'After a year of doing only that, I started to suspect that what I was really doing was just plain hiding out.' He decided it was time to go back to singing. 'If you build up the kind of thing that Paul and I had, it's really kind of perverse to completely turn your back on it.'

The obvious course was a solo album, something he had been considering for the past year. In April he booked some time at San Francisco's Columbia Studios. He didn't feel particularly nervous. 'I have my talents and I can do quite a lot on my own,' he said. As soon as he stepped back into the familiar studio environment, he realized how much he had missed it. 'I like to make music. I have some experience doing it. I felt it behooved me to relate to all of this. I had to put it all together and try an album.'

His first task was to find some material. He didn't approach Paul for any. 'I didn't think there were any free-floating Paul Simon songs that were available.' There were a few writers whose work he had always liked, one of them being Randy Newman. 'Actually,' he said later, 'that part of the project wasn't at all difficult. Once I'd cut the first four tracks, I really knew the kind of material I needed to round it off.'

One person Art did approach was Jimmy Webb, the phenomenally successful songwriter whose career began in his early twenties with such well-loved classics as 'MacArthur Park', 'Gal-veston', 'Witchita Lineman', 'Didn't We' – songs that established him as one of the age's greatest songwriters. His other activities have been equally fruitful: composing scores, writing, arranging and producing entire albums for Richard Harris and the Fifth Dimension. He has worked on albums with Glen Campbell and other major artists. He won many Grammy Awards for 'Up Up and Away' and 'By the Time I Get to Phoenix'.

Clearly, Jimmy Webb was an excellent choice for Artie's first solo album. Jimmy recalled: 'Artie called me and said he was looking for material. I went up to San Francisco and played him everything I'd written, and some I hadn't. The Beach Boys and Baptist hymns. I played him "All I Know", and he turned to his engineer and said, "Well, Roy, do you think I could make a hit out of that?"'

As it turned out, the song was a hit. And it was the beginning of a fruitful collaboration and a good friendship. It was a very gradual process. Jimmy recalled: 'It wasn't instantaneous. Artie isn't one to do anything without a lot of thought.'

The same amount of thought went into the sounds he wanted. Reverting to his tried and true method of the portable tape recorder, he went to San Francisco docks to record the sound of an ocean liner. He'd arranged for the harbour-master to let him know when a big liner would be in the area. On the day, he went out in a tugboat, accompanied by Linda, and while the engine was kept quiet, he captured on his stereo recorder the sound of the captain blowing his whistle. It was a sound that thrilled Art. It eventually ended up on the album in 'Feuilles-oh'.

He discovered another interesting sound during a visit to Paul's apartment in New York City. Paul was playing some of his songs that he'd been working on, and his dog Carolina was panting on the couch, only inches away from Linda's ear. After the song, Linda remarked that the dog had been panting in rhythm. Art mentally clocked up the idea as one he could use later; it ended up on 'I Shall Sing'. 'There's a lot of things all over the album,' he said later. 'Didn't Orson Welles say that a child's best toy is a movie studio? That's what it's like.'

The beginning of recording was the hardest, as beginnings often are. He found himself in the studio with no budget restrictions, no time limit, and every kind of technical facility and expertise at his disposal. It was an enviable situation, of course. 'But where do you begin? The possibilities are enormous, but you get blinded by them. So initially you try to restrain yourself in order to find a suitable groove. And I can tell you, I went through a painful first month and a half.'

One problem was actually getting into the routine of work. Art found himself deliberately stretching out lunch breaks, simply because he dreaded going back to work. Those first weeks had no direction, and as he put himself through the motions of recording, he had no clear idea of where it was all leading. It was mechanical, 'like working all day in a factory'. He began to wonder if the joy would ever come back.

He persevered. And in time, it all fell into place for him. 'The gears started to mesh and I soon found myself going through the same familiar process as the albums with Paul.' Once on the crest of this feeling, Art worked slavishly. He was in the studio five days a week, all day long. He took only a rare week off. He had found the suitable groove.

In June '72, Columbia released a Simon & Garfunkel *Greatest Hits* in the USA, and in Britain a month later. It was a huge success, perhaps partly because it seemed to be the last chance to have the duo on record. But also, it gave a generous number of songs. In the USA, it was the number 1 chartbuster for a week, remaining in the charts for 131 weeks (over two and a half years). In Britain, its success was quite phenomenal: number 1 for ten weeks, remaining for 179 weeks in the charts (and that's three and a half years). This was the longest time any album had been in the charts.

Greatest Hits was awarded a Gold Disc as early as 6 July 1972. This was the duo's seventh Gold Disc; Simon & Garfunkel

were the only artists to have earned one for every album they had
released. The cover shows them standing together, smiling into
the camera, dressed in summer clothing. On the back, they sit in
front of the East River – another reminder of their New York
origin. It seemed appropriate that, while they were involved deeply
in their separate musical projects, they were reunited here on an
album to celebrate their incredible success.

For one concert appearance in June Paul and Art were truly
reunited. This was the McGovern for President Rally at Madison
Square Garden in New York. Organized by Warren Beatty, it was
an impressive show, reuniting other acts of the sixties: Peter, Paul
and Mary and also Nichols and May. Artie confessed that he
didn't feel particularly committed to the political cause. 'I do
believe in the lesser of two evils,' he said, 'and in that spirit, I
became a McGovern supporter.' But the show itself enticed him
on to the stage. 'It appealed to my showmanship. I loved the idea
of those three acts. I thought it would be a terrific show.'

Art and Paul were glad to see each other. It was the first time
they had sung together on stage since the farewell concerts two
years earlier. Art felt that in some way, he was retracing the past.
'It was a strange non-experience. We had ostensibly broken up,
and here we were doing this thing together. And I did think
beforehand that it would be a kick, some kind of novel experience.
And yet, after about three bars into the first song, I had a very
strong feeling – well, here we are again. This is where I left off.'

To the surprise of everyone, Paul sang the final verse of
'Bridge' with Art, something he had never done before. Inevitably,
the press latched on to it and asked Art about it. He told them it
was Paul's idea, something he wanted to try. 'I don't know what
you want me to say,' he concluded. When they asked him if he
and Paul enjoyed being together again, he replied without flinching: 'Yes. We're anxious to see each other when we see each
other.'

The concert was a great success, though you could say the
campaign wasn't. In November, only months after the benefit,

Richard Nixon was elected President of the United States by a huge majority. At that point, no one could know the world-shattering scandal which would follow his appointment. Even though Watergate was still firmly lodged in the future, some Americans had misgivings. Paul was one of them. He told *Rolling Stone* how he reacted to the Nixon victory. 'I remember putting on the TV set in the morning and I saw he was coming down to make his acceptance speech. Tears started rolling down my eyes. I didn't know what was going to happen in the next four years.'

Closer to home, in September '72, Peggy gave birth to a baby boy, named Harper James (Harper being her maiden name). Paul became immediately occupied with his son, spending as much time as possible with him. He alternated between his two homes on the East Coast, the New York apartment and the farm in Pennsylvania. He was very much a family man now.

Meanwhile, Artie was deeply involved in the album he was making on the West Coast. In October, however, the duo was reunited socially for the wedding of Art and Linda Grossman.

In the autumn of '72, Paul had planned to go on tour. But he caught flu and couldn't sing. Then an accident which damaged a bone in his left index finger prevented him from playing the guitar. It didn't heal quickly. Paul started having cortisone injections to numb the finger for a day or two at a stretch, because it was too painful for him to play.

Work carried on to the end of '72. Then in March 1973, Artie returned to acting; he appeared in the television play *Acts of Love* in which he played the unfaithful boyfriend of Marlo Thomas. Still, he worked on his album. And enjoyed his new marriage.

The new year of 1973 would bring new directions for both men; it would bring solo albums and performances. It would enable them to move further and further away from the duo status of Simon & Garfunkel.

Chapter Sixteen

RHYMIN' SIMON

The early months of 1973 brought Paul back into the studio working on his second solo album. Once again, he drew from very diverse sources, musically and rhythmically. This album took just over six months to write, and four months to record in studios in New York, Muscle Shoals (Alabama), Jackson (Mississippi) and London (England). His reason for travelling was simple: 'Always for musicians. Wherever the musicians are, that's where I go.'

This time his producer was Phil Ramone, who had done 'Me and Julio' with him on the first album. There were two reasons for switching from Roy Halee. Art was already working exclusively with Roy on his album in California; also, Paul liked Ramone. 'He's in New York, he's accessible and he's good.'

Much of the musical backing on the album was done by a group of musicians Paul first heard on a Stax record called 'I'll Take You There' by the Staple Singers. He called Al Bell at Stax Records, asking who the musicians were. 'He told me about the guys in Muscle Shoals.' So Paul went to Sheffield County, Alabama, to see for himself.

He was delighted with what he found. 'The Muscle Shoals group have their own studio and it fits like a glove.' Originally, he'd intended to record only 'Take Me to the Mardi Gras' there, a white reggae number, similar to 'I'll Take You There' in style. He booked the studio for three days, the usual time it took to complete one track.

As it happened, he finished the track on the first day, to his utter astonishment. 'They're sensational musicians,' he said. 'Very friendly. Very comfortable studio. It's easy to work and I can work very rapidly.' He ended up by doing five tracks, instead of just one. He asked them which one they wanted to take next and they opted for 'Kodachrome', so that was put down the following day. Eventually, they did 'One Man's Ceiling', 'St Judy's Comet' and 'Loves Me like a Rock'.

Paul was full of praise for their skill. They worked out very sophisticated arrangements in their heads, then wrote down changes with incredible speed. 'It's something to see; it's spectacular,' he said. Their versatility was also marvellous, enabling them to produce an amazing diversity of sounds in those five tracks.

Paul greatly enjoyed the trips to Muscle Shoals. 'That was peaceful. There's nothing to do but go into a recording studio.' He would spend three or four days there at at time, then he'd go back to New York to work on the vocals. 'I think, to a degree, you can get different sounds out of different studios. But I don't go for studios. I go for the musicians,' he said.

Another musical contributor was Alan Toussaint, with whom Paul had never worked before. 'He was great. Very nice guy, very musical.' Most of Toussaint's recording is done in Atlanta, and Paul hoped to work with him one day. 'I'd like to see what's going on there.'

The concept of this album was very different from that of *Paul Simon*. For one thing, Paul wanted more emphasis on voices this time. On his first album, he used no harmony, either by overdubbing or with other singers. He'd felt people would wonder why he'd split up with Art, if he still wanted harmony. Now, further away from that split, he gave full rein to his love of the richness of voices. He contacted the Dixie Hummingbirds and the Rev. Claude Jeter, lead singer of the Swan Silvertones – all black gospel singers. He also enlisted the vocal talents of Maggie and Terre Roach, two students from the songwriting class he had taught at New York University.

A neat and clean-cut Tom and Jerry in 1958 (Micheal Ochs Archives/© Redferns)

Above: Paul on the English folk circuit, London 1965 (courtesy of Judith Piepe)

Left: The famous tour of one-night stands when Paul was paid £12 a night – received here from Jack Froggatt (courtesy Jack Froggatt)

Paul and Art pausing for
an off-stage discussion
in London 1967
(© David Redfern)

Paul and Artie riding on the subway, but soon to be phenomenally famous with 'Bridge over Troubled Water', 1969 (Gems/Redferns)

Above: Paul and Artie taking a break at the Monterey Pop Festival, 1967 (Colin Beard/© Redferns)

Below: Simon and Garfunkel reunited at the triumphant Central Park concert, September 1981 (Victoria Kingston)

Paul and Art, reunited and optimistic at a press conference,
announcing their 1982 tour (© David Redfern)

Onstage on the Summer Evening with Simon and Garfunkel tour 1982
(Victoria Kingston)

Paul Simon solo – performing
on stage in 1987
(Victoria Kingston)

Paul signing autographs for fans in England during his Graceland tour of 1987 (Victoria Kingston)

But vocal style isn't the only difference between this album and its predecessor; there's also a marked thematic change. On *Paul Simon*, the overall mood was introverted and troubled. In *There Goes Rhymin' Simon*, even the title is more light-hearted and playful. The second solo album burst upon the public as a joyous celebration of family life and the bonds of family. It included a love ballad to his wife, a lullaby for his son, and songs about friendship and childhood. When the album emerged in May 1973, it was evident that here was yet another aspect of Paul Simon, as a musician and composer, but also as a man.

Even the album sleeve was consistent with a more relaxed person. It is a collage of images which symbolize the songs in a tongue-in-cheek way: a plaster cast for 'Learn How to Fall', pebbles for 'Loves Me like a Rock', a picture of Paul as a sleek rock 'n' roller for 'Kodachrome', and a touching picture of Paul holding his infant son to illustrate 'St Judy's Comet'.

This light-hearted angle on his work suggested a more confident artist at work here. He had proved with *Paul Simon* that his audience was still there for him, receiving him with open arms, as he had hoped. Now he was well into his stride with this superb album.

It opens with the upbeat 'Kodachrome' which obviously proclaims the superiority of the colour film, but also uses colour to symbolize vitality and imagination. It has a compelling rhythm and some humorous touches as a man looks back on his youth from the standpoint of a stable maturity.

This is followed by 'Tenderness', a fifties type ballad, addressed to a friend. Paul croons softly, backed by the Dixie Hummingbirds. The soulful, subdued horn arrangement is by Alan Toussaint; Roy Halee produced the track with Paul. The lyric explores the thin line between being honest and inflicting pain in a relationship.

'Take Me to the Mardi Gras' captures the joy and exuberance of the New Orleans Festival and of music itself as a healing, purifying process. The track fades out with the uninhibited sound of Dixieland Jazz, played here by the Onward Brass Band.

A complete change of mood is signalled by 'Something So Right', an exquisite love song, a tribute to Peggy Simon. The tone is conversational, but the declaration is solemn and eloquent. It presents an ironic, painful revelation – that the singer is the first to admit when something goes wrong, but always the last to know. The song also gives an insight into the writer's need for privacy and isolation, and Paul returns to the wall metaphor which he first used in 'I am a Rock'. The strings come courtesy of Quincy Jones.

Side one closes with 'One Man's Ceiling Is Another Man's Floor', a very underrated song. Paul told Jerry Gilbert: 'It's based on New York paranoia.' It's another of his tough, graphic portraits of city life. What the song represents is starkly realistic, horrifying, so casually told by a cynical New York tenant who takes a grim satisfaction in relating the bloody details of local violence. There have been fights in the building and the elevator man doesn't work there any more (and Paul's broad New York pronunciation of 'woyk' should be noted) – but our tenant is crouched behind closed doors, in terrified safety, while the elevator man is beaten up, no doubt calling for help. The implications of this throwaway line are profoundly disturbing.

Side two opens with 'American Tune', musically based on a Bach chorale piece which Paul had played for many years. He recorded the track in London, which is where he wrote the lyric, and where it was co-produced by Paul Samwell-Smith, known, among other triumphs, for his work with Cat Stevens. The string arrangement is by Del Newman.

This song is arguably Paul's finest achievement. He muses on the loss of his ideals, dreams that are broken. Then the musing broadens out to look at his friends and their dreams. One of the most haunting aspects of the song is the dream sequence, where America is put into perspective; an American far from home has the vision of his own soul rising before him and smiling reassuringly – an ominous vision, without doubt. The Statue of Liberty sails away towards the sea, abandoning its people and all their former ideals.

The final verse broadens yet further into political fears. The glorious arrival of the Pilgrim settlers is neatly understated – simply a ship they call the *Mayflower* – and it's linked to its modern equivalent of space exploration. But the legend lives on, in spite of all cynicism, in spite of everything that has failed. The American tune persists.

The song ends on a superb anti-climax; the broadened theme abruptly narrows again, moving from world issues to something acutely and ironically personal: he's tired and has to go to bed, because tomorrow is a working day. The critics received this song with abundant praise, and justifiably so, because it's a masterpiece in every sense. Just as Paul captured the mood of the sixties with 'The Sound of Silence', so 'American Tune' epitomizes the seventies.

'Was a Sunny Day' is a contrast in style, a slow blue-beat song, playful and light, but with some cynical touches: the word economy of the high school queen who has nothing really left to lose. There's a reference to Earl 'Speedoo' Carroll, the lead singer of the Cadillacs, one of the best black vocal groups of the fifties. The vocal backing here is by Maggie and Terre Roach.

This lyric actually began life, in a rougher, more fragmented form, as the lyric to the tune of 'Mother and Child Reunion'. Paul discarded these words for the time being when he wrote the lyric about his dog's death. He then resurrected them to use with this Carribbean track.

'Learn How to Fall' is a stringent piece of wisdom, with a clear message. It says you have to be ready to take the rough with the smooth, certainly Paul's philosophy. It's true and wonderfully concise, sung with a joyous kind of optimism.

'St Judy's Comet' follows, a lullaby to Harper, the Simon baby. Paul played this a couple of years later on the children's programme *Sesame Street* to a small audience of children, which included the now mature Harper of three years old. Paul explained to them that he wrote it because his little boy found it hard to go to sleep, and would stay awake far too late. It gives us a brief, touching glimpse of a private Paul Simon. Maracas and vibes create the gentle percussion, to back Paul's acoustic guitar.

The album closes with 'Loves Me like a Rock', a joyous celebration of devoted, undying love. It's a gospel, exuberantly sung by Paul with the Dixie Hummingbirds doing the responses. It celebrates the love of a mother which sustained him as a child, and the adult love of his woman, equally sustaining. It's a hand-clapping, rousing affirmation of love, a fine ending for an album so obviously rich in love.

There Goes Rhymin' Simon was received ecstatically by critics and the public. It was awarded a Gold Disc right away. It earned a Grammy nomination for the Best Album of 1973, and *Rolling Stone* chose 'American Tune' as Best Song of the Year. Any doubts anyone may have entertained about Paul's solo status were completely disspelled with this album. It was obvious from the moment the stylus fell into the groove that he was still at the top. After all the unsettled, doubt-filled years, that was a very good feeling.

Simultaneous with the release of the album was the single 'Take Me to the Mardi Gras' / 'Kodachrome'. Paul would have preferred something else. 'I felt it would be nice if I had a single out that was one of the prettier ballads on this album, because I feel that I'm at my best when I'm writing ballads.' But Clive Davis, then president of Columbia, felt strongly that the first single should be more commercially appealing. Paul accepted his choice. He told the press: 'I do my best to make the record as valid as I can musically, but once it's finished, then Columbia goes and sells it. That's what I want them to do, so I'm finished now.'

Because of the reference to a brand name, the BBC didn't give 'Kodachrome' any air play, since it conflicted with their policy of no advertising. But that didn't seem to affect sales, for the single was a big hit.

After the release of the album, Paul and Art talked on the phone. They hadn't seen much of each other lately – not since Art's wedding the previous October. Now, Artie was in San Francisco, still working on his album. He told Paul he'd been to the Kentucky Derby, and Paul laughed: 'You're crazy. Too many people.'

Paul asked Art's opinion of *There Goes Rhymin' Simon* and Artie said he liked it very much. At this stage, they were still amicable towards each other. According to Paul: 'We have all those experiences in common. We're not close friends at the moment, but we're not enemies either. We grew up together and we had, obviously, that whole Simon & Garfunkel thing. But it's drifted apart.'

To coincide with the release of his album, Paul embarked on an eleven-city tour of the USA and Europe, which would conclude in London's Royal Albert Hall in June. He realized he wouldn't be able to create the same sound live as he'd done on record. 'It's impossible. I'd have to be pulling elements from all over the globe to reproduce it. I don't think it's necessary. Guitar is enough.'

He was to take a backing group: Urubamba, a South American group that included two members from Los Incas, now involved in a lawsuit over that name. Urubamba took their name from a river that runs through Peru. Also on the tour was a quintet, the Jessy Dixon Singers, a gospel group comprising three female vocalists, a male bass player and Jessy Dixon, who played the organ and sang. Paul first heard them the previous summer at the Newport Jazz Festival and had been eager to work with them. As additional backing there was Paul's brother Eddie, who made a few appearances with his guitar. All told, Paul was travelling with fifteen people. He was thrilled. 'All I've ever worked with is one other voice and a guitar. This is great. I get off easy because I have a group to play with.'

This was Paul's first tour since splitting with Art. In fact, it was his first real solo performance of any kind, apart from a few spots on McGovern benefits the summer before. Two questions were dominant in the music press at the time: why he had chosen now to go on tour, and why he had waited so long. Paul told *Melody Maker*: 'I think I just decided to do something so I'd be getting off my ass. I just like to be nervous, that's all. I'll be very nervous because I haven't done it for so long.' He wasn't apprehensive about the audience response. 'I'll go out and I'll sing my songs and I'll try to sing in tune. And basically, that's what I have to offer. People either want to hear me sing my songs or they don't, so I feel that nobody will be expecting any more of me than that.'

As to why he had waited so long: 'I didn't have anything to go on the road with. I didn't want to go out with a whole repertoire of Simon & Garfunkel. I wanted to be an artist of some stature on my own, and now I think I'm approaching that status.' He was looking forward to being on stage again. 'I have a touch of the exhibitionist in me,' he laughed.

Even so, he had a 'very uncomfortable two weeks at rehearsals', worrying about going back on tour. He had always suffered this way, before performing, particularly before a major tour. He described how, even in the Simon & Garfunkel days, he would have nightmares before it started, especially after a long absence from performing: 'Dreams like, we come on stage and there's only one mike, no mike for my guitar, and it's too high for me and too low for Artie. And my guitar has a broken string. And I say, "Excuse me, I have to get another guitar." And I go backstage and scream at our manager. Panic dreams like that.'

As always, once the tour had started, he relaxed and began to enjoy it. His basic act opened with five or six songs that he performed solo. Then he brought on Urubamba to back him for 'If I Could' and 'Duncan', as they had done on studio albums. A new version of 'The Boxer' closed the first half.

In part two, Paul did another five or six solo songs, before introducing Jessy Dixon and the group to sing 'Mother and Child Reunion' and very different versions of 'The Sound of Silence' and

'Bridge'. Both groups slipped in a couple of numbers without Paul, and the finale of the show brought everyone on stage together.

A lot of the material was taken from his new album. Originally, he'd intended to do only four new songs, but he added another because the audiences responded so well to them. He was surprised and pleased to find out that they liked his new material as much as the Simon & Garfunkel songs. The tour ended in London, with Paul playing to three packed houses at the Albert Hall. It was immediately sold out and Paul was greeted each night by a standing ovation.

On 7 June Paul arrived a little late, having been detained by traffic in Park Lane, where he was staying at the Dorchester Hotel. He came on stage, a solitary figure, and launched straight into 'Me and Julio'. He was overwhelmed by the applause, and often showed this by applauding the audience. At the end of the show, they wouldn't let him go, but went on clapping until he came back for three encores: 'Take Me to the Mardi Gras', 'America' and 'Bye Bye Love'. Gavin Petrie wrote in *Disc*: 'With or without the musical embellishments to the show, it was a good one.'

After the tour, Paul went back to New York, glad to be home. 'I grew up here,' he said. 'It's my home town. There's a lot of action. I'm comfortable with the pace of New York, although when I went back to London, I really loved it. And I thought I ought to live there for a few months of each year.' He planned to take the rest of the summer off. He was going into the country to relax and to teach his son to swim. He was also thinking about his career, the next project, perhaps a movie score. 'I'm ready to take a plunge into anything,' he said. 'Something different is what I'd like to do. Something that would make you a little nervous. Something that pushes you and makes you stretch out a little bit.' It was a characteristic goal.

In July, 'Loves Me like a Rock' / 'Learn How to Fall' was

released. In the USA, it was number 1 for a week and in the charts for seventeen weeks. In the UK, it only made it to number 39. It was awarded a Gold Disc on 9 October 1973 – a nice birthday gift, because it was Paul's first solo million seller since parting with Artie. Things were definitely getting better.

Chapter Seventeen

ANGEL CLARE

In September 1973, CBS launched Artie's first solo album, entitled *Angel Clare*. Art chose the title with deliberation. 'It's a name I like. Comes from literature. The English majors will know. In a sense, I wanted to play right into, rather than back off of, this description of me as sweet.'

Angel Clare is an important character in Thomas Hardy's great tragic novel, *Tess of the D'Urbervilles*. He is a rector's son with a great passion for farming, and for Tess. When she confesses to him her 'tainted past' – her seduction by her cousin – Angel rejects her and is unable to forgive her. This sets off a series of tragic consequences, and when he returns to find her, it's far too late. Angel is man doomed to the terrible fate of his own guilt.

The album cover presents a golden, autumnal close-up of Artie, wearing an open-necked shirt (with a tiny hole under the collar), photographed by Jim Marshall. The cover represents the solo quality of the artist, just as Paul's did, but it's warmer and lighter.

Angel Clare is a collection of traditional and contemporary folk songs, chosen and placed for the diversity of sound and style. It was produced by Artie and Roy Halee. The overall production was painstaking; Art estimated that he spent 80 per cent of his efforts on the instrumental parts. 'For me,' he said, 'the recorded sound is the record.' And it shows. *Angel Clare* is lavishly orchestrated. Art used some old friends among the musicians: Joe Osborn on bass and Larry Knechtel on keyboards, both from

Bridge. Also mentioned among the 'other musicians' is a guitarist who was a particularly old friend – Paul Simon.

It opens with 'Travellin' Boy', a Paul Williams / Roger Nichols composition, one of those with a wanderer theme. Some critics felt the grand orchestral arrangement was too lush and heavy, but it's actually a spectacular opening.

'Down in the Willow Garden', a Charlie Monroe song, is linked to the album's title in theme. Here, though, it's a man facing the gallows because he's committed murder, rather than Tess. Then Van Morrison's 'I Shall Sing' is very appropriate for an artist who so loves to sing. It's a light contrast to the heavier songs, though it doesn't really show Art's vocal range.

Randy Newman's 'Old Man' is a powerful song, which personalizes old age and death. By 1973 Randy Newman was already a songwriter of distinction, well known for his ironic statements concealed by an ostensibly callous throwaway lyric. There is much pain in this song, and the full-bodied quality of Art's singing here emphasizes it. A piano arrangement paying tribute to the Randy Newman style, it's one of the high spots on the album.

Side one closes with 'Feuilles-oh' / 'Do Space Men Pass Dead Souls on Their Way to the Moon?', a medley that combines a pretty French ballad sung traditionally with a collaboration between J. S. Bach and Linda Grossman, then Mrs Garfunkel. The music is Bach's and the lyric is Linda's.

Side two opens with Jimmy Webb's 'All I Know', surely one of the finest songs on the album. It's a sensitive and realistic analysis of the inevitable hurting that goes on in relationships. The man and woman bruise each other, but are united by their love. This track, the first in a long line of Jimmy Webb songs for Artie, shows his voice at its best, giving scope for passion and vocal skill.

'Mary Was an Only Child' is a collaboration between Jorge Milchberg, Albert Hammond and Mike Hazelwood. It was Paul who discovered the song and told Art about it. When it was to be recorded, Art returned the compliment by asking Paul to play guitar on the track. It's a strange song, with skilful overdubbing which gives it a ghostly sound.

'Woyaya' is an unusual track, by Sol Amarfio and Osibisa. It blends Art's multi-layered voice with the voices of ten-year-old Chinese children from St Mary's Choir. It's a singalong, full of optimism.

This leads us into the traditional folk song 'Barbara Allen', a song that is poignantly sweet and painful. Art captures both the sweetness and the pain, rising to the climax in notes of seemingly effortless perfection. It would be interesting to hear him do this in a traditional way, with just a guitar for accompaniment. The same could be said of the closing song, another Jimmy Webb composition, 'Another Lullaby', which is perhaps too heavily orchestrated for a lullaby, but is nevertheless sung with tenderness.

Critics were divided when the album was released. Some complained that its production was too lush, too sweet. There were even one or two who felt that Artie had nothing to offer without Paul Simon. He was criticized for not writing songs – for just singing. It's surely ludicrous to dismiss his talent, simply because he isn't Paul Simon. The point is that he has an excellent voice. On *Angel Clare*, he was experimenting with how to use it as a solo artist.

Art was pleased with the work he'd done. 'It's the album I wanted to make,' he said. It sold very well in America, leaping straight to number 20 on the Billboard Chart in only its second week. Undoubtedly, it would have had better sales worldwide if he'd promoted it with concerts. All the same, it won a Gold Disc. Art watched the sales slightly anxiously: 'If this album hadn't succeeded at all, I would have been desperately disappointed,' he admitted later.

To coincide with the album, CBS released 'All I Know' / 'Mary Was an Only Child'. The single was a hit in the USA. After the album's release, Art was asked the old, old question: if and when he would record with Paul again. He was decisive in his answer:

'I have an investment along the path that I'm on, and for someone to lift me off and put me down on another course would feel like a terrific jarring of the gears.'

He attended a short round of promotional parties at Columbia Studios. Then in October he performed at the Columbia Records Convention. His reasons were partly to promote his new album, and fortunately the convention was held in the city in which he'd been working. 'I was very high on the album and it was just a skip across town,' he said. But he had another reason: 'For future reference, I thought it would be interesting to see how I felt on stage.' Altogether, he did four songs. He didn't enjoy the first three at all, because he felt physically uncomfortable and out of place. 'But I tried to say, "That's cool; it's been a long time. It'll take a couple of shows." And by "Bridge", I got into it. I felt good. It's that encore thing; it's after the fact.'

Paul was in the audience, but that didn't make Art feel nervous. Paul's response after the show was characteristic of him and of their close friendship. According to Artie: 'Paul always gives you a critical run-down. I respect his opinion. He said, "You really have to work on your speaking, Artie. Got to think what you're going to say and prepare your sentences." '

After the convention, Art was asked if he would tour again. He admitted that he sometimes wanted to. The yearning was still there for a live audience, for the nights when everything went well. But he added: 'I think I'd rather make another album.'

In autumn '73, with no further commitments, Art took off with Linda on a house-hunting trip to Virginia. Things were looking good for him now. He had a solo album out and it was selling well. His marriage was making him very happy. He felt that married life suited him.

He had started to look at his life and get it into perspective. He analysed, among other things, his attitude to money. His middle-class upbringing had left him with a gut feeling that it's wise to save money, to invest for old age, to provide for sickness and accidents.

'Pursuing a lot of money is a foolish waste,' he said. 'I have a very strange relationship to money. I don't know how to spend it. I don't really feel it leads to much happiness. I can't develop a real interest in material goods. Money mostly means convenience for me – cabs. I like getting out of a movie if the movie is boring in the middle, and not feeling I've wasted the rest of the money I spent.'

During the next months, his probing self-analysis extended to the Simon & Garfunkel days, and to the psychological effects of such huge success. 'I sometimes look back at those years and realize that there was a tremendous amount of immaturity, or self-seduction, of glorying in the kind of reinforcement that comes with all ego strokes. I suppose I did lose my equilibrium. I should have been able to put away the dope about four years before I actually did. There were changes I had to make that somehow got delayed.'

In February 1974, Paul released 'American Tune' / 'One Man's Ceiling Is Another Man's Floor' from his album. It was another hit in the charts. A month later, Art released 'I Shall Sing' / 'Fueilles-oh', which was also successful.

That same month, Paul released a live album, appropriately entitled *Live Rhymin'*, consisting of a selection of the performances from the '73 tour. The sleeve has pictures from the tour – of a dynamic Paul, poised for action. Interestingly, 'American Tune' is improved by the omission of strings; this acoustic version captures the sense of solitude and isolation.

There's also an interesting change in 'Duncan'; in this live version, it's the girl who creeps to Duncan's tent with the flashlight. It makes me wonder which came first in Paul's mind. In 'The Boxer' there's an extra verse, a retrospective glance at the passing years, and the resigned conclusion that things don't change much after all. It's rare for Paul to add extra verses, and he must have liked this one, because he has stuck to it faithfully ever since.

Side two focuses on gospel versions of his songs, most strikingly of 'Bridge', which no one thought Paul would ever do.

It's extended to a full seven minutes, and it almost becomes a different song. The album closes with a solo 'America'. It's easy to forget it's a live album, the audience is so quiet.

Paul pervades this album with his more relaxed style and approach. When a voice from the audience entreats him to say a few words, he feels at ease enough to make a joke: 'Well, let's hope we all continue to live ...' and the expected 'happily' remains ironically unsaid, because living is hard enough to do these days. The album earned Paul another Gold Disc.

In May, two songs from the album were released on a single: 'The Sound of Silence' and 'Mother and Child Reunion', both featuring the Jessy Dixon Singers.

Naturally, after the release of *Live Rhymin'*, the press were anxious to find out how Art reacted to Paul's solo 'Bridge'. He answered them cautiously: 'I know if I say anything at all and it's not tactful, you'll lift it out of context and it'll be the headline. You want me to say something that is in the least possible taste.' Art grinned good-naturedly, then added: 'Well, I like our version of "Bridge over Troubled Water" better than Paul's solo version.'

In September '74, Art released a new single, 'Second Avenue', a fine version of a Tim Moore song, backed by 'Woyaya' from the album. He was now thinking of his next move, realizing that a tour was the logical step. In the meantime: 'I had a real good time recording and my next move will be to get some more songs together and go back into the studio and see what gives.'

Once more, he had been thinking of writing his own songs. The urge he had felt in the early sixties was still with him. 'I think that, eventually, I might just have it in me,' he said. 'But then, I may be quite wrong. And if I am, then I'm willing to accept that. To be quite honest with you, all the attempts I've made so far have fallen short of my standards.' And he commented on Paul: 'I miss him not writing songs for me to sing, although I never felt he was writing for me specifically in the past. I miss the quality of his lyrics and his chord changes and melodies. I still have a great regard for his writing.'

Chapter Eighteen

STILL CRAZY AND BREAKING AWAY

During 1975, the lives of Paul and Art were strikingly parallel. Both would have a hit album and reunite as a duo for a hit single; both of them would have a traumatic year in which their marriages, once sources of great joy and satisfaction, would collapse and end in divorce.

It's always impossible to assess a relationship from the outside. But in all relationships, problems are deeply rooted and nothing really happens suddenly. Looking back, it's generally possible to see how, where, why it all went wrong. As outsiders, we can only speculate. We can see that both marriages were subject to the same pressures. They were classic cases of men who couldn't find enough hours to devote to careers they loved and women they loved. Paul and Art had outstandingly successful and absorbing careers, into which they had channelled all their energies from the very beginning.

Paul suggested as much, later: 'I'm much less adept at working out my personal life than my career life. It's not like I spent fifteen years on my relationships. I didn't, and you can see I didn't. The ones that I had didn't hold.' And Artie also implied that show business might have contributed to his divorce. 'My wife attacked the tinsel, the glitter and the trivia of the music business, although that was what had attracted her in the first place. She developed a hatred of the life.'

As the marriages were disintegrating, both men responded to the emotional turmoil in the same way – positively, by working.

The year 1975 opened for Paul with a single cut from his album: 'Something So Right'/'Tenderness'. He was writing some new songs, and they would inevitably reflect the pain he was feeling in those months. And he was thinking about doing a tour and a television special.

When his divorce came, it was, he said, 'relatively pleasant, as far as that's possible. There was no bitterness.' He shook off feelings of self-pity, telling the press: 'I'm not the only guy in the world who got a divorce.' No, he isn't. But clearly, his trauma generated the creativity which produced *Still Crazy after All These Years*. At the same time, Art was in another studio, working on his new album, which would be the bestselling *Breakaway*. As he suffered the crumbling of a marriage that had once made him so happy, the sounds he produced in the studio were melodic and tranquil.

'It would be easier, I suppose,' he mused, 'to lose the tensions in rock 'n' roll where the sounds are louder and more fraught, but I don't like that. So when I sing, I remove my nature from my music and subtract my nerves from my voice. And when the tape is good and the music flows, the elation is like making love.'

Throughout 1975, work continued in different studios and with very different patterns, reflecting Art and Paul's personalities. Art's album was produced by Richard Perry, well known for his work with Barbra Streisand and Ringo Starr. A collection of excellent musicians was featured: Larry Knechtel again on keyboards, Jim Keltner, Klaus Voorman and Andrew Gold, who according to Art 'plays everything'. The talents of Graham Nash, David Crosby and Bruce Johnston were displayed on background vocals. Art worked on through 1975, alternating between extended holidays and periods of intense creativity.

Paul's new album was also a new direction for him. His producer was again Phil Ramone, and he gives us some insight into Paul's work pace during those painful months. 'To work successfully with Paul, you must live in the pace he comes into the studio with. A lot of times during the album, we had to stop for a month or so, because there was nothing flowing from him. Once they're written, each song matures technically at its own individual speed.' The album took about nine months to complete. 'Just like a baby,' Ramone laughed. 'I guess you could call it natural childbirth.'

Paul worked with singer Phoebe Snow on 'Gone at Last', and she regarded it as 'super exciting. All of a sudden I was in the studio with a genius whose songs I'd loved for years, singing this joyful gospel tune. That session was so crazy. It went by so fast, like an Amtrak.'

It was fast indeed. The vocals took only a few hours, a rarity for a Paul Simon track. The two artists built up a professional rapport and, in time, a personal friendship. Phoebe Snow talked about Paul in the studio: 'He understands all the emotional levels of the artistic process. I think he understands what's at stake. We were in the control room one day, listening to the final version of "Gone at Last", and he suddenly turned to me and said, "Isn't it nice to win?"'

On 11 May, Paul took a break from the studio to join in an End of War Rally in Central Park's Sheep Meadow. In a sense, it was an historic event, to celebrate peace in Vietnam and Cambodia. The sun shone brilliantly throughout the afternoon's carnival of songs and speeches, as the crowd of over fifty thousand recalled the losses and tragedies of the long war. Other major stars who appeared that day included Joan Baez, Pete Seeger, Tom Paxton and Phil Ochs.

In September '75, Art emerged with a new single, the thirties hit 'I Only Have Eyes for You' by Harry Warren and Al Dubin, a number which had been a US hit for the Flamingos in 1959. For Art it was a smash, escalating the charts and reaching number 1 on 25 October, and staying there for two weeks. Produced by Richard Perry, the song is arranged slower than usual and Art sings it with tenderness. Side two of the single is 'Looking for the Right One', a ballad by Stephen Bishop, which Art sings wistfully, rising to a dramatic climax.

The next single was released by both Art and Paul, a one-off reunion which would also appear on both albums a month later. 'My Little Town' is a cynical view of life in a respectable and stifling town, where it's hard to nurture a dream because there's so little imagination there.

The song is filled with childhood memories: the boy saluting the flag on the classroom wall, with the ominous feeling that God is watching everything he does. The climax of the song presents a remarkably concise portrait of a youth, impatiently and restlessly dreaming of his future. In a few brilliant words, with the finger on the gun simile, Paul conveys that reckless, potentially explosive energy. Inevitably, the song reminds us of the young Paul Simon.

Paul originally wrote the song for Artie to sing. 'I volunteered to give him that song. I said, "Because you're singing so many sweet songs it's driving me crazy. So I'm going to write a really nasty song and that's my present for your album."'

Art liked the song, partly because he remembered it in its early, embryonic form. He explained: 'I told him I'd take it, because I was making an album culled from all forms of music. And certainly, a Paul Simon song would be of interest to me. I started working on the song, knowing all the while that Paul Simon, not being too prolific a writer, was probably going to need the song himself.'

While Paul was teaching it to him, Art realized how effective it would sound with their harmony. 'I thought the middle part was ideally suited to the old S & G blend, and I felt like harmonizing with Paul because I hadn't done that in years.'

And so it became a song for the duo. It was recorded by both artists simultaneously on both albums. According to Paul: 'I think it was Artie's idea. He felt it wouldn't be fair to put it out on one. We figured there would be a certain amount of commotion about our not having sung together in the studio for five years.'

Sure enough, there was a commotion. As soon as the single came out, reporters speculated about a permanent Simon & Garfunkel reunion. They seemed particularly pressing in interviews with Artie, insisting that the single indicated a reunion in the pipeline. He handled all questions of that nature with perfect detachment. 'Yes, it would seem to indicate that. I'm going as far as your statement and it's perfectly logical. There is a chance that we might get together to record an album, but I can't say any more, because there is no more answer. It was good to work with him again because I like him and I think he's talented.'

In October, Art made a three-day visit to England, during which time he recorded a video of his single for *Top of the Pops*. He gave press conferences at the Savoy Hotel in London. By all accounts, he conducted himself during the conference with diplomacy and adroitness, obliging photographers by posing with some pigeons. Above all, he carefully parried all the usual, worn-out thrusts about Paul Simon. When asked: 'Are you fed up of people asking you questions about Paul Simon?', he replied calmly: 'Yes. I'm fed up of people asking me questions about Paul Simon.' Still they pursued that line with questions which seemed designed to irritate or embarrass him. Would he and Paul team up again? Art replied: 'I see nothing to block an occasional get-together.'

When one persistent reporter asked: 'Have you fixed a date?' Art drily parried with: 'Are Paul and I dating?' The general consensus was that Art had handled the confrontation with skill. All the same, he must have been getting tired of it.

A week after that flying visit to London, two new albums were released by CBS: Art's *Breakaway* and Paul's *Still Crazy after All These Years*. They came out on the same day in October and so inevitably, there was still more speculation about reunions. Paul and Art were concerned that this shouldn't be the implication. Paul took steps to prevent it. 'As far as I could control what they did, I stopped that. But I can't stop them from running ads in papers that say Simon. And Garfunkel.'

Everyone played up the simultaneous release. Advertisements appeared side by side in the newspapers and magazines. Record stores displayed the albums next to each other in the windows. All this inevitably invited comparison of the albums from the critics. It would have been naive to suppose anything else would occur in those circumstances.

Paul insisted: 'They're two very different species.' When he was asked whether the publicity had helped Art commercially, he said: 'I don't know that it helped him any more than it helped me. He had a hit record on that album. It was number 1 in England and it's done well here too. I don't think it hurt either of us that we did a track together.' And he admitted: 'Working with him was pretty easy after the initial tension of getting back.'

The cover of *Still Crazy after All These Years* shows Paul on a New York fire escape, looking confident and relaxed. And why not? This album proved, if any still doubted it, that *Rhymin' Simon* was no fluke.

The opening bars of the title track are magical, and the lyric gives us loneliness and turmoil constructed by a craftsman. How many lyricists, in rhyming 'years', would sidestep the predictable 'tears', 'fears' – and choose 'beers', 'ears', then marvellously 'peers'? The rhymes are unselfconscious, seemingly accidental.

Eddie Simon described this song as one that 'any thinking, feeling human being can understand. My brother's saying, "Look, I'm working every day; I'm trying to do the right thing and get through the best way I know how. I've been famous and not famous, badmouthed and broken up inside. I've travelled and I've seen a shrink. I've been in love and got married, and that bottomed out too. And you know something – after all that work, all that pain and trouble all these years, I'm still crazy."'

After 'My Little Town' comes 'I Do It for Your Love', a wistful song about the disintegration of a marriage. When asked if it was about his own marriage, Paul said it was 'all partly true, but not literally true'. It's profoundly painful, but not sentimental, a recollection of the touching moments they shared, now seen ironically in the light of their present unhappiness. In the interlude, the rug metaphor is a starkly original and effective image.

Paul commented on the song's brevity to *Newsweek*: 'That's a big emotional coming and going. I'm aware of that, but I'm not attempting to analyse it or sum it up, because I don't understand it. Writing songs is cathartic. It's a way of saying what I don't say to people.'

'Fifty Ways to Leave Your Lover' is a cynical look at a familiar situation. Apparently, Paul woke up one morning and the opening words were in his head. He captures the clichés of speech, using them for ironic effect. Paul was always skilful with natural speech patterns – listen to 'America'. Here we endure the woman's politeness, are irritated by her repetition of the refrain and feel uncomfortable when he allows her to seduce him. Then there's that interlude, with its chanted instructions and a man's name attached to the end of each one. The crude rhymes jar, and they're meant to because it's all slightly offensive. Slipping out the back and dropping off the key, presented with such detachment, are fairly callous deeds. According to Eddie, Paul wrote the interlude when he was playing children's songs with Harper. 'Paul loves to play these little improvisational rhyming games. Harper James laughs like crazy when he does it. I think that's where the song came from. I know it's Harper James's favourite.'

The music was written with a Rhythm Ace, an electronic drum machine. This helps to create the tense, jerky effect. The constant drumbeat, which fades away at the end, suggests someone marching away, walking out of a relationship. It's unnerving, and as it dies away, we feel the sudden silence – the kind of silence we feel when deserted by a lover.

'Night Game' is a mournful song about the death of a baseball pitcher. Paul captures the sombre, funereal mood in the music. Lyrically, he fills the song with details about baseball. He described the theme as 'ritual death': 'Like in Roman times, when they used to send people out in the arena to fight to the death. And it would have this cathartic effect on the crowd. Well, today in our stadiums, people don't get killed, but they fight, and there's a winner and a loser. They're the descendants of those arenas, those games.'

'Gone at Last' is the fast-moving gospel sung with Phoebe

Snow, which has an optimistic message – to share a trouble is to ease it. Originally, the track was cut with Bette Midler, but it wasn't released because of contractual obstacles between the record companies. 'The version with Bette had more of a Latin, street feel,' Paul said. 'I changed the concept with Phoebe and tried a gospel approach because she was perfect for it.'

'Some Folks' Lives', a complete change of mood, is a superb song, which doesn't receive the acclaim it deserves. In some ways, it takes us back to 'Blessed', though with a different musical and lyrical style. The narrator, again challenging God to account for injustice, is now less confident, more apologetic. Orchestrally, it's magnificent, and Paul's voice swells with the music.

'Have a Good Time' shows a man who is depressed because he's another year older, and is getting thoroughly drunk, trying to convince himself that he's having a wonderful time. It's also a serious song, because he confronts himself with very disturbing doubts. These doubts are echoed by the repetition of the hollow reassurance that dominates the song – have a good time.

In 'You're Kind', we have an ostensibly sincere extolling of the woman's virtues – how she has been good to him, expanding his social life. In the interlude, he undercuts this ironically, revealing that he feels stifled and smothered. They have opposite personalities and, moreover, he feels trapped. Paul's window metaphor conveys this wonderfully, but also echoes an Ogden Nash line in a poem which humorously points out that men and women have irreconcilable conflicts within marriage. The final irony comes at the end of the song, when his refrain of 'so good' turns into 'so goodbye'.

'Silent Eyes' is the magnificent climax to the album, a song quite unlike anything he'd written. While 'American Tune' looks at what it is to be an American, this song profoundly explores Paul's Jewish heritage. In 1968, he said: 'Sometimes I'm American, sometimes I'm Jewish. But mostly, I'm Jewish.'

The song's title reminds us of those haunting photographs of people being ushered into trucks and railway carriages, to be taken to concentration camps. We think of their eyes, dark and sunken from hunger, staring lifelessly out of lean, gaunt faces. The eyes are silent because the suffering was silent.

The song personifies Jerusalem as a woman, grieving alone for the misery inflicted on her people. That misery becomes a personal burden, urging him to take action, calling his name. In that sense, the memory of the injustice becomes a race memory, a flame that is never extinguished, a torch passed from one generation to the next. The climax of the song comes with a stirring vision of Judgement Day, when the Jewish people will stand up, united in their anger. Dramatically, it cries for retribution and atonement, even though there can be none in any satisfying sense.

Connected threads of imagery run through the song: images of sight, blended with those of sound. The title itself is literally almost paradoxical – but it conveys, with great clarity, generations and centuries of passive and terrible suffering. The whole song is a metaphorical and thematic unity, a masterpiece.

The two dominant themes of the album are death and the disintegration of relationships. Critics pointed out that the album reflected the recent trauma of Paul's personal life. 'I write about the past a lot,' he said. 'My childhood and, the last couple of years, my marriage. Not intentionally though. I didn't set out to write about the disintegration of a marriage. It's just that, that's what was happening at the time. I guess I have an easier time expressing myself in a song than in real life. I can say things in a song that I would never say otherwise.'

Still Crazy after All These Years got a Gold Disc and also received two Grammy Awards: Best Album of the Year and Best Vocal Performance by a Male. The album was received with rapturous praise by the critics, as it shot up to number 1 in the charts. It confirmed Paul's solo status and it re-established him as one of the greatest songwriters of his age.

The cover of Art's album *Breakaway* was indeed a break from his previous style, and from the image that went with it. It's a stark, blue-tinted photo of Art, flanked by two women. The one on the left was Laurie Bird who starred with James Taylor in the film *Two Lane Blacktop* in 1971, and who became Art's girlfriend for several years. The cover challenges the sweet choirboy image that had hounded Artie for so many years.

The album opens with 'I Believe (When I Fall in Love With You It Will Be Forever)', the Stevie Wonder classic, co-written with Yvonne Wright. It's optimistic, and Art bursts into the chorus with energy. Larry Knechtel beats dominantly on the piano, strong sounds that take us back to 'Bridge'. Andrew Gold plays electric piano and both acoustic and electric guitars.

'Rag Doll' is a Steve Eaton song, again featuring Larry Knechtel on piano. It uses the full range of Art's voice, the lower register as well as the famous high notes. He croons with intimacy and captures the sexuality of the relationship as well as the tenderness.

The title track is a version of the Gallagher and Lyle hit, which was also the title track for their album. Art has a very different arrangement but it works well. It blends his pure, high notes with guitar and synthesizer (Steve Cropper and Bill Payne respectively). Helping out with harmonies are David Crosby and Graham Nash, as well as ex-Beach Boy Bruce Johnston.

Then 'Disney Girls', Johnston's own composition, is a glowing and nostalgic view of youth, about recapturing that feeling by returning to a simpler way of life. It extols the virtues of living peacefully with a local girl who wants to have a family, early nights and a small town life. Art takes a slow wander through the melody, fitting for the lazy summer days of wine and friends that the song depicts.

The next song, 'Waters of March', is by Antonio Carlos Jobim. It's a stream-of-consciousness string of unrelated things, sung in a chant-like monotone. Jobim's style of writing often uses all the notes on the chromatic scale, most notably in 'The Girl from Ipanema'. Art liked the song as a celebration of the ordinary things that we take for granted.

'My Little Town' is followed by 'I Only Have Eyes for You',

then 'Looking for the Right One', all of which appeared on singles. Then we have '99 Miles from LA' by Hal David and Albert Hammond. A man is driving to his lover and thinking of her as he drives. Lyrically, the juxtaposition of thinking and doing, linking the physical act of driving to the act of making love, creates a kind of tension. Musically, the scale descends with each sentence, underlining the monotony of driving and the tension of waiting to see her. Del Newman arranged and conducted the strings, flutes and horn.

The album closes with 'The Same Old Tears on a New Background' by Stephen Bishop, a vocal delight. The piano is by John Jarvis. It's mournful and dramatic, marvellously controlled.

When *Breakaway* was released, the critics were very divided in their views. Most of them felt it was a superb album, that Art was becoming more versatile and ambitious in his choice of material and arrangements. Some said that it was the work of a craftsman, both vocally and musically. The production was also praised. On the other hand, some critics attacked it for being a middle of the road album, claiming that Artie would never be more than a romantic background singer. They seemed to be ignoring the success of 'I Only Have Eyes for You', a song that dominated the charts that autumn, especially in Britain.

Paul responded defensively to the claims that Art's songs were too romantic and sweet. 'Artie's not all romance. He's got brains, bitterness, pain and scars. He just happens to have a voice like an angel and curly hair like a halo. But he's a grown-up.' *Breakaway* wasn't just the work of a grown-up; it was the work of a very accomplished singer. A lot of people bought the album and it soon received a Gold Disc. Clearly, he wasn't doing so badly, for a romantic background singer.

Chapter Nineteen

BACK ON THE ROAD

On 18 October 1975, NBC presented *Saturday Night*, their late-night show, with Paul hosting a line-up of celebrated guests. This very popular show could boast household names on their guest list every week, and regulars such as the late John Belushi, Chevy Chase, Jane Curtin, Gilda Radner and Dan Ackroyd. It soon became compulsive viewing for its political and cultural satire, breaking down barriers in style and content. In many ways, this very New York kind of show paved the way for others; it was the model for a British series of the same name which launched such stars as Ben Elton and Harry Enfield.

The comedy highlight of this show was the one-on-one basketball game between Paul and Connie Hawkins of the Atlanta Hawks. Paul's dry humour is evident in the pre-match interview when, with dead-pan face, he admits that Connie's one-foot-four-inch height advantage would definitely be a factor in the game. He muses: 'He's got me on speed and shooting ability. I've got to stay with my strengths . . . basically, singing and songwriting.' It could only happen on *Saturday Night*. The game was played to 'Me and Julio down by the Schoolyard', conducted in a dubious fashion with lots of pushing and grabbing. Amazingly, the victory is Paul's: believe it if you can.

The show was a landmark for Paul. He was trying his hand at comedy, something he would pick up again later. It was also the beginning of his association with Randy Newman, which would later become a musical partnership. Paul introduced Randy on the

174

show to sing 'Sail Away', graciously admitting that he'd like to have written it himself. Phoebe Snow also sang on the show, obviously very pregnant. They performed the duet 'Gone at Last', backed by the Jessy Dixon Singers.

But without doubt, the highlight of the show was the reunion with Art, introduced by Paul simply as 'my friend, Art Garfunkel'. After entering to thunderous applause, Art and Paul sang several of their hits. After 'The Boxer', Paul remarked in something of an understatement: 'It's good to sing with you again.' Art had a solo spot for his new hit, 'I Only Have Eyes for You'. Then Paul closed with a gentle acoustic version of 'American Tune'. Unsurprisingly, that edition of the show received very high ratings.

Also in October, Paul went into rehearsal for his forthcoming tour with the Jessy Dixon Singers. He would be accompanied by a group of top session musicians, including David Sanborn on saxophone, Richard Tee on keyboards, Hugh McCracken on guitar, Steve Gadd on drums and Toots Thielman, the famous jazz harmonica player.

Wearing a tracksuit and carrying a Saul Bellow novel, Paul arrived at Constitution Hall and went through the show with his band. At the end of the rehearsal, he glanced around him at the empty seats and the few ushers who had been watching. 'I want to thank you all for coming out tonight,' he said, vamping to an imaginary audience. 'Artie will be here for the second half of the show. He'll be a little disappointed there's only nine people here, but I promise we'll get to all your requests.'

The way it turned out, of course, was entirely different. After the release of his album, Paul set off on a national tour and played to packed houses right across America. He closed at the Avery Fisher Hall in New York on Thanksgiving Night. Artie came on stage with him to do a few numbers: 'My Little Town' and, in the finale, 'The Sound of Silence', 'Scarborough Fair' and 'Old Friends'.

Once again, this led to speculation about a permanent reunion. But Paul remained adamant. 'I can't go back and do anything with Artie. I'm not meant to be a partner. I don't know if Simon & Garfunkel would be that popular if they did come back. Artie came out on stage with me three times on this tour and the reaction was intense and astounding, but if we'd done a forty-minute set, there wouldn't have been that reaction.'

The reviews were very good, not just because of the reunion element, but for Paul himself. David McGee wrote in *Rolling Stone*: 'An appropriately joyous, memorable event, marked by Simon's masterful control of the proceedings and by the unerring proficiency of Simon's band members, by the overall cohesiveness of the show, and most of all by the emotional impact of the material.'

Immediately after the US tour, Paul and co. set off for a tour of Europe. This closed in England in early December: at the Manchester Palace on the 8th, Birmingham Hippodrome on the 9th, and finally at the London Palladium for three sell-out concerts on the 11th, 12th and 13th.

These were concerts of diverse musical styles, bringing together the best of jazz, blues, gospel and folk. Paul gave his musicians great scope in the arrangements. In her review, Penny Valentine noted how 'My Little Town' was left wide open for a Hugh McCracken solo on lead guitar, and 'I Do It for Your Love' included a stretch of Toots Thielman on harmonica.

Moreover, Penny Valentine wrote: 'His songs are written with a clarity and precision and put together with a fine steel hand. There is nothing extraneous or indulgent about Simon's work. It is stark, tight, sparse. He is a man who knows how to use music to make the notes count, to make each musician a clean, cool maestro of his instrument. And now on stage, his powers as this kind of organizer, a producer of quality goods, are what come through. Paul Simon was immaculate.'

Derek Jewell wrote in his review: 'Sheer perfection it surely was. No wonder the audience stood and stood, cried and cried to win encores. Absolute unmatchable triumph. Yet it was not only

Simon they applauded, but the exquisite texture of the whole. A concert in a class of its own.'

And Ray Coleman summed it up: 'Above all, Paul Simon is a musician. At the London Palladium, Simon gave a concert so majestic, so enthralling and rich that it is difficult to pitch any other recent event against it in comparison. His was the ultimate performance of the anti-star, obviously diffident about selling himself, but utterly convinced that his songs would pull him through.'

After the Palladium, Paul returned to New York and started work on a television special to be shown on BBC TV on New Year's Eve. He was thinking about where to go now, looking for a new challenge – not easy to find when he'd already conquered so many musical fields. Tracing his musical roots back to the songwriters of the thirties, he said: 'I'm trying to get closer to Broadway and Tin Pan Alley. It's no fluke that me, Berlin and Gershwin and Kern are all Jewish guys from New York who look alike.'

Also in December, the single of 'Fifty Ways to Leave Your Lover' was released in the USA, though not in Britain until a month later. It was a big seller; in the States, it was number 1 for three weeks and twenty weeks in the charts. In Britain conversely, it only reached number 20 for a week and spent seven weeks in the bestsellers. It was awarded a Gold Disc in March '76, and was Paul's second million-selling single as a solo artist.

The year 1976 opened with another concert tour, again produced by Phil Ramone. He handled the sound mixing for the whole tour, just as he had done for the previous two. Paul booked the shows into concert halls with approximately 3,000 seats, and no more. Clearly he wanted a more intimate atmosphere.

He travelled and performed with a large backing group, which included the Jessy Dixon Singers. Moreover, he insisted that the sound equipment should be of the highest studio quality. All this meticulous care meant that, financially, he could hope only to break even at the box office, since his overheads were sky high. But that didn't worry him in the slightest.

In February, Paul gathered his two Grammy Awards – Best Male Vocalist and Best Album – for *Still Crazy*, bringing his total to an incredible nine. In fact, Simon & Garfunkel were nominated for Best Vocal Performance by a Group for 'My Little Town', but they were ousted by the Eagles with the great 'Lyin' Eyes'.

By spring, Paul was getting anxious about his productive pace. Since going solo, he had spent a lot of time touring, something he had never enjoyed much anyway. But it had been necessary, in order for him to be accepted by audiences as a solo artist. The difficulty was, whenever he performed, he found it hard to write. He hadn't written anything since the album in early September. Now, in spring, having taken two months to unwind from the tour which had ended in January, and it was taking him yet another month to get the creative flow back. 'I don't like this period,' he said. 'It doesn't scare me now, but right before it ends, I'll panic. I always panic. Invariably, the first song will come because I lower my standards, which are always too high. I'll write a blues.'

He was right, of course. His standards were too high, but the constant quest for perfection was the source of his energy. He was still working hard at his study of advanced music theory. He told Paul Cowan: 'I don't think it matters what question you start with. As long as you start with a question, it's going to lead to something interesting. When I've finished an album, I can't begin to work again unless I get some new input of information. Otherwise, I wind up doing exactly what I did before.'

He was encountering some serious physical problems, but responding to them positively. His finger, with that old injury, now had calcium deposits in it. Every so often, it would swell and become discoloured. He could no longer take cortisone, so he was trying another drug 'which tears my stomach apart'.

Sometimes, the pain prevented him from playing the guitar, from using his left hand at all. He made use of these times by having voice lessons, so that he could sing for longer periods in the studio and could extend his top range. Also, faced with the horrifying possibility that his finger might get worse, forcing him to give up the guitar, he was learning to compose on the piano.

The spring of 1976 also saw him readjusting to being a single man again – a single man with a three-year-old son. He moved into an elegant, eight-room duplex apartment overlooking Central Park on New York's West Side. He surrounded himself with the art treasures he had been collecting over the years. One of his favourite possessions was in the living room – a Deco Steinway piano, built for George Gershwin's teacher.

Apart from his art collection, Paul was living relatively simply, considering he was a multi-millionaire, earning the highest royalties in the business. He had become a shrewd businessman, but not a tycoon in the true sense. 'Outside my own field, business interests are an unnecessary diversion. Nor is my self-image being very wealthy, even though I am.'

He could afford anything he wanted – boats, planes, chains of houses – but he didn't want them. 'I'm not living even near the true economic level I can afford. My values are still what I grew up with, tempered with my nouveau riche experience.' He was making substantial contributions to charities.

The usual army of servants of a man in his position were absent. He engaged a Czech housekeeper to do the cooking and shopping, to send his clothes to the cleaners and to look after Harper while he was working. And that was all.

His son was a constant source of happiness to him. The boy lived most of the time with Peggy, a few blocks away. But he stayed with Paul at the apartment several nights each week. Paul had constant contact with his ex-wife, whenever one of them collected Harper. They were amicable and reasonable with each other, and there were no custody battles. 'I think we're both good parents,' Paul said. 'It's just too bad we weren't compatible enough to present a united, nuclear family.'

Paul's relationship with Harper was a very close one. In a

Rolling Stone profile, Paul Cowan described how, during rehearsals for the Madison Square Garden concert, Harper was
present. Wearing a vivid red Superman T-shirt and a red and
yellow cape, he darted to and fro around the sound system, while
his father quietly sang 'American Tune'. Obediently waiting until
the song was finished, Harper approached his father, asking him
excitedly: 'Did you see me?' Paul replied quite seriously: 'I saw a
shape, but it was going so fast, I couldn't figure out what it was.
Was it you?' And Harper responded by hugging his father.

After the musicians left, Harper, with his red cape flowing
behind him, hurried over to the microphone and sang in a loud,
clear voice: 'Still crazy after all these years, still crazy after all
these years.' Peggy watched the proceedings with amusement. On
the way down in the freight elevator, she said, 'A star is born.'
And Paul, with his penchant for choosing exactly the right word,
added: 'A star is duplicated.'

At this time, Paul did a series of numbers for the American
children's TV programme *Sesame Street*, performing with a group
of children which included Harper. There was something enchant-
ing about Paul and his son, sitting on stone steps, singing the
Beatles song 'Get Back'.

Summer '76 was busy for Paul. He had organized the Madison
Square Garden Concert, in order to raise money for New York's
public libraries. In the early days of June, he was doing his final
rehearsals and he insisted on having no ragged edges, nothing left
to chance on the night.

He rehearsed with his usual session musicians with an intensity
and precision that were characteristic of him. Paul Cowan was
there at the last rehearsal and described Paul's method of working:
'He was clearly in charge, but he exercised his control in a loose,
good-humoured way. That afternoon, the almost compulsively
verbal man communicated most of his emotions, most of his
ideas, through gestures, smiles, phrases.'

Phoebe Snow arrived to practise 'Gone at Last', which she and
Paul were to perform with the Jessy Dixon Singers. Paul had her

rehearse the exchange with Ethel Holloway, one of the singers, a total of six times so that their parts were perfectly syncopated.

Similarly, he wanted his own set to be right. It should last exactly forty-six minutes, no more and no less. So he went through his act by himself, timing it as he sang and played the guitar, nodding encouragingly to anyone working particularly well, but continually glancing at the clock on the studio wall. It was exactly forty-six minutes.

On the night, the concert was a huge success, playing to a packed house of fifteen thousand who applauded wildly. So great was the response that Paul did an unplanned second encore of 'Me and Julio' and 'Bridge'. As Paul Cowan wrote, the applause was not only for that night: 'It was for all the songs that had poured from him for the past ten years, for all the experiences he'd helped to shape. He was one of us. More important, his music was part of us.'

After the second encore, the applause continued relentlessly, and Paul, obviously moved by it, applauded in response. He explained to the audience that if he stayed for another encore, the Garden's workers would go into triple overtime, and that would cut into the profits so badly needed by the libraries. He thanked them and hurried off stage, as though embarrassed by their warmth.

After the show, he was clearly thrilled. For tonight, not only had he been accepted on his own terms as a solo artist, they had also paid him a joyous, spontaneous tribute. At last he could say: 'It's been a long time since I've heard those cries of "Where's Artie?" from the audience. It took me five years to get there,' he said.

He talked to Bruce Pollock about his future. 'Today, I'm functioning on a value system that is well defined in my head, and it doesn't matter what somebody says about my work. I feel I know how far away I am from what I could potentially be. It's nice to be praised, but my eye is on a place further down the line. It will require more work, and either I'll get there or I won't. Check back in ten years and see if I've done anything.'

Chapter Twenty

'BRIGHT EYES'
AND MORE

Early in 1976, songwriter Mike Batt was asked to write a song for a film. Mike Batt was already well known in Britain as a record producer and composer, notably of the hit songs for the popular television series *The Wombles*. Director John Hubley and producer Martin Rosen were to make an animated cartoon film, *Watership Down*, based on the bestselling novel by Richard Adams. They approached Mike Batt.

I was fortunate enough to interview Mike Batt in his London offices in the early eighties; he is a very clear and thoughtful speaker, who recalls details with accuracy. He told me how he became involved in the film. 'I was with John Hubley, who sadly died during the making of the film. The producer, Martin Rosen, took over from John as director. They were briefing me about the writing of the music and the songs. And the dramatic place that "Bright Eyes" was to fill was the place where the rabbit Hazel is supposed to be dead. They just asked me to write a song about death, which shocked me a bit. I couldn't imagine what you could write about death without being morbid. But I went back to my house and I started to write.'

Actually, he came up with three songs: one for a female singer and two for a male voice. One was called 'Losing Your Way in the Rain', and ended up on an album Mike did called *Tarot Suite*, with Colin Blunderstone singing it. The second song, 'Run Like the Wind', also appeared on *Tarot Suite*, sung by Barbara Dixon, who recorded it again some years later. The third song was the classic 'Bright Eyes'.

For the two male songs, he had in mind a voice of approximately the same weight as his own, a light tenor. 'The best light tenor I could think of was Art Garfunkel, because he's got that fantastic tone and control, which is important. And so while I was writing, he came into my mind. I really did write them for his voice.'

He took the songs to John Hubley and Martin Rosen, who liked them. They asked him if he would like any particular singer. 'I told them, "Well, I'd really like Art Garfunkel, but I'm sure we won't get him."' Mike gave them a list he had compiled of seven singers who could achieve a similar sound, with his own name at the bottom.

He told me: 'They said, "Well, forget about the list. Let's try and get the real thing." So they asked me to make some demos, which I did with great care, because it's very important that you do the demo as well as possible, to attract the interest of whoever you're trying to get involved. I spent about two nights doing these demos and Martin Rosen took them to the States.'

In the States, Rosen saw Goddard Lieberson, for many years the head of CBS. Ironically and sadly, he would also die before the tracks were finally recorded, so he never saw the end of the project. Mike recalled: 'Goddard was a very talented person, a very witty person. He more or less started CBS Records. Therefore, he knew Art Garfunkel very well, and Martin Rosen knew him. So Goddard introduced Art to the tracks.'

Art heard the songs and liked them immediately. He talked to Mike on the phone, working out some of the details. It was agreed that Mike should arrange and produce them, and they fixed up some dates when Art could come over to record. At this stage, Mike didn't know which key Art would sing in, and it was hardly feasible to work that out on a transatlantic telephone call. But Art felt it would be roughly the same key as Mike's voice on the demo, possibly a semitone higher.

Artie arrived in London on the day before the session, utterly exhausted. Mike recalled: 'He had a terrible day that day. Everything went wrong for him. I think his plane was late and he had to change hotels.' Consequently, he missed the scheduled meeting with Mike at 1 p.m. and didn't arrive until 1 a.m. Somehow, in the dark, he found his way to Mike's house in Surbiton.

Mike had spent the previous day recording the Barbara Dixon song, which was never actually used in the film. Now Art was here, just hours before another day in the studio. It was their first meeting. Art didn't know much about Mike, who was not yet well known in America. As he entered Mike's music study, he was astonished to see a row of Gold Discs on the wall.

Despite both being very tired, they set to work on the songs, running through them and discussing the arrangements. Art then went back to the hotel to snatch a few hours of sleep. Mike stayed up to do the arrangements, so he had no sleep at all.

The recording day was similarly fraught with setbacks. Mike had booked a special piano because he wasn't entirely sure that the studio piano would be in tune, and they had no time to wait around. Mike left at nine o'clock for Wessex Studios in north London.

The Steinway piano he had booked arrived at the studio a little late, and slightly out of tune as a result of being moved. There was no one there who could tune it. Because time was limited, Mike started the recording. He had guitarist Chris Spedding and other good session musicians, and he intended to overdub himself on the piano later.

But that didn't work out either. When the tuner finally arrived, they had already started recording, minus piano, so he wasn't allowed to enter the studio while recording was in progress. Mike told me: 'He said, "Well, I'm not staying here. It's more than my job's worth to stay here for ten minutes." So he didn't wait to tune the piano, so of course I couldn't use it. And that is the reason there is no piano on the track to this day.'

Art arrived to do the vocals, and worked with Mike through the rest of the day and all through that night. Art had flown across the Atlantic and was suffering from jet-lag; Mike had worked for two nights and days without any sleep.

Naturally, the session was crowded and tense. There were decisions to make about style and arrangements. Mike told me: 'It took us a while to get to know each other. There were all sorts of pressures. Don't forget we had a control room full of people: a director, producer, sound editor. There must have been ten people in that control room, which doesn't make for a relaxed session. But we actually enjoyed the sessions despite the tension. It took a few hours before we could really relax with each other. But it did happen. At the end, we parted company very satisfied and on very good terms.'

I asked Mike what it was like to work with Art. His answer was thoughtful: 'The thing about Arthur, and I would say the same about me, is we're both perfectionists. We're both very keen that everything we do should be of the highest quality. And I don't think it's a bad thing at all that two people should come together and try to influence each other, to spur each other on to greater heights. I know that I demand a high standard, but with Arthur, he was demanding a high standard of me, which perhaps I would demand of myself anyway. But it's nice to have someone else watching you, making sure you do your job really well.

'He's a very meticulous person. You can tell a lot about people by their handwriting and by the way they speak. Art's handwriting is extremely meticulous, almost like a very fine script. And he speaks very meticulously and in a very controlled way. And it's also reflected in the way he works.

'When you have an artist who is singing and a producer in the control room, you have to have a rapport so that the artist is safe in the knowledge that the producer's not going to accept anything less than the artist's best. But also, the producer has to work, demanding the best, but not making the artist neurotic.

'If you're working with someone who is very good at what he

does, where you're delighted to be working with him – and Art Garfunkel is one of those people – he still needs to know, however brilliant he is, that there's somebody in the control room who is listening to what he's doing and applying the same standards that he'd apply himself. And there's a relationship you have to develop. Sometimes it takes days, or weeks. But we managed to do it in a few hours, which is quite a thing really.

'It's a kind of atmosphere that's struck up between the two of you. The artist has to feel comfortable that you're applying enough quality control. At the same time, you've written the song, so you've got to be brave enough to say – well actually, would you try it a bit louder or a bit softer. It's rather like directing a movie in a very small way.

'An artist who is confident and good is usually better at taking direction than an artist who is insecure. But if I said something to an artist that he really hated, he might be big enough to try it, but might also reserve the right to say, "Look, I know we tried that, but I don't think it's a good idea." And then of course, I've got to have the humility to say, "Fine, let's do it your way." It's a compromise, but you mustn't compromise too much if you feel you're right. It's part of being a producer, and part of being a singer. But Art has produced records as well, so he has a knowledge of the problems, and therefore a sensitivity to try to solve them.'

Mike considered carefully before summing up his ultimate response to his work with Art. 'It's something that I remember with a feeling of achievement. We knew we were both trying for something of really high quality, and I think we ended up with it. It's a phrase I've used before about recording, but I think you could say it was a painful birth of a beautiful child. I mean, I can't speak for him, but at the end of the session, I was very pleased. He had done a great job.'

Art went back to the States, leaving 'Bright Eyes' shelved in England for the time being. During summer '76, he enjoyed a long vacation and kept a low profile, dodging the publicity in Malibu,

California. He had worked hard and felt no guilt about this period of rest. He had a well-balanced equation of work and leisure: 'A lot of my colleagues pursue it hot and heavy, 95 per cent style. But I try to keep it 75 per cent. To me, that seems human. You can figure I'll keep a proportion of 75 per cent for decades to come, hopefully.'

By December, he was restless and longing to be working again. He started a new album. It was typical of his style that, once having begun on it, he devoted all of his time and energy to it. It entirely dominated 1977.

Chapter Twenty-one

RECORDING SONGS AND MAKING A MOVIE

The year 1977 opened for Paul with an appearance at the Inaugural Eve Gala Performance in honour of Jimmy Carter's election as President of the United States. The show was held in the Kennedy Center for the Performing Arts in Washington, but was televised to the whole of America. Paul appeared with a crowd of stars, including Shirley MacLaine who appropriately sang 'It's Not Where You Start but Where You Finish', Aretha Franklin, and Leonard Bernstein conducting the National Symphony Orchestra.

While Art worked on his album in California, Paul arrived there to take part in a film, his very first. Until now, his only involvement in film had been writing and performing the score for *The Graduate* and the ill-fated Warren Beatty film, *Shampoo*. Now, in 1977, Woody Allen persuaded him to take a cameo role in his brilliant movie *Annie Hall*.

Besides Woody himself, the film starred Diane Keaton in the title role, Tony Roberts and Shelley Duvall. Indeed, it was during the making of the film that Paul started dating Shelley. In the film, the part of Tony's girlfriend is taken by Laurie Bird, Art's real life girlfriend.

Paul played tycoon record producer Tony Lacey, a man with a lifestyle strikingly opposite to Paul's own. He lives in a lavish, luxurious house in LA, complete with swimming pool and private cinema. He is surrounded by pleasure-loving hangers-on and gorgeous women. With promises of recording contracts he turns

Annie's head, and she leaves Alvie in search of a glamorous singing career.

It might seem strange that Paul, so intensely serious, should play an obviously shallow and superficial man. Tony is the typical satirized Hollywood mogul: have you seen my swimming pool, have you seen my bedroom. He collects things that are expensive and people who are trivial and bored. Woody Allen drew the character with perceptive accuracy, but the character is definitely not based on Paul Simon.

Paul didn't show the acting promise that Artie had shown; perhaps because he is an introverted person, acting is more difficult for him. But at the same time, Paul is good as Tony Lacey because he underplays the role. When we see Tony tempting Annie, he seems plausible, a quiet man. Like Annie, we want to believe in him, even though we can see no evidence. And we identify with her sense of disappointment when all his promises come to nothing.

Meanwhile, Art continued to work on his album, which was to be a new direction in several ways. It was much more eclectic musically than the previous two albums. He travelled to Alabama to work with the Muscle Shoals Rhythm Section, the musicians who had recorded with Paul a few years earlier. He crossed the Atlantic to Dublin to work with the Chieftains, the famous Irish instrumental group who play traditional folk music. He went to New York to cut one track, but the rest of the work was done in various studios in California.

Another difference from previous albums was that, apart from one traditional song and a fifties standard, all the tracks were written by the same composer, his friend Jimmy Webb. Artie paid tribute to Jimmy's talent with a selection of love songs which he presented with lavish orchestrations. 'I've been criticized for being too lush,' he said. 'But what that really means is that my leaning is more legato than percussive. I happen to like smooth, connected notes more than choppy, staccato ones. I find some songs too gritty, too sophisticated. My style is to sing bloody, from the heart.'

Art employed the skills of old friends on the album: Jimmy was accompanying him on keyboards; Stephen Bishop, David Crosby and Leah Kunkel (sister of the well-loved Cass Elliot) were doing background vocals; Joe Osborn played bass and Bill Payne played synthesizer; Barry Beckett did some work on keyboards and was associate producer. Later, Artie said: 'This time, my partners were more supportive. That tilts it more in my direction in terms of allowing me to express myself more fully.'

Another factor was that he produced the album himself, so it reflected his love of the musical sound and the joys of the mixing room where, by his own estimation, he spent 80 per cent of his studio time. 'I respond more to notes than to lyrics,' he said. 'I'm interested in their richness and power. What I get caught up in is texture and sonority. The sound per se.'

In the autumn of '77, CBS released a Paul Simon single, 'Slip Slidin' Away' / 'Stranded in a Limousine', which became a hit in the following year. 'Slip Slidin' Away' is a carefully structured song, presenting people in conflict. The third verse, about a man torn between the love of his son and the circumstances which keep them apart, would seem to be autobiographical. The song is unified in structure because each verse progresses through life: the first tells of a sexual love that's all consuming, the second of a marriage that's not working, and the third of a divorced parent poignantly trying to communicate with his child.

'Stranded in a Limousine' is a hard, funky number, very evocative of New York streets, capturing the excitement in the neighbourhood as a gangster is spotted in his car, stopping at traffic lights. Tiny details build up to an atmosphere of tension: the children run to tell their parents and the adults decide how to 'divvy up' the reward money, then there's a frantic rooftop search and the inevitable photographers.

The single heralded the arrival of a new album, *Greatest Hits etc.*, in November. It's generous on songs, opening with both sides of the single and including all the solo hits. 'Duncan' and 'American Tune' are both live versions. The critics loved it. Barry

Cain wrote that Paul possessed 'a bionic eye which sees through the dirt, and an undeniable talent actually to sculpt songs. One of the few albums deserving the name *Greatest Hits*.' It was highly successful commercially, a certified million seller, receiving a Platinum Disc.

Early in December, both Paul and Art appeared on television. On the 8th, NBC presented the *Paul Simon Special*, an hour-long show of music and comedy, which featured most of the talents from the *Saturday Night* team. It was written by Paul and Lorne Michaels, with improvisations from Charles Grodin and back-up from Chevy Chase and Lily Tomlin. From the public's point of view, the most eagerly anticipated guest on the show was Art Garfunkel, who joined Paul to sing, appropriately, 'Old Friends'.

On the 11th, NBC presented the Billboard Number One Music Awards, hosted by Kris Kristofferson and the Bee Gees. Paul appeared with Leonard Bernstein and Marvin Hamlisch, paying a warm musical tribute to the late CBS President Goddard Lieberson.

By the end of 1977, Art was in the final stages of his album. The last few months had been gruelling, as he blended sounds together, checked and rechecked every tiny detail himself. He was striving for perfection in every aspect of the album. 'I work a lot on crafting,' he explained. 'It's exhilarating at first and then very painful. I get caught up because I think it takes a special love for the music to make it work.'

He did make it work, and the album was finally completed in the studio on 23 December 1977. The relief was enormous. Art took off immediately for a skiing holiday in Aspen. He was exhausted but very satisfied with the work he'd done.

It was while he was on holiday that he realized how much he wanted to tour again. Columbia executives had been urging him to set up a tour in the new year to promote the album. Now he felt ready to face the challenge. With three albums to his credit, he felt confident enough to consider the prospect of a major tour.

Art returned from his holiday refreshed. In this mood, he told

Columbia not to release his album but to hold on while he re-recorded one or two tracks. Then, in the early spring of 1978, he felt it was finally ready. It was to be called *Watermark*.

The cover photo, taken by Laurie Bird, is strikingly different from the starkness of *Breakaway*. We see Art reclining on a sun deck in the California sunshine. It suggests a new optimism and confidence, and Art was aware of this: 'I was after a photograph with no mystique. I wanted to come out from the masks, to get away from the shadows, including my own.'

The first track, 'Crying in My Sleep', traces how a man passes an evening, trying to forget his lover: he calls in at a favourite café, runs a bath, watches television, drinks too much and takes sleeping pills. And all for nothing, because he wakes from a disturbing dream in which he reaches out for her and knocks the phone off the bedside table. His assurances to the operator – I just had a bad dream – are poignant. Art's phrasing is skilful, important in this song.

'Marionette' is a fascinating song. The puppet he has created is likened to the woman he loves, and musically, her jerky movements are suggested by the jaunty melody. Art sings it more slowly than Jimmy Webb does on his own album *And So On*, but he still maintains the puppet-like feel of the song. An interesting difference is the added line which refers to Brandenburg Gate, presumably in honour of Bach's Brandenburg Concertos. The texture of Art's voice is wonderful here; it conveys a sadly resigned old man who recognizes her despair and addresses her with simple tenderness. Then he puts her back on the shelf to wait for the next man, and hope for better luck.

'Shine It on Me' is a love song with unusual and difficult phrasing, which is controlled here with ease. The song is simultaneously sweet and powerful, and Art alternates between light and shade of texture. It's very dramatic.

'Watermark' is a tribute to a childlike and elusive lover, described with similes that convey her idealized and enigmatic qualities; she is like a watermark, never really there and never really gone. Art's vocal is lightly backed by acoustic guitar and overdubbed to get a husky sound.

'Saturday Suit' urges a lover to forget the daytime problems and go on the town, even though it's a weekday. Vocally, it's interesting because it gives Art a chance to use some mellow, lower register notes.

'All My Love's Laughter' is haunting. The lyric is one of Jimmy Webb's finest – a portrait of a woman who is all too easy to love but who has ambitious goals. She is physically lovely but unattainable, the wearer of many faces, possessing mysterious charm but little substance. Jimmy's own version on record is angrier and more sexual, and we know that he did try to hold on to Satan's proud lady. Art sings it sweetly, and perhaps that's ironic because the woman, like the song, isn't as sweet as she seems.

Side Two begins with 'What a Wonderful World'. This song, the Cooke/Alpert/Adler classic of the fifties, is recorded here with Paul Simon and James Taylor, and produced by Phil Ramone in a New York studio. A well-balanced track, it blends the individual styles of the three artists into a tongue-in-cheek humour. It's a very nostalgic song, informally recorded as though three friends have got together one afternoon. The Simon & Garfunkel blend is still magic, and James Taylor is hypnotic as always.

'Mr Shuck 'n' Jive' is a re-titled version of Jimmy's 1972 song 'Catharsis'. The slow and mournful piano notes enhance the sense of failure and bitterness. Peter Reilly wrote of this track: 'Garfunkel manages to infuse a generous compassion that gives heart to the final lines.'

'Paper Chase' is a serious lyric with lively music, describing sexual games that are tantalizing and irresistible, ultimately leading to rejection. This is a good example of Jimmy Webb's skill in using a metaphor that's imaginative and apt, then sustaining it through the song. It's a skilful analogy to show a woman's elusive and frustrating sexuality.

'She Moved through the Fair' is a traditional folk song,

beautifully recorded with the Chieftains. It maintains the authentic Irish feel, and it reveals not just the purity of Art's voice but also its control.

'Someone Else' is a very sad song, tinged with bitterness. It presents an inevitable cycle of pain, as one affair leads to another – a favourite theme of Jimmy's. Art sings with empathy, and the result is emotionally charged.

The album ends with 'Wooden Planes', a recollection of happy, uncomplicated childhood, now seen in contrast to the turmoil of adulthood. The lyric works in simple, direct statements, underlined musically with a series of disturbing diminished chords to express conflict and anger. Vocally, it's a minefield, but Art lifts his voice to a passionate climax which also marks the close of the album.

Artie had good reason to be proud of *Watermark*. After a huge investment of time and energy, he had produced a finely balanced, flawlessly sung album. To date, it was his own favourite. 'I'm in *Watermark* more than I have been in any album.' But the critics were divided in their views and old labels are hard to get rid of. To some, it was once again evidence of his skill as a background singer and no more; others felt that his choice of material did him credit and that he'd interpreted Jimmy Webb's songs with sensitivity.

Anyway, the public liked it, and it soon reached Gold Disc status. Artie was asked if he was sorry it hadn't sold even more. 'No, I'm not disappointed,' he said. 'Enough people bought it. Enough for me.' But he also felt: 'Frankly, my records are something less than Simon & Garfunkel's. There's a certain combustible energy in partnerships, I think.'

Art has deep feelings about duality, the combining of talents and ideas. For this reason, he works very well in partnerships. And for this reason, *Watermark* was an album he liked particularly, for here he had combined outstanding talents – those of a highly gifted writer and those of a superb singer.

Peter Reilly threw light on this in *Stereo Review*: 'Garfunkel has exactly the right spare, intelligent vocal style for Webb's intense, deeply felt lyrics, and the nonchalant but enormously secure musicianship the elusive music demands. In song after song, Art Garfunkel brings to performing completion the work of one of America's best writers of popular music. It is the fusion of the two major talents, Garfunkel and Webb, that gives the album its glow.'

Chapter Twenty-two

WARNER BROTHERS AND A TOUR

For quite a long time, Paul had been considering an entirely new venture, writing a musical. He felt he had gone as far as he could with albums of unrelated songs, and the logical step forward was to write a show, either for film or for Broadway.

On 15 February 1978, he signed a contract with Warner Brothers Records. It was a new leaf indeed, after fourteen years with CBS. In *Rolling Stone* Michael Tannen, Paul's lawyer and business manager, was reported as saying that CBS had originally been offered Paul's movie soundtrack and that they had declined it. CBS made no comment.

The contract with Warners guaranteed Paul a great deal of money. It was estimated that he would earn somewhere between ten and fifteen million dollars for his next three albums. He would also have total artistic freedom, as specified by the contract. Nevertheless, according to Michael Tannen: 'Paul didn't want to leave CBS. What it came down to was that Warner Brothers wanted Paul more than CBS did. The money difference was not that great. Warners didn't steal him. Money was not the reason.'

Presumably Warners' connection with the movie industry was a significant factor in Paul's decision. What he had in mind was more than a musical album: he was writing a script which he wanted to make into a film. It was a massive project, and it was obviously convenient that Warners would be able to release both the album and the film.

In the spring of '78, Art embarked on a major tour of the

USA, his first since the final S & G concerts of 1970. He explained why he'd waited so long: 'I felt I didn't have sufficient material to give people the full value they deserve. Now I feel I can fill out a show.' And he told *Rolling Stone*: 'I was busy with other things. It's in the last few years that I've begun to think, and very subliminally, that it is pleasurable to sing for people when the sound system is right.'

Obviously, he was feeling nervous about it. He was, after all, stepping out from his former duo role and presenting himself on stage as Art Garfunkel, solo artist. 'In essence, this tour is dominated by a successful overcoming of something I shied away from for a long time,' he said. But in a characteristically balanced way, he accepted that the anxiety was a necessary part of the developing process. For he certainly was developing, and that involved stretching himself and taking risks. He felt ready for the challenge. 'Readiness, in fact, is very central to this tour,' he told the press.

He set off with his band, consisting of a guitarist, pianist, drummer, and vocalist Leah Kunkel, on a forty-city tour of the States. He was delighted to be on the road again, and he radiated his enthusiasm to his audiences in performances that were polished and professional. 'I'm finding the tour incredibly satisfying,' he told journalists.

Rich Wiseman reviewed Art's thirty-third date at the Dorothy Chandler Pavilion in Los Angeles. The previous night, Art had been suffering with a lingering sore throat, the nightmare of every singer. In spite of this, Art was at his best on stage. Wiseman described the event in glowing terms. Art was totally relaxed, even joking with the audience after his spirited rendition of 'Cecilia': 'I'm beginning to think the old duo shouldn't have split up after all.' He included five other Simon & Garfunkel numbers which he performed impeccably and confidently. He received two standing ovations. After the show, thrilled by the response, he said lightheartedly, 'It sure is nice being stroked.'

But it wasn't all stroking. The day after the triumphant show, he was disturbed by an article in *The Times*, the result of a long-distance, ninety-minute telephone interview several days earlier. Art described it as the kind of interview that is 'so off-putting that you vow you'll never do it again'.

And with good reason. The journalist had laboured the point that Art didn't write songs, referring to 'his aversion to composing'. Now, with the newspaper in his hand, Artie told Rich Wiseman: 'I should have asked, "Do you water-ski?" He would have said no. I would have said, "Why?" And then I would have invited him to consider how it feels being asked that same question, twice a year, every year for the last six or seven years.' As if that weren't enough, the journalist had also commented that Art had done 'nothing' since the album *Bridge over Troubled Water*. Art told Wiseman: 'It hurts my feelings. It puts me on the defensive. You mean, "Hard work in similar endeavours with a lesser degree of mass acclaim." That is not the same as nothing.'

Art agreed that his band was scaled down in comparison to the Simon & Garfunkel days. Nevertheless, while he realized that his solo act had lesser proportions than his duo act, he felt positive about the challenge that presented. 'Two people are inherently more interesting than one. The loss of Paul Simon is a loss of great talent. Naturally, it's something I can't enjoy dwelling on. Give me a break and I'll take it from there.'

He did just that. The last dates of his tour were equally successful, closing at New York's Carnegie Hall. Paul joined him on stage to sing 'My Little Town'. Another highlight of the show was Jimmy Webb as a special guest. Art closed the show, after several encores, with a moving version of 'Bridge'. After the show, CBS marked the end of the tour by throwing a party for him at Tavern on the Green, with an impressive guest list that included Paul Simon.

The following day in the *New York Times*, Robert Palmer reviewed Art's Carnegie Hall show. 'Mr Garfunkel has become a compelling song stylist and an understated, but remarkably musical vocal technician. He has the rare ability to put a song over with a maximum of feeling, a minimum of fuss and an admirable control of pitch, timbre and phrasing.'

The tour was a significant turning point in Art's career. He had at last emerged triumphant as a solo artist. For some time, he had been reflecting on his position as the other half of Simon & Garfunkel. He was eager to shake off that image. 'I don't always want to play the vulnerable one,' he said. '"Is he strong enough to be a person, or is he, in fact, a sack of potatoes?" That's a little bit of an embarrassing pose.' And once again, he gave his answer to the old familiar question about Simon & Garfunkel getting back together. He told the press: 'If I never said another word on that subject, I'd be pleased.'

While it was true that there was no Simon & Garfunkel reunion in the pipeline, there was a personal reunion of Paul and Artie during the summer and autumn months of 1978. Art was back in New York now and found himself seeing a lot of his old friend. 'I started hanging out with Paul and it seemed the most natural thing in the world. We reminded ourselves of the humour we shared, the jokes, the similar concerns, the similarity of our lives.'

Their shared interest in making music was still there, a major part of a thirty-year friendship. Art told *Newsweek*: 'I'm still friends with Paul and I can imagine getting together with him one evening, starting to sing and realizing that it sounded good when the sun came up the next morning and we were still singing.' Quite unconsciously, Artie was echoing those words in Paul's song in which all of the nights they harmonize till dawn.

By late autumn, Paul had made some progress on his soundtrack but was running into legal problems. When he signed with Warners, Paul still owed CBS one more album, as stipulated in his contract. He planned to release an album of songs by other writers whose work he admired. It's a great pity this album never appeared.

On 29 November Paul filed two lawsuits against CBS in the New York State Supreme Court. He was seeking release from his contract with them, or a ruling that any album he delivered consisting of songs previously unrecorded by him should be accepted and promoted by CBS as the one he owed them. This should therefore fulfil his obligation to them. He also claimed damages of around ten thousand dollars, on the grounds that CBS hadn't promoted his single or *Greatest Hits etc.*, and that royalty payments had been irregular – which CBS denied.

CBS Records Group President Walter Yetnikoff, in a letter to Michael Tannen, claimed: 'The concept of recording an album of songs by writers other than himself is, under the circumstances, inconsistent with Paul's contractual obligations to us.' And they went to court.

Paul was shocked and hurt by the attitude of CBS. 'Their reaction was unpredictably severe,' he said later. 'And I felt they were hostile to me on a personal level. I've never in my entire career had an enemy, and it was all very upsetting to me.'

Eventually, Paul bought back the album he still owed them, and was thereby released from his contract. Ultimately, relations between him and the company became more cordial. Paul later cast CBS executive Bruce Lundvall as an extra in his movie.

Work went on with his new project. He had decided to make it a film, because filming seemed closer to the process of making an album and thus was partly familiar ground. Also, if he did a film, he could present the soundtrack as an album; with a Broadway show, other people would be singing his songs.

The screenplay was taking a long time to write. It was more or less his first experience with prose since his college days. 'I felt nervous about it, but I wanted to feel nervous about it. That's what I call the "good scared", where you bite off more than you can chew – and learn to chew bigger.'

Chapter Twenty-three

MAKING MOVIES

Movies would dominate Paul's and Art's work in 1979, and the year opened with a burst of creative energy from both of them. They each had important projects on hand – projects that would bring a sense of achievement but also some disappointment.

Paul was still working on his screenplay. He'd emerged with a story about Jonah Levin, a rock 'n' roll musician whose career is declining and whose marriage breaks up. Paul had set himself an ambitious goal. 'I thought I would tell the story of my generation of musicians and I thought I would explore the crevices of my marriage and divorce, but the closer I got, the further away I got. So whatever autobiographical bits are let in are just information that clings to the intestine as it passes through. That's not exactly the metaphor I would choose for my marriage but . . .'

His involvement in the project was enormous. He had conceived it, written it and scored it. Indeed, Warner Brothers agreed to finance it only because he was so deeply involved at every level. Michael Tannen was the executive producer, so the whole venture was tightly controlled.

There was the question of who to cast as Jonah. It's difficult to find actors who can sing rock music convincingly. Paul discussed the role with Richard Dreyfuss, who was a viable choice in many ways. But there were practical problems. According to his contract with Warners, Paul had to give them the soundtrack of the film to be released as an album. Paul felt it would seem odd to have Dreyfuss acting in the film and miming to Paul's voice.

In any case, Warners wanted Paul to star in the film. He was dubious about it; apart from a small role in *Annie Hall*, he had no acting experience. 'I didn't know if I wanted to be so far out there, to be so vulnerable to criticism on a personal level,' he said. 'And I thought, "Well, if I write it and I write the music, that's plenty. But if I go and star in it . . ."' But in the absence of a better solution, he agreed.

Then he looked for someone to direct. He approached several directors, but some were wary of Paul's massive involvement in it; they felt they would be in a difficult position creatively. Paul understood their reluctance. 'They all wondered if there was going to be room for them to direct.' But one director, Robert M. Young, didn't share that feeling. According to Paul: 'His ego didn't get in the way. He saw room for him to function as a director and be of help to the movie and still feel that he was, you know, in charge.'

Paul took his leading role very seriously and went to learn his craft, taking acting lessons from Mira Restova, former teacher of the legendary Hollywood actor Montgomery Clift, and suggested to Paul by Charles Grodin. He learned some of the techniques he needed: to cry in front of the cameras, tears induced by inhaling menthol.

He spent several weeks in Chicago, where the action takes place, mastering the mid-American slang and dialect of club entertainers and waitresses. He explored the background of the film, striving to make it accurate in every scene. The same drive for authenticity had taken him to Jamaica in search of musicians almost a decade earlier.

He worked hard, redoing difficult scenes with the same relentless spirit that had been characteristic of his album recording. Afterwards, he said he'd enjoyed it, but 'I don't want to be a movie star, and being a celebrity undermines the seriousness of your work. I'm not an exhibitionist. No, I'm not ready for summer stock companies and *Streetcar Named Desire*.'

Co-starring as Jonah's wife Marion was Blair Brown, a

respected and versatile actress who achieved one of her greatest triumphs playing the enigmatic Jacqueline Kennedy alongside Martin Sheen's JFK. Jonah's band, Stuff, was made up of the session musicians who had toured with Paul and appeared on his albums over the years: Richard Tee on keyboards, Eric Gale on guitar, Tony Levin on bass and Steve Gadd on drums. Jonah's son, Matty, was taken by eight-year-old Michael Pearlman; Paul's own son Harper had a tiny part in the film as the boy Jonah, a sequence that appears over the credits. In a cameo role, Lou Reed took the part of an incompetent record producer, one of Jonah's many burdens.

The film takes an honest look at the world of rock music. It focuses on the ugly side, the realization that you're not making it any more, that maybe you're past it now. And what do you do when you can't give it up, and it appears to be giving you up? What do you do instead?

In the *Rolling Stone* review of the film, Dave Marsh points out the conflicts that run through it: between Jonah's rock 'n' roll dream and Marion's wish that he'd grow up; between the dual role of musician and employer to the band; between the urge to make music and the need to accommodate the people who market it; between the joy of artistry and the necessity of working for a living. As in Paul's songs, the conflicts are restrained and understated.

Elvis Presley pervades the film, and also Jonah's life. There are three references to him: Marion urges Jonah to grow up, pointing out that he's wanted to be Elvis since he was fourteen. When the band is on the road in their van, they play a morbid game to pass the time, where each of them names a dead pop star; it's even suggested that they have two separate categories for overdoses and plane crashes. Jonah names Elvis, adding sadly, 'Yeah, he's dead all right.' Elvis features for the third time when Jonah recites to Marion two lines from one of his more sentimental love songs.

The picture of Jonah builds up through these images of Elvis. Jonah emerges as a failed rock 'n' roller who dreams of being another Elvis Presley, something he can never be. Paul himself, of course, had lived with such a comparison for most of his life. By now, he was evaluating not only the success of Elvis's great legend but also the personal tragedy. He told *Playboy*: 'As much as I idolized him, the lesson of his life – what happens to people with tremendous gifts in their youth – was terrible. His lesson was that you go to Las Vegas and stop thinking and live in an insulated world where you can get as many drugs as you want. That's very destructive.'

Despite the surface similarities, Jonah certainly is not Paul Simon. Admittedly every writer uses his own life in his work, reshaping it and turning it into fiction. But there it ends, because Jonah is quite different from Paul in some important ways. Their careers are far from parallel: Paul is famous and successful and Jonah isn't; Jonah plays in a band, which Paul did briefly as a teenager. Paul was in a duo, of course, but essentially he is a solo artist, and his only experience with a band is with session musicians and backing groups. 'I was never part of that life in that way,' Paul admitted. 'And that is an essential part of rock 'n' roll. I only know it by being with people who are in it. But I never lived it.' It would be true, I think, to say that it's really Jonah who's the typical rock 'n' roll performer, rather than Paul.

Most importantly, perhaps, their lives are financially poles apart. Paul pointed this out: 'Jonah Levin doesn't have the luxury that I have of sitting back and thinking about strengths and weaknesses. He's out there hustling a buck, and I'm not.' As journalist Dave Marsh so aptly puts it: 'For Jonah, just making a friend is a luxury.'

The parallels are there in the depiction of Jonah's personal life, most obviously in his relationship with his son. Also, we feel that in Jonah and Marion, Paul is exploring much of himself and Peggy. That is by no means a weakness in the film; rather, it lends authenticity and realism.

The year 1979 opened for Art also with the prospect of a movie. He stepped back into his film career when British director

Nicolas Roeg cast him as the lead in his new project *Bad Timing – A Sensual Obsession*, an original screenplay by Yale Udoff.

Best known for his direction of such controversial films as *Walkabout, Don't Look Now* and *The Man Who Fell to Earth*, Roeg is a man with a lifetime of filming behind him. He has been described by Philip French as 'possibly the most extraordinary cinematic talent to have emerged in Britain since the departure of Hitchcock'.

Bad Timing is the story of a love affair between Dr Alex Linden, an American psychoanalyst and lecturer at the University of Vienna, and Milena Flaherty, a tempestuous, fiercely independent woman played by Theresa Russell. Their affair is doomed from the start, perhaps, to bring them both frustration and heartache. While they are sexually attracted to each other, they are irreconcilably opposite in character. In the passionate clash of wills, they destroy each other with jealousy, anger and hostility.

From the first moment, Roeg liked the script. 'It touched a major chord in my emotion and I wanted to make it very much,' he said. And Art would later describe the director's attention to detail: 'From the first week, Nick began to get interested in how my character moves, speaks, ponders, asks and the faces he makes. And I began to stretch out with this lovely feeling that he was really giving me an open shot.'

Art realized he was facing his most challenging role so far. He was to portray a man who is drawn, almost against his will, to a relationship that is inevitably destructive – the attraction of the moth to the flame. The part was very demanding. As the love affair of Alex and Milena unfolds, we have to understand the intensity of their passion, which goes beyond jealousy, beyond reason, and finally beyond control. It's a relationship constantly in turmoil, alternating between love and hate, pain and ecstasy.

Art welcomed the challenge this presented. 'It is nerve-shredding to go on stretching yourself in work, but to rest on past successes or coast on present achievement would become so boring. It is better to be scared than bored.' In the same spirit as his director, Art became totally absorbed in the character, devoting his days to acting the part and his nights to preparation. 'I'm here to make a film,' he told the press. 'and I have no time for anything else. Acting and music are my jobs and I have to do them as well as possible.'

In the four exhausting months on location in London and Vienna, he became physically and emotionally drained, but kept his eye firmly on the goal. 'It's the process of being a person on screen so that other people can look at him,' he said. 'You are hired to search your soul and come up with aspects of who you are, for presentation. So it behooves you to find out who you are.'

It was during those location shots in the spring of 1979 that Art worked with Daniel Massey. His part in the film, described in something of an understatement as a 'foppish man', is a delightful and intriguing cameo role. It lasts only a few moments, in which he has an exchange with Alex in a crowded café.

Daniel Massey comes from an established acting family, and is one of Britain's finest actors, with a distinguished stage career. But he's more popularly known for challenging roles in TV dramatizations; most memorably, he was in Jean-Paul Sartre's *Roads to Freedom* on BBC, in which he played a gentle, cultured intellectual who is tortured by the guilt of his homosexuality. He also gave a fascinating, impressionistic performance as Noël Coward in the film *Star*, in which Julie Andrews played Gertrude Lawrence.

Daniel told me about his first meeting with Art on the set of *Bad Timing*, when they were introduced by Nicolas Roeg: 'I only met him for literally ten minutes and I liked him. I was intrigued as to how he worked because I'd been aware of him as an actor prior to the film, in *Carnal Knowledge*, and I thought he was wonderful in that.'

They started work on the scene at about ten thirty in the morning and spent some time rehearsing together. There was very little opportunity to socialize, since it was a realistic location and there was a lot of background to set up. Nevertheless, shooting was completed by about four in the afternoon.

I asked Daniel Massey about Art's method of working. He told me: 'I think he's a man who prepares a lot. So what I noticed on the set was really rather free, and I thought he was comfortable in front of the camera. I think he has an empathy for the camera, which is evident from the way he performs.

'I liked meeting Art. He was very sympathetic, not at all pulling a star job on you. He couldn't have been. He was rather retiring. When we weren't in front of the camera he would go away and I think he was on his own. Everyone liked him very much. He seemed to be a sympathetic soul. And very unactorish, which I like.'

Daniel talked about how much he enjoyed Art's solo albums, particularly *Breakaway*, which he plays a great deal, his favourite track being 'Waters of March', which he described as 'the quintessential Garfunkel number'. He told me: 'He's got a marvellous sense of rhythm in popular music. It has that wonderfully elusive, ambiguous quality that I find is one of the chief pleasures that he projects. Your responses are multiple; you say, "I like that, but I don't quite understand why."

'What's fascinating to me about Art is that you can't pin him down. He's acutely intelligent and extremely sensitive. I would think he's not a Top 20 merchant, and I'm always drawn to that sort of figure because what makes them interesting is precisely that they make you work in your responses to them. And so he's a much richer confection.'

Denholm Elliott also co-starred in the film, in the role of Milena's Czech husband across the border. He's a tired, disillusioned man who is only too aware that his marriage to a sexually attractive young woman is irreconcilably over, and tries to content himself with occasional visits which give him fleeting and bittersweet consolation. He's an important character in the film because it is he, and not Alex, who really understands Milena. He loves her for what she really is, and Alex never truly comes to terms with that. He lets her come and go without recrimination; she will always belong to him in some elusive way, simply because of the freedom he allows her.

Denholm Elliott's death from tuberculosis in October 1992 was a tragic one. His career had been impressive, centred almost entirely on character roles, often of English gentlemen. He was a master of world-weary, sardonic, intelligent, sophisticated men of the world, notably in *Alfie*, *King Rat*, and the BBC's production of *Hotel du Lac*.

Denholm talked to me at some length about Art's dedication to the role of Alex. 'His acting is very contained; I think that's the word,' he said. 'He goes very much for truth rather than effect. I think he's a very good actor of that school where you've got to really be inside the character and you've got to really feel the scene. In the final scenes, he had to appear totally exhausted and haggard, and I believe that he actually didn't sleep for two nights, so that he could look and feel the part. He's very realistic and it comes out marvellously.'

Interestingly, Denholm gave some insight into Art's lifestyle during those weeks. 'He's very reclusive and has enormous energy, I thought. His needs were very small. I think he was staying in one room with a bath. There wasn't anything very grand. He could put his hand on his hi-fi on the one side, and on the telephone on the other side.'

In just that spirit, Art spent the rainy nights in his room, playing his tapes of Bach and thinking about his own life, his past experiences and the nature of love itself. He had embarked on a course of self-discovery and was searching for something that would help him get nearer to the complex and ambivalent character of Alex Linden.

In April, journalist David Lewin talked to him in Vienna and found him analysing show business and the pressures that were inevitably put on a star. 'There is the problem of finding people you can trust, whose advice is honest,' he said. 'You have to be able to sort out who is flattering you from those who are telling the truth. More than anything else, it's not having anyone to trust that destroys people in this business.'

He also talked about those reckless years when he had witnessed the premature and tragic deaths of Jimi Hendrix, Janis Joplin, Brian Jones. While Paul was exploring just this subject in his new screenplay, Art was going through it in his mind. So many young artists, he realized, had died needlessly from drug overdoses. He explained how it had affected him and Paul, making them more cautious, more disciplined and, to some extent, more isolated than many of their peers.

During those months on location, Art was thinking about marriage. Now, four years after his divorce from Linda, he was considering a second marriage, to his girlfriend Laurie Bird. He was cautious about it; it was all too easy to step back into a situation that had been so devastating the first time around. 'I still have the scars of failure, because I didn't take marriage as something you changed, but as something that would last a long time. It's difficult telling your parents that your marriage hasn't worked. It's more difficult telling yourself.' And he told another reporter: 'I'm reluctant to marry again because my first marriage went wrong. But I did think I would marry again one day; I'd like children.'

Then, in May 1979, *Watership Down* burst into public view, and would affect Art's career greatly. The film was released along with 'Bright Eyes' as a single. Almost three years after they recorded it in those exhausting hours in the London studio, Art and Mike Batt saw its release with a sense of satisfaction.

It's unfortunate that some disc jockeys and reporters viewed 'Bright Eyes' far too simplistically, as a song about rabbits. Presumably they began with the idea that the film is about rabbits – but of course it is more than that. As an allegory, it endows the animals with human powers of expression and human experiences. We can identify with them on every level. The journey of the rabbits into their Promised Land symbolically represents the escape of all persecuted groups of people from danger into safety, from war to peace, from hunger to plenty. The human parallels are endless.

In spite of this, Mike Batt spent many a frustrating interview explaining what ought to have been obvious – the more profound implications of the song. He told me: ' "Bright Eyes" is an adult song. It's not a song about rabbits, just as *Watership Down* isn't just a book about rabbits. It's a story about people, about human qualities. And "Bright Eyes" is a song about human emotions. It's a question I ask myself quite often: what does happen when you die? It's a feeling you get when someone has died; how can that lively person not be there any more? Where have they gone?'

There can be no doubt that Mike's song and Art's performance of it contributed greatly to the commercial success of the film. The haunting theme song underlined the essentially serious aspects of the novel: the elusiveness and mystery of death. 'Bright Eyes' captured the imagination of a huge audience and subsequently became a classic. Art's performance of it remains the definitive version – majestic and poignant, rich in emotional power.

The single was a huge success, climbing the charts rapidly in both America and Europe. In Britain, it was number 1 for two weeks, and it stayed in the charts until early July. It was awarded a Gold Disc almost immediately. Moreover, it won three of the coveted Ivor Novello Awards: Best Film Song, Most Performed British Work and Best Selling British Record. Mike Batt was correct; though it had been a difficult birth, 'Bright Eyes' was indeed a beautiful child.

Chapter Twenty-four

FATE FOR BREAKFAST AND TWO FILMS

With 'Bright Eyes' came a new album from Art, *Fate for Breakfast*. It was recorded and mixed in different studios on both sides of the Atlantic, and produced by Louie Shelton. The album displays an impressive crowd of session musicians, mostly tried and true. The cover shows a relaxed Art, seated at the breakfast table, surrounded by brightly coloured kitchenware. He was obviously very much at ease with his audience.

Side one opens with a love song, 'In a Little While' by Dennis Belfield, who also plays bass on some of the other tracks. It's lonely, but optimistic. Vocally, Art achieves a strangely taut, vibrating effect which captures a sense of urgency.

'Since I Don't Have You' is in a slower mood; Art sings with pathos which rises to intensity in the third verse. The tenor saxophone solo, played by Michael Brecker, echoes the torch songs of the forties. It's musically well balanced, very different from the fifties version by the Skyliners.

'And I Know' is a Michael Sembello and David Batteau song, restful and dreamlike. Billy and Bobby Alessi provide the distinctive background vocals, along with Leah Kunkel.

'Sail on a Rainbow' is by Stephen Bishop. Vocally, the echo is effective, giving Art a chance to use his falsetto range. The tenor sax interlude is played here by Tom Scott, and gives a contrast to the overall lightness of the track.

'Miss You Nights', a Dave Townsend song, which closes side one, is a high spot on the album. Art's voice stands out in all its glory, controlling the pathos with subtle light and shade, alternating between gentle regret and strong passion. The orchestration is also very strong, particularly in the dramatic piano by Larry Knechtel. There's a light string arrangement by Del Newman. It's hard to follow up the well-known version by Cliff Richard, but Art's rendering stands beside it without flinching.

After 'Bright Eyes' comes 'Finally Found a Reason', a pretty song, also from the Sembello–Batteau team, with help on the lyric from Rick Bell and Craig Bickhardt. It's a light, refreshing love declaration, with pleasant background voices including that of Stephen Bishop.

'Beyond the Tears' is a direct contrast, a Bob Grundy–Jeffrey Comanor composition with the theme of unselfish, undying love. It's dramatic, powerful, with Artie's singing truly 'bloody, from the heart'.

'Oh How Happy' by C. Hathcet, is jaunty and gives scope for the versatility of Art's voice. The overdubbed backing blends neatly into the vocal; he shifts tempo and phrasing with dexterity. The overall sound is reminiscent of the resonant clarity and sweetness of chiming bells.

'When Someone Doesn't Want You' is a Jeffrey Staton composition – a slow, aching song. This also has a tenor sax interlude, a style which suits his voice and which he obviously favoured at this time. Steve Gadd's regular, heavy drumbeat is effective – like a pounding heartbeat.

'Take Me Away' closes the album, a song by Lance and Grant Gullickson; it's a heavy track orchestrally – and the orchestration is dominant here. Art sings all too briefly. Overall, *Fate for Breakfast* is an interesting album, on which Art experimented with different effects, vocally and musically. While it probably contains some of his lighter, weaker work, there can be no doubt that it also features some of his most powerful singing. It wasn't a milestone album, but it sold respectably and broke some new ground.

By June, his work on *Bad Timing* was almost over. The

company returned to New York to finish shooting. It was on arrival that Art received the horrifying news that Laurie Bird had committed suicide in his penthouse apartment where she had been staying.

Like many victims of the show-business treadmill, she had taken a overdose. Large amounts of drugs were found in her body and it was concluded that she had been taking them for some time. Police found her suicide note in the apartment; it indicated that she had been depressed for a long period.

Art was shattered by grief and by the senseless waste of her death. But in truly professional spirit, he managed to hold himself together long enough to complete the work on the film. *Photoplay* reported: 'The pain was showing on the face of Art Garfunkel as he walked in front of the cameras. Art looked pale and drawn.' It was with huge relief that Art finished *Bad Timing* and was able to give way to his feelings of utter devastation and loss.

He couldn't make himself return to the empty apartment where she had died, so he took a suite in a hotel on New York's Upper East Side. It was there that he spent the next few months, alone with his grief and endless questions. What would make a young and lovely woman take a fatal overdose of drugs?

When a journalist sought him out, he said: 'For months, I've been sympathetically feeling the depth of the pain that must have led her to take her own life.' He was devastated by loneliness: 'Laurie was the greatest thing I ever knew in my life. There are many yearnings we have as human souls, but to me, the paramount yearning is intimacy with one person. It hurts me that I'm the only one who knows how great she was.'

His grief was aggravated by press releases which placed the blame for Laurie's death with Artie. It was suggested, even stated in some cases, that she killed herself because of his reluctance to marry her. Reading such items in the press was a particularly cruel blow to Artie, not least because it wasn't true. He had been reluctant to marry only because he wanted it to be a success this time. He was clearly in love with Laurie and she knew that.

Anyone with any insight into suicide knows that there must be more of a motive, that the taking of a life is driven by a very strong force. It's a profoundly destructive act.

Although we can reason that the blame for Laurie's death should not be placed on Artie, guilt nevertheless took its toll. Years later, he talked about the effect it had: 'I asked myself constantly why I didn't marry her, because surely she was the apple of my eye. She was everything I was looking for in a woman. But I was very hurt by my first marriage, so as far as marriage to Laurie was concerned, I was extra scared.'

The press grew tired of the story in time, but Art remained alone with his sorrow. 'I was heartbroken,' he said later. 'It laid me low. I used to get very sad when the sun went down. The nights were very lonely for me.'

In the early winter months of 1980, he was struggling to come to terms with her death. After a long and bitter fight, he had reached a point where he felt he'd gained some insight. 'I feel I've learned a lot about the way living works on this planet,' he said. 'If there is an architect, I've got some clues on his moves now.'

He found himself remembering the words of prayers which had meant little to him, and now gave him some comfort. And he found some comfort in his friendship with Paul, with whom he was spending more time now. 'When a man doesn't have his woman, as I haven't since Laurie died, he's more open to his men friends,' he said.

He returned from a reclusive vacation in Hawaii in March, determined to throw himself back into his work. All the same, he stayed in the hotel that would be his home until he felt able to return to the apartment which was so full of memories.

When *Bad Timing* was released in London in the spring of 1980, Art was still haunted by Laurie: 'I'm still groping as to why she did it,' he said. 'I find it impossible to have a relationship with anyone else.' Years later, he was able to analyse this feeling: 'She was so wonderful and so unknown to anyone except me,' he said. 'But what really stopped me from seeing and getting involved with new women was the fact that I just couldn't forget Laurie. I hated the thought that the way to get over her was to put her out of my mind. It was the one thing I didn't want to do to her.'

Meanwhile, in the last days of summer 1980, Paul was putting the finishing touches to his movie *One Trick Pony* in the cutting rooms at West 54th Street, wedged almost unnoticed between 7th and 8th Avenues. Phil Ramone worked with him, finishing the soundtrack engineering. Already, 'Late in the Evening', the first single from the album and the theme to the movie, looked likely to be a hit, and was being played on radio stations throughout the country.

Simultaneous with the release of the film was the album release. The cover shows Paul turning back to glance at the camera, symbolic perhaps of Jonah's living in the past. Side one opens with the fast, upbeat 'Late in the Evening', Paul's tribute to the rock 'n' roll he loves. It evokes an atmosphere of being with a crowd of friends, summer evening streets filled with a cappella music, girls sitting on the stoops watching.

'That's Why God Made the Movies' is a very complex song, strewn with Freudian imagery. Paul merges the loss of the mother in infancy with the adult fear of losing his lover; this blending reinforces the child–lover connection with powerful, stunningly beautiful imagery that suggests childhood and sexual love simultaneously. The interlude is a plaintive cry, childlike in construction, and the title itself is something a child might have said, but of course it's also an adult feeling: God made movies because life and reality are so painful.

The song explores more than this; it also shows a young man going out into the world, as Paul Simon's young men usually do, quite unprepared, armed only with courage, determination – and, above all, hope. The reference to the wolves' adoption of him alludes, of course, to Kipling's *Jungle Book* and to various legends, heightening our sense of the hostility and danger he faces, as well as the kindness he sometimes encounters. In this sense, we are taken back to the prostitutes of 'The Boxer' and the girl who befriends Duncan.

'One Trick Pony' is another of those seemingly flip songs that are actually profoundly painful. It's built on a sustained metaphor – the horse that can do only one trick. Some critics have assumed that Jonah is referring to himself, that he's the one trick pony, but that's obviously not correct. It's a cry of envy: see how the other guy manages to get by, much more easily than I do. There's a cleverly controlled bitterness in the description of the other man's gliding movements, the excitement he generates, his pride, his style. He can do only one thing well, but it will be enough to see him through, and that's what matters. It's caustic and makes us wince, but it never descends into self-pity.

'Oh Marion' is addressed to Jonah's wife; it's about the process of forcing yourself to be detached, and hopefully invulnerable. Jonah speaks of himself in the third person, which distances him from us and from himself. It's an enforced and deliberate isolation – shifting your heart in order to protect yourself. By the way, how many songwriters could use words like 'phenomenon', 'abstain' and 'auditioning' so neatly, and with such incredible ease?

'How the Heart Approaches What It Yearns' is, by any criteria, a beautiful and poignant song. Capturing the aimless wandering and hollow futility of a man's thoughts and journey through a melancholy evening, it's probably one of the loneliest songs Paul has ever written. The imagery is well controlled: sustained metaphors of heat and fever to convey sexual longing.

The song was important to Paul because it was a new direction for him musically. 'This tune has a very simple chord structure, but an odd time signature,' he explained. 'It's 10/8 and I keep this part very simple in terms of what I'm saying. Then I change the time signature to 6/8 and I use imagery. My teacher pushed me into that. He said, "Why don't you get into some new time signatures?" I don't expect other people will notice it. But at least I know it.'

'Ace in the Hole' opens side two and it's a hard, funky number about the ways in which a person can get relief or keep sane:

religion, money and music. It makes concise statements which are irrefutably sensible and familiar to all of us who have known despair; also, the message is characteristic of Paul's tense discipline: if you're crazy and you know it, you can compensate by keeping your self-control. The interlude is completely different from the rest of the song in style and tempo, and it glances at one of Paul's many city landscapes: visions of the moon rising over the smoke stacks of the cities they pass through. In the bus they are enclosed from the outside world, but not from their own memories and loneliness.

'Nobody' is a truly exquisite song, opening with a prayer-like tone coupled with startlingly vivid imagery. It reminds us of John Donne's poetry. The series of questions which makes up the song leads us always to the same answer: nobody. And this becomes nobody but you. It reminds us of 'Kathy's Song' in that it equates sexual love with the sacred.

'Jonah' portrays the life of a touring musician in marvellously economical opening lines. It also conveys the all-consuming power of music in one brilliant metaphor – Jonah being swallowed up by his music. A weary, desperate, aching song, it's one of his best.

'God Bless the Absentee' centres on the disruption of family life caused by being on the road. The singer misses his wife and son and the comforts of home. It explores music as an influence on his life, but here it's a cleansing, healing process, here though by implication also a painful one, symbolized by the surgeon's knife.

The climax of the album is the superb 'Long, Long Day' which reiterates the themes of the other songs: weariness and sexual longing and loneliness, here epitomized by the slow and wandering melody. His chance encounter with the woman in the bar is dramatized poignantly as they realize with a shrug that they're both alone and might as well be together.

The final verse is ironically undercut with a reference to the mechanics of writing where Paul hesitates before using an old cliché like the title of the song. It is typical of him that he avoids embarrassing extremes of sentimentality, and makes a cut that is sharp and clean. Those lines stand as a tribute to Paul himself, I feel, because he hates to abuse words. Only a writer with a profound love of language in all its complexity could have produced the lyrics to the album *One Trick Pony*.

The album was very favourably received. In *Stereo Review*, Peter Reilly wrote: 'What makes this such an interesting, challenging, chance-taking album is that it is evidently an attempt to communicate with an audience that the experts say no longer listens to pop music, to tell them that though the long pop summer is over, it's okay. Who else do you know of, who has had the courage to ask his audience to grow up along with him? There are, of course, one trick audiences too, those who will reject the offer out of hand. Pity.' And Martyn Sutton wrote: 'Every melody and every lyric is impeccably constructed. Without doubt, one of the best albums of the year.'

In September 1980, the films *Bad Timing* and *One Trick Pony* were both released in the USA (though *Bad Timing* had been premiered in London earlier, in April). In a blatant publicity gimmick – not a new one for Simon & Garfunkel – the two films were released together, even shown at the same cinema.

Art later described how he learned about that, from Paul himself: 'He got off the telephone and said, "My movie's opening at the Gemini One Theater. Guess which movie is opening up at the Gemini Two?" And I couldn't think of it. If somebody wants to make money from bringing up the old Simon & Garfunkel connection, that's okay. But my people haven't been pursuing it.'

They did not need to. Art received excellent notices for his performance as Alex Linden. According to David Sterrit of National Public Radio: 'Art Garfunkel gives the best performance of his career.' Philip French reported in the *Observer*: 'Art Garfunkel accurately hits off that precise combination of emotional immaturity and narcissistic brilliance that makes a certain kind of New York intellectual.' French went on to praise the technical skill of the film: Tony Richmond's camera work and Tony Lawson's editing. He added that, on a second viewing, he was 'fully convinced that it was a film of the very first rank, a work of great originality'. In *After Dark*, Norma McLain Stoop wrote: 'One of the year's best films. Dazzling. Exceptional acting by Art Garfunkel.' And Fred Yager of Associated Press: 'Art Garfunkel displays a keen acting ability in the most challenging and complicated role any actor could undertake.'

Such critical acclaim was gratifying, of course; the film also won Best Film Award at the Toronto Festival. Despite all this, it wasn't the commerical success it deserved to be. While Art must have felt satisfaction that his acting talent was recognized by the critics, he was nevertheless disappointed to watch the movie fade into the background. He had worked hard on the characterization and considered it to be his best film so far.

Ironically, Paul's life was again to run parallel to Artie's, as the release of his movie bought disappointment. *One Trick Pony*, which ended up one million dollars over its budget (already six million), brought widely diverse comments from the critics. In fact, they're so diverse that it's hard to realize they're talking about the same film.

Some saw it as a praiseworthy attempt that hadn't quite come off. Paul Gambaccini wrote: 'Unfortunately, Simon was an occasionally amusing, but not attention-grabbing actor. There wasn't enough meat in the plot, and too many shots of being on the road – literally the road, motorways, backroads, city streets.' But he called it a 'noble, but failed experiment'. There is much justice in this appraisal.

Other critics felt that it succeeded in presenting a truthful look at the world of rock 'n' roll. The *Los Angeles Times* called it 'perceptively and ruthlessly honest. An intimate film of much wit, style and impact. It ranks as one of the year's best.'

Paul's acting came in for much adverse criticism – that it was lukewarm, listless and uninteresting, and that the film lacked emotional substance. Naturally, Paul was hurt by such notices: 'I should do what Woody does, ignore them. But I'm curious. I don't take it well, either for my music or for the film.'

Some critics complained that Jonah was a failure and therefore uninteresting as a character. 'I feel that I tried to tell the truth in *One Trick Pony*,' Paul said. 'My point was that there are a lot of people with talent who don't succeed. I wasn't trying to draw a portrait of a guy who didn't have any talent. He just wasn't succeeding any more. The major difference between Jonah and Paul Simon is that I'm just lucky, because people like what I do.'

To make matters worse, Paul felt the film was poorly promoted with insufficient advertising from Warners and that it wasn't widely distributed. Certainly, in Britain it was almost unknown. Perhaps this is why interest waned after a couple of months. It was distressing for Paul, to say the least. Later, he told Stephen Holden: 'It was a very hard thing for me to accept. My feeling at the time was, well, I've made a failure. I'd had a pretty good history of successes. And here was this project that I'd put more effort into than any project I'd ever done. I had a lot of years tied up in it, and it came and went just like that.'

It had been an important step in his development as an artist, too. He was approaching forty, and realized that the mass audience of record buyers is largely made up of young people. As a writer, his lyrics had always kept pace with his own life and growing up, from the youthful anger of 'I Am a Rock' to the mature pain of 'I Do It for Your Love'.

Over the years, more than any other artist, he had avoided repeating himself, avoided the trap of regurgitating old themes from his youth. For this reason, his writing pace had been slow, more so in the seventies than the sixties. He told Jon Landau: 'I was a beginning writer then. So I wrote anything I saw. Now I sift. Now I say, "Well, that's not really a subject I want to write a song about."'

All this was admirable and has set him apart from most of his peers in his pursuit of excellence. But it also left him with the dilemma of how to address an audience of youngsters – or, more accurately, how to continue to address his audience of contemporaries. 'If you're working in an area where most people aren't interested in what you have to say when you've lived fifteen years past adolescence, you get bored with trying to talk to those people,' he said. 'I thought that film was a field where I could be accepted by my peer group.'

Now ironically, for the very first time in his career, Paul Simon was being convicted by his peers. It would lead to a period of great turbulence and depression, in his public and private life. He would make a lot of changes. But before then, he was going back on the road. If the film was a failure, he would go back to the thing he knew he did well, performing his songs.

Chapter Twenty-five

TOURING AND ANALYSIS

Before the release of the film, Paul had been planning a tour. Now, in the midst of its release, the show had to go on, or rather the rehearsals did. They were exciting and intense periods of work. Paul spent those late summer and early autumn days of 1980 taking his band through the programme on the huge soundstage on 52nd Street.

Dave Marsh witnessed the last rehearsals and described them as 'streamlined chaos'. There were huge packing cases piled up to the ceiling, Phil Ramone's children picking out notes on Richard Tee's keyboards, secretaries constantly answering telephones and crew members testing and re-testing equipment. In the middle of it all, Paul was working on a medley of 'Kodachrome' – a slightly more reggae version – and Chuck Berry's rock 'n' roll hit 'Maybelline'.

Perhaps because the work was so gruelling, perhaps because of *One Trick Pony*, or perhaps because it was yet another tour, Paul started to have his panic dreams again, a couple of weeks before he went away. One in particular stuck in his mind: he dreamed that some of the band were late, and they had to go on stage without rehearsal. Paul, resourceful even in his dreams, suggested they do 'Me and Julio' because it was easy for them, in the key of A. And typically with a nightmare, things went from bad to worse. When he started to play, the guitar was out of tune, and the strings were loose. Paul described the horror of that moment: 'Everything was in total chaos, and I had to stop and say, "I'm terribly sorry." And I was thinking, "Maybe this isn't the right tune. Maybe it should be 'Slip Slidin' Away . . .'" And then I looked up and a couple of people were leaving.'

But, as always, the reality was quite different. In October, Paul set off on his US tour – six weeks and twelve cities. He took along enormous amounts of sound equipment and a thirteen-piece band. Consequently, he was sure to lose money. He described the tour as 'virtually sold out and way in the red', adding with a shrug: 'There's no way I can even come close to breaking even.' It was estimated that the tour could lose him as much as three hundred thousand dollars. But then he hadn't made a profit on any solo tour.

His motive for touring wasn't profit – far from it. 'I'd like to go out there. I'd like to take this band and have a record of it. You know, these guys at this particular moment, 'cause I don't know if we'll all be together again. It's the movie, it's the album, it's everything.' That feeling of comradeship and warmth sustained them through the tour.

One concert, at the Tower Theater in Philadelphia, was released by Warners as a sixty-minute video. It shows Paul relaxed, responsive to his audience. On his birthday, 13 October, he did a concert at Fort Worth in Texas and was joined on stage by his girlfriend Carrie Fisher for a duet of 'Bye Bye Love'. That was appropriate because he was embarking on a tour of Europe: a whirlwind tour of thirteen cities in only two weeks.

It was phenomenally successful. Copenhagen and Oslo were rapturous in their responses. In Vienna, much to everyone's surprise, Paul was given a standing ovation. He did encore after encore, unable to leave the stage, so tumultuous was the applause. Finally, he went backstage and brought on the Jessy Dixon Singers who had changed into sweaters and jeans and were on the point of leaving the theatre; with him, they performed the final encore.

The European tour closed triumphantly with concerts at London's Hammersmith Odeon, where audiences greeted Paul ecstatically, demanding encore after encore, and getting them. On the last night, Paul expressed his gratitude for such a warm reception. Someone called out: 'Well, buy us a drink then.' To everyone's amazement, Paul did. He put one thousand pounds behind the bar, a drink each for the entire audience. Fittingly, someone shouted: 'Keep the money. Just come back next year.'

Not surprisingly, the concerts were hailed by the critics. Simon Tebbutt of *Record Mirror* wrote: 'Paul Simon is more self-assured and less self-absorbed than ever before – the fully fledged artist at the height of his creative powers. Tonight he finally asserted himself and blasted the past away in a thrilling set which barely made any reference to the Simon & Garfunkel heyday of the sixties.' Ralph Deyner commented: 'Simon's deft string arrangements and orchestrations [were those of] a master of understatement.' And Ray Coleman: 'The magnificence of Paul Simon's London concerts last week, which will be hard to top as the most perfect concerts of the year, showed a writer of brilliantly crafted songs surrounded by master musicians, at the peak of performance.'

While in London, Paul gave an interview to Ray Coleman at the Savoy Hotel. He talked about his film: 'Unless you go out and take some gambles and fall on your face, you won't learn. If you keep succeeding, it means the steps you are taking are too small. It is necessary to take big steps. It was scary and out of my natural reach. It was something I'd never done before. I knew that whether I succeeded or failed in popularity terms, I would acquire a whole lot of information and skill. Even if I never made another movie, I could use that information and my other work would benefit. It will not be a smash hit. Artistically, I'm proud of the fact that I stayed with it and made it. It's a flawed piece of work, but I'm still proud of it.'

When Paul returned to New York a few days later, he was shocked to learn that Warners didn't intend to release the film at all in Britain. This was surely a mistake on their part because it couldn't become popular if people didn't have the chance to see it. 'I do not work for people to leave it on the shelf,' Paul told the

Daily Mail. 'I intend to buy the film rights from Warners and sell the thing myself.'

He couldn't know it at the time, but interest in the film would be revived later when it was shown on American cable television, first in Los Angeles, then in the other major cities including New York. This would be a consolation to him. 'It has a life that's going to go on,' he said, 'and now that I realize that, I feel much better.' It has since been shown on British television, too.

But for now, that was far ahead. By the close of 1980, Paul was aware only that he'd spent a long time making a film that wasn't appreciated, not even, he felt, by the company he needed to promote it. He fell into a period of severe depression and began to wonder if he would ever come out of it. On the other hand, he had everything going for him: wealth, status, interesting work, a son he loved dearly and a relationship with his girlfriend Carrie Fisher, the talented and beautiful daughter of Eddie Fisher and Debbie Reynolds.

Carrie was deeply rooted in show business, almost from birth. 'I was born into something much larger than myself,' she said. While she was still a child, her father, popular singer and heart-throb Eddie Fisher, left Debbie Reynolds and married Elizabeth Taylor. Carrie and her brother Todd grew up in the Hollywood world of glitter and scandal, accustomed to the trappings of wealth, fiercely loyal to their mother, wary of reporters and their questions, obsessively camera-shy. 'We grew up on the Map of the Stars,' she said later. 'We played games on the tourists. If they shot stills, we ran. If they shot films, we stood still. I developed a phobia about being photographed that I didn't get over until *Star Wars.*'

Despite such fame and luxury, Carrie never became self-satisfied or over-confident. She was saved from such a fate by the security of being loved and by her own indomitable sense of humour. 'We were products of a broken home. No, a broken mansion,' she said with a smile. 'Mom was away a lot on location or in Vegas. The place was wired for security into the police.

Teams of people brought us up. Millions kept it clean.' In an interview with Clive James, Carrie referred to her philosophy of life as 'gallows humour'.

She soon learned that show business isn't just glamour, that it has its cruel side; she understood that it is a tough environment to survive in, and that survival is a right of the fittest. Not surprisingly, she chose it for herself at a very young age. At fifteen, she left Beverly Hills High School to study acting in London. She had already done some singing and dancing in her mother's Las Vegas act. While still a plump teenager, she took a small role in Warren Beatty's film *Shampoo*.

The rest followed quickly. At nineteen, she was literally rocketed to fame as Princess Leia in the blockbuster movie *Star Wars*. She was young, but she knew from experience what stardom was all about. She jokingly told Jim Jerome that she tended to be associated with the famous princesses Caroline and Stephanie of Monaco: 'As soon as one of those princesses does something incredible, forget it, I'm asked to be in the TV movie about it. It's weird but that's how I'm typecast, that's who I am. Princess Anyone.'

Now, after two years of living together, she and Paul were having difficulties with their relationship. He openly admired her talent: 'She's really got the goods and the Force is with her. She'll emerge as a gifted comedienne.' At the same time, the long separations forced on the couple were taking their toll.

Carrie was filming in Los Angeles with Chevvy Chase, the comedy *Under the Rainbow*. Much of her work was in California, while Paul was based in New York. Paul was finding that the pressures of work demanded a huge sacrifice of his private life. 'My personal life isn't a mess, but it could use more time,' he admitted. They were both stars: one of them had to give way, and neither wanted to.

Certainly, some of the tension was caused by temperament. Paul would later admit this: 'Faced with a problem that made us uncomfortable, we were inclined to say, "Hey, I don't need this."

We were spoiled, because we were both used to being the centre of attention.'

With the failure of his movie and the difficulties with Carrie, Paul knew he had reached an emotional crisis. He was suffering from writer's block, more seriously than ever before. Later, he told *Playboy*: 'The movie came out to mixed reviews, and the soundtrack album didn't do nearly as well as I'd hoped. It was a period of great depression for me. I was immobilized.'

A friend recommended that he see Rod Gorney, a lecturer and psychiatrist in Los Angeles. Paul called him from New York, then flew out to California to see him. He went directly to his house from the airport. He felt an urgent need to work out why, given all the facts of his life – that he was young, healthy and famous, with talent and money – why he was so unhappy.

They sat down to talk. Paul told him about his life and his recent inability to write anything; this was a serious writer's block and, for the first time in his life, he was unable to overcome it. He talked about Carrie, about his work and the recent feeling of failure he was trying to cope with. Gorney listened and was interested. He suggested they meet again to talk more. He lent Paul a guitar to take back to the hotel.

Paul took it away, but he didn't open the case on the first night, so convinced was he that his creative powers had gone. It was only after further prompting and encouragement from Gorney that he sat down to try, and the result was a piece of paper and a few scribbled lines which later became 'Allergies'. He was thrilled.

The bigger problem remained, however. He now felt it made no difference whether he wrote anything or not. He had no financial incentive to work; now with the lack of interest in *One Trick Pony*, he had lost all other motivation. His drive, once such an integral part of his character, had evaporated. He was sinking more and more deeply into himself.

Paul described to *Playboy* how Gorney helped him through this: 'He was able to penetrate someone whose defences were seemingly impenetrable. Of course, the reason I'd been blocked was that I felt what I did was of absolutely no importance. He was able to say, "The way to contribute is through your songs. And it's not for you to judge their merits, it's for you to write the songs." For me, that was brilliant. And liberating.'

A few days later, Paul flew home. Slowly he started writing again. He also looked at his life, determined to get it into shape, and took his health very seriously. He was on a strict diet that forbade dairy foods, red meat or sugar, prescribed in the '70s to help dissolve the calcium deposits in his hand.

He toned up every day by jogging in Central Park and by working out in his private gymnasium, a room in his luxurious apartment which cost five thousand dollars to equip. Consequently, he was looking tapered, having dropped his weight to 117 pounds. He felt that physical discipline was vital in his life: 'Control is one of the essences of art. There is a controlled tension in my work and it is very much like me.'

He still had only one housekeeper who took care of him and Harper. 'My life is pretty organized,' he said. 'I'm sort of spoiled. She worries about my health, which happens to be perfectly adequate for my age and temperament. But it's nice.'

For Artie meanwhile, there was much room for speculation. By autumn 1980, his career was in limbo. After the release of *Bad Timing*, he found himself once again forced to deny reporters' questions about a reunion with Paul. 'I have certain ideas,' he told the *Daily Mirror*. 'But I'm reluctant to put them into words. I can see the film side becoming more important for a while, but it depends on the scripts. If there are no tasty projects coming up, I'll fall back on music, which is closest to my heart.'

In October he went back into the studio to start work on a new album, which would take over six months to complete. Again he was co-producing with his old friend Roy Halee. As with his previous albums, Art's search for good material led him far afield, this time to Britain. Richard Kerr, an English songwriter living in the United States, showed a song to Roy Halee because he thought it might suit Artie.

The song was 'A Heart in New York', written and sung by the successful Scottish duo Gallagher and Lyle. Art had already recorded their 'Breakaway', and, when he heard this one, he liked it. He telephoned the publisher in London and spoke to Graham Lyle about the arrangement. He wondered whether Graham would be able to change one or two things in the lyric to make it more suitable for him to sing. It was agreed that Graham should go over to Miami where Art was recording.

Since his successful partnership with Benny Gallagher in the seventies, Graham Lyle had become equally successful writing songs for other artists, as well as producing albums. He is knowledgeable about music of all kinds, open and friendly, easy to talk to. He spoke of how he had met Art in a hotel where they had a meal and talked about their backgrounds. At first glance, they seemed to have no common ground, because Graham grew up in a suburb of Glasgow. But they found parallels, especially in their musical influences: the artists Graham had listened to on imported records were the very ones Art had gone to see in New York clubs.

They liked each other instantly. Graham told me: 'I found him really kind. He made me feel quite relaxed, coming into that situation where I was a total outsider.' They started work on the song and Graham tried to rewrite it in several different ways. The problem was that, as he had originally performed it, the plane arrives from London just as the dawn is breaking over New York City, a romantic and evocative image. As a New Yorker, Art knew this wasn't practical because flights from London don't arrive at that time. Also, the song describes seeing the Manhattan skyline before the plane lands; in fact, planes coming into Kennedy Airport from London don't normally fly over the city. The only reason Graham had done that on his flight was that, owing to technical problems, the plane had been instructed to circle in the air for some time. Maybe it seems like a small point, one that could be covered by poetic licence, but as Graham said: 'He's such a perfectionist and he wanted to get it right. He has to believe in the song he's singing, and he went to a lot of trouble for it. But we ended up using more or less the lyric of the original, with slight alterations.'

Art asked Graham to play acoustic guitar in the session, along with Pete Carr. They put down the basic track there in Miami – the two finger-style guitars and Art's vocal. The other instruments were to be added later in New York. It's something Art often does, having the composer of a song play accompaniment or sing on the record. I asked Graham if he thought there was a specific reason for this. He told me: 'Probably because the atmosphere of a song often comes well from the person who wrote it. The dynamics, the ups and downs of it. And Art recognizes that. That's experience. You get some artists who do songs and they discount the original feel. They don't think it's important. Sometimes, they can lose the whole song.'

Art strove for ten days to achieve a song that had both the writers' concept and something of his own. He worked hard at the vocals, with an approach that was characteristically dedicated and professional. Graham told me that Art would go into the booth alone to do the singing. 'He's very serious about his music and he cares about details. He cares about music. It's certainly not just a business to him.'

I asked Graham, himself a skilled and experienced performer, to give me some insight into Art's technique. He told me how impressed he was during those ten days, watching Artie record. Particularly impressive was Art's tracking – putting a phrase of vocal on record and then singing it again on top to give a fuller, warmer sound. 'A lot of people do double track vocals,' he said. 'But it's difficult to get it spot on. He can do it exactly. He can do that three or four times. He's got it to perfection. I thought his vocal technique alone was impressive; I'd never seen anything like it. His care over each line and the performance of it, and his use of the microphone in the studio, especially close mike work, that was something. I've been singing all my life too, but I learned an awful lot just watching him. He's musically aware. He knows what you're talking about. He knows the note he has to go for, without even touching an instrument. He can hear it. He has a good ear.'

Personally, he described Art as a very serious man, dedicated to his work; a great reader of books, analytical about people and life. 'He's quite private. He's been a star for so many years, all of his adult life, and that fame has continued. Now he's part of American popular history. In spite of that, I found him amazingly sane.'

For Artie, still reeling from the shock and grief of Laurie's suicide, and now wondering which direction his life should take, that sanity surely lay in doing his work. At that difficult time, the work saved him.

Chapter Twenty-six

COMING TO TERMS

In the early months of 1981, Paul was getting his life into perspective. He had stopped going to the analyst so regularly, but was still calling in for an occasional chat. All things considered, he was feeling much better.

'I'm freer personally,' he said. 'I've been through all these traumas in the last ten years, and you know, after you get beat up a couple of times, you're not so afraid of being beat up. I'm not interested in hiding any more. I don't want to be that guy any more. I don't know that I ever did want to be that guy. I guess I was. I just feel disconnected from who I used to be. My life is so different. I certainly can't imagine it without my child.'

One of his regrets since beginning the absorbing project *One Trick Pony* was that it had taken him away from Harper, now eight, for such long periods. For this reason, he spent as much time as possible in New York, leaving only when his work absolutely demanded it. 'I don't like to go away because I like to see my son. I see him every other day when his school's in session.'

Harper, now a third grader at a private school in the city, spent half his time with Paul and the other half with Peggy, an arrangement that had worked out well since he was a toddler. Paul had always felt a strong sense of fatherhood, and now he was becoming aware of how swiftly time was passing.

He told Jim Jerome how, on a visit to the dentist, he had looked at the X-rays of Harper's teeth, with the macabre feeling that to see a skull X-rayed is like seeing someone dead. 'So I'm looking at Harper's skull, his baby teeth, and behind and below and on top of them, I can see his next age and then the space for wisdom teeth. This is my little boy. A whole life in those X-rays of his teeth. Yeah, it's flying. Time's flying.'

He was trying to make the most of that time by sharing a large part of it with his son. 'It's a great thing in my life to be a father,' he admitted. 'I always wanted to have children and be a member of a nuclear family. The molecules exploded, however, in a manner I couldn't predict at the time of my marriage.'

Nevertheless, his ex-wife still meant a great deal to him. They had a friendly relationship, especially with regard to Harper. But he also hoped for her personal happiness whole-heartedly. 'It's not just that we share a child. You don't fall in love without a reason. That feeling is rare, and those people who meant that to me, still mean a lot.'

His friends were also important. He went out in Manhattan quite a lot, and owned a Mercedes, but found it impractical to drive much in the city. If he went to the theatre or had to make several stops he generally preferred to go by hired limousine. But he often went about on foot.

He still liked living in New York, and thrived on its pace and variety. He rented a house in Long Island for summers, but preferred to stay in the city the rest of the time, partly because of Harper but also because he felt happiest there. 'I'm not your basic walk-in-the-woods guy. I'm not overwhelmed by sunsets,' he said.

Socially, he was keeping a low profile, avoiding publicity as much as possible. Despite his star status which made him both instantly recognizable and in demand, he still managed to achieve a certain degree of personal liberty. 'Manhattan is a congenial place to be. People do come up to me and say hello and shake my hand, but very seldom have I been annoyed or abused by anyone. When I was young, I fantasized about being famous in just the way I am.'

Over the years, it had become customary to invite close friends to his apartment overlooking the spectacular Central Park. He had plenty of room there, and most of his entertaining took place in an upstairs den-study, with an adjacent bathroom with a luxurious, tiled hot tub. He told the press that he socialized very little with other musicians, but saw a lot of his parents and brother Eddie. And he was spending a lot of time with Artie. He and Carrie were sometimes seen out socially with Art and his new girlfriend, actress and later director Penny Marshall, the first steady date since the death of Laurie Bird over a year earlier.

Another of Paul's close friends was Lorne Michaels, ex-producer of *Saturday Night*, who lived down the hall in the same apartment building with his girlfriend Susan Forristal, who later married him. According to Michaels: 'Paul's one of the people I go to for advice. He's direct and clear-headed. He assesses your situation with kindness and compassion.'

Paul's business commitments were less of a burden now. Since the mid '70s, he had been slimming them down to a manageable size. In the early days, he had invested his royalties in the stock market. But that soon became too intense; he was depressed if the market went down but not particularly elated if it rose. Now his finances were more straightforward: his money was in treasury notes. He gave some to charities and then forgot about it. 'I don't think about it because I don't live on a level that approaches my income,' he said.

All the same, the Simon empire was vast. Having retained all his own publishing rights, Paul annually reaped the royalties of a long string of hits which had been covered by other artists: by 1980, 'Bridge' alone had been recorded by two hundred other artists. He also received massive royalties from his single and album catalogue (previously released records), from sheet music and from air play. To quote Michael Tannen: 'Paul has probably the most valuable self-owned publishing catalogue anywhere.' What is incredible is that he had become a self-made millionaire in so few years: five prolific years as half of Simon & Garfunkel, then only nine years as a solo artist.

It was hard for him now to realize that only sixteen years

earlier he had been busking on the streets of Paris, and working in folk clubs for a few pounds a night. Paul admitted that he found it difficult to reconcile his middle-class upbringing with his current wealth.

It had taken him years of analysis to arrive at a frame of mind where he could accept it. 'Entertainers are paid disproportionately high sums of money for their contribution to society. I used to feel guilty, but now I accept that gratefully. When someone tells me, "You've given me a lot of pleasure in my life," it all seems like a gratifying, very pure way of making money.'

By spring 1981, his life was reaching a point of balanced contentment. He didn't have everything he wanted; he was still trying to reconcile his problems with Carrie with the great love he felt for her; he was striving for perfection – a higher goal, another challenge. He was daunted by the passing of time, but determined to keep pace with it.

More than ever, he realized he had a lot to be thankful for, and he was learning to appreciate that: 'I have options. I've got brains, health. I'm thinking now of the best way for me to live my life. Yeah, I'm happy. I'm busy. It's exciting now. I've got a kid. I've got friends who love me and whom I love. My parents are alive. Yeah, I'm happy. It's not going to last for ever, but this is a precious moment.'

Chapter Twenty-seven

CENTRAL PARK

In the summer of 1981, Paul got a call from Ron Delsner, possibly the most important concert promoter in New York City. He said that Gordon Davis, the Parks Commissioner of New York, had suggested a free concert in Central Park in aid of the city's parks. Would Paul be interested?

Warren Hirsch, Italian sportswear mogul, told the *New York Times* that he hoped to raise over a hundred thousand dollars through the sale of T-shirts and badges. The venture won the approval of Gordon Davis because, although it would obviously promote sportswear, it was essentially a non-commercial enterprise which would benefit the city and would cause no damage to the park itself.

Paul's immediate answer was yes, he was interested. But then he had second thoughts. Remembering his negative feelings after *One Trick Pony*, he began to doubt himself. So he decided to ask Artie to come on stage with him and do a few songs. He phoned Art who was on holiday in Switzerland, and Art was enthusiastic. As they talked, the idea expanded. Paul suggested that Art should join him for the second half of the show, perhaps for ten of their best known songs.

Art returned to New York and they began the planning. They soon realized that it wouldn't work. Art summed up the problem: 'It didn't seem right to either of us that Paul should be the opening act for Simon & Garfunkel. And for him to follow Simon & Garfunkel didn't make show-business sense.'

Close friends suggested an entire Simon & Garfunkel concert. It would mean more to the public. So they started to consider it. Maybe the timing was right for a one-off reunion; both men were between projects at the moment, and they were amicable towards each other. On the other hand, it would certainly be a large undertaking, and not without risks. They weren't at all sure how the public would respond to Simon & Garfunkel after eleven years. A whole new generation had emerged since their split. But in the end, they rose to the challenge. As Paul put it: 'I thought – what the hell – let's just do the whole concert.'

The practical problems were considerable. Lorne Michaels was called in and his company, Broadway Video, was set to tape the event, to be televised later. A massive, 160-foot stage was built, with a set designed by Eugene Lee, symbolically to represent New York's skyline. It took a week to construct. And the costs were high – over $750,000 to stage and record the show, much of the money being put up by Paul himself.

When they started, both Paul and Artie were in high spirits. As they discussed the show, they began to disagree again, first about the musical backing. Art felt that their own voices and an acoustic guitar would be most appropriate. 'I just felt that the more variables you control in an open air show, the better,' he said.

Paul was adamantly against this: 'I said, "I can't do that any more. I can't just play the guitar for two hours." First, my hand had never fully recovered from when it was injured a few years ago, when I had calcium deposits.' Also, many of his more recent songs weren't written for acoustic guitar. 'Still Crazy' was an electric piano song; 'Late in the Evening' needed horns. In addition, he argued that, with the size of the park and of the expected audience, one guitar wouldn't put out enough sound. 'Besides, I love working with a band,' he said. 'I love it when it starts rocking.'

He assured Art that it would work. 'I kept saying to him, "Artie, the band will jell, and when it does, you'll want to sing.

You'll like it."' In the face of such enthusiasm, Art relented and agreed to the band, eleven of New York's finest session musicians, who had all worked with Paul before, several on the *One Trick Pony* tour.

In an empty Manhattan theatre, they began rehearsals in earnest. Paul described it: 'The weeks before the concert were so tense that there were times when I really regretted having agreed to do it. It was very rushed. Artie had to learn a lot of new material very quickly.'

From a practical point of view, Art's situation was far from enviable. Since many of Paul's solo hits were included in the programme, he found himself with a collection of songs that he had never sung, which had to be learned lyrically and musically in a short time. Paul had adapted some expanded orchestrations from the *One Trick Pony* tour to save time, and Art had to work on some new harmonies for the songs.

With such a daunting task before him, Art faced some moments of doubt. But Paul's faith in him was unshakeable. 'It's well known that Artie's a great ballad singer,' he told the press. 'Artie's worried that he can't sing rhythm, but I know he can because that's how we grew up.' And Art would justify that faith on the night, adapting his voice to some of Paul's funkiest numbers and adding a new dimension to the hard rock 'n' roll of 'Me and Julio', 'Kodachrome' and 'Late in the Evening'.

As for harmony, they soon found themselves in the familiar groove that was so comfortable for both of them. As Paul said: 'My experience with Simon & Garfunkel is that, no matter how long a layoff there's been, within about an hour, we can get the blend back. Basically, I guess the blend we get is just an outgrowth of our friendship.'

The day before the concert, Paul and Art were interviewed by the *New York Times* while they took a short break from their rehearsal. Paul summed up their feelings about the performance and the chances of a longer Simon & Garfunkel reunion. 'If this concert turns out to be enjoyable, then maybe we can plan to do a few more. We're just going to do it and see what happens.'

What happened was greater than either of them expected. On 19 September 1981, half a million people arrived in Central Park to see a reunion concert of two men whose careers had spanned one and half decades. It was musical history before their eyes. But for all the event's awe-inspiring magnitude, the atmosphere was relaxed. Paul addressed the crowd, tongue firmly in cheek, and said, 'It's great to do a neighbourhood concert.' In one sense, it was just that. Two old friends had come together to sing a few old songs.

There were no outbreaks of violence or disturbances of any kind, despite the size of the crowd. There was only one difficult moment. Paul was singing a new song, 'The Late Great Johnny Ace', an autobiographical tribute which links the gun deaths of fifties star Johnny Ace, President John Kennedy and Beatle John Lennon, whose New York shooting was still fresh in the mind. While Paul was singing, a youth leapt over the barricades and on to the stage. Within seconds, a security guard carried him off, as the youth called out to Paul, 'I need to talk to you.' Paul recovered quickly, stepping back to the microphone to finish the song in truly professional spirit. Obviously, it had startled him, but it was only a moment, and the show continued on without further incident.

The performance went very well. Paul later described it: 'We just did what we'd done when we were an act in the sixties. We tried to blend our voices. I attempted to make the tempos work. I talked a little bit too, but I found it impossible to hold a dialogue with half a million people. In a certain sense, it was numbing. It was so big and it was happening only once. I didn't have much time for an overview while I was performing.'

They sang some of their best loved classics for an hour and a half of blissful nostalgia as one hit followed another. But it was more than just a nostalgic trip: it was a show that proved, if any doubted it, that Simon & Garfunkel still had that magic. Watergate had happened, John Lennon had been tragically murdered a few hundred yards away, punk rock had arrived, peace and love and flower power had vanished for ever – but Simon & Garfunkel could still blend their voices into a sound of absolute perfection.

There were many musical highlights: superb renditions of old favourites such as 'America', 'The Sound of Silence' and 'Mrs Robinson'. There were Paul Simon numbers rearranged for the duo: most beautifully transformed was 'American Tune', to which Art's voice lent a special pathos. There was joyous rock 'n' roll music: 'Late in the Evening', 'Me and Julio' and 'Wake Up Little Susie', the tribute to the Everly Brothers which reminded half a million people where Artie and Paul had come from.

Paul's solo moments were intimate; though delivered to such a crowd, they still had the quality of a private monologue. His 'Fifty Ways to Leave Your Lover' was quietly cynical, while 'Still Crazy after All These Years' was filled with loneliness.

Art's solo songs were mellow; he produced notes of purity in 'April Come She Will'. In Gallagher and Lyle's 'A Heart in New York', delivered as a tribute to the city, Art reached a dramatic climax, raising his arm to symbolize the Statue of Liberty. At the reference to Central Park, 'Where they say you shouldn't wander after dark', the crowd roared its approval, because they were there and it was after dark, but tonight they felt safe, sharing a sense of unity.

Art's finest solo moment was of course 'Bridge over Troubled Water'. Accompanied by Richard Tee on piano, he stood at the microphone and rendered sounds of stunning power and control. In the open air, the sound reproduction cannot be what it is in the studio. Having seen Art's perfectionism in the studio, I know he would find fault with his performance of 'Bridge' that night. But for the audience of half a million who listened in silence, it was truly wonderful as he reached for the famous last note. The applause was tremendous, dying down only when Paul's guitar chords announced the next number.

For the duo, there was nothing to top 'The Boxer'. As Paul and Art sang together for the climax of the show, a hush fell over the audience and a mood of reunion filled the air. The duo blended into the familiar harmony, now and again exchanging glances of pleasure. As they sang Paul's added verse, they looked at each other across years of friendship that had been both private and public. As they took their bows, each man put an arm around the other, a spontaneous gesture of warmth that was shared by the audience.

There was a feeling, as the evening ended, that nothing could ever compare to that concert. In spite of all their differences, Simon & Garfunkel were together again. Perhaps it wouldn't last, but it had happened. As they stood together on the vast stage, set in a park even more vast, it was as though they were celebrating the end of an era. And that feeling was awesome.

Paul described their feelings after the concert: 'Afterward, our first reaction was, I think, one of disappointment. Arthur's more than mine. He thought he didn't sing well. I didn't get what had happened, how big it was, until I went home, turned on the television and saw it on all the news, the people being interviewed, and later that night, on the front pages of all the newspapers. Then I got it.'

Art went directly back into the studios to finish the vocals for his new album, *Scissors Cut*. He had decided to issue 'A Heart in New York' on a single. He was briefly reunited with Graham Lyle, who was involved in doing a master tape of three songs with Mark Griffiths, a singer-guitarist and a member of Matthew's Southern Comfort. Roy Halee was producing it. Graham was delighted when Art volunteered to come into the studio and do the vocal harmonies for it. He told me: 'He did it, I suppose, to return the compliment of "A Heart in New York". And I was thrilled. It was great.'

Just weeks after the Central Park triumph, Art released *Scissors Cut*. The cover is a stark, black and white portrait of Artie, dressed immaculately in evening wear. Just above the bow tie, a tiny plaster indicates a little cut, so near to the jugular vein. The inner sleeve gives two more pictures: Art as Nately in *Catch-22*, and one standing in front of a class, holding a piece of chalk.

The album is dedicated to Laurie Bird, an indication that, notwithstanding his happy relationship with Penny Marshall, Laurie's tragic death was still very much in Art's thoughts after more than two years.

The title track is by Jimmy Webb, a poignant song which uses the children's game metaphorically to show the destructiveness in the worst moments of a man–woman relationship. The guitars are by Dean Parks and the strings arranged by Del Newman and conducted by Teo Macero. The opening bars of this song give us some truly magnificent moments – dramatic, moving, astonishingly clear.

'A Heart in New York' comes next. According to Graham Lyle, it is based on an experience he had while staying with some friends in their Manhattan apartment which overlooked the river and gave a breathtaking view of the city. 'It was fantastic,' he told me. 'If you have someone there that you know, it makes such a difference. New York can be so alien for an outsider, like any city, but with someone there, there's a relationship. New York really has got a heart.'

The track captures the excitement, not only through the lyric, but through the arrangement. There's a tight guitar beat and a tenor sax passage by Michael Brecker, and Crusher Bennet's percussion – these all combine to suggest vitality. At the close of the track, we hear the swell of the crowd's response to a winning team and the exultant cry: 'The last ball's in the air.'

'Up in the World', by Clifford T. Ward, is a strange, slow number with a lyric addressed to a successful woman by the man who loved her in hungrier, happier days. This isn't a new theme, but it's brought to life by specific references – her condescending ways, her frequent nights alone. The abrupt ending when Art sings into echoing silence, is very effective. The string arrangement is by David Campbell, and Joe Osborn plays bass.

'Hang On In' by Norman Sallitt brings a change of mood. It's foot-tapping, with dominant guitars which provide a suitably strong backing by Jeffrey and Michael Staton and Dean Parks. Then, 'So Easy to Begin' is a Jules Swear song which moves wistfully through a relationship that isn't working out, but isn't easy to let go. Art sings plaintively, with utterly perfect phrasing. Leah Kunkel's background vocals are especially effective in this one.

'Can't Turn My Heart Away' by John Jarvis and Eric Kaz isn't so different in theme from the preceding track, but a contrast in style. It emphasizes the heavy rhythm of the piano, here played by John Jarvis.

'The French Waltz' by Adam Mitchell is a romantic ballad, sung in the traditional style of an English verse with a French chorus. Art sings well in French. The arrangement blends acoustic and electric guitars to get an interesting light and shade of tone.

'The Romance' is by Eric Kaz, a slow and gentle song which rises in intensity at the chorus, where Art's voice soars to convey the ecstasy of mutual love. Art's vocal is skilfully overdubbed with the background vocals.

'In Cars', by Jimmy Webb, moves wistfully through the idyllic teenage years of romance and cars. With a few brief lines, it captures car worship which rises to poetic intensity. Jimmy's own vocal of this, on his album *Angel Heart*, is a very strong track, more of a singalong than this. Art gives these happy memories of youth a sacred quality. For the last four lines, Art is joined by Paul Simon in the vocal – fittingly. In the fade-out we hear Art singing the opening lines to Bob Dylan's 'Girl of the North Country', which has its origins in the traditional English folk song, 'Scarborough Fair'.

The album closes with 'That's All I've Got to Say' by Jimmy Webb, written along with the score for the film *The Lost Unicorn*. Lyrically, it's an example of Jimmy's ability to say so much in a few words. The opening lines describe the writer's frustrating peculiarity of being unable to write about what is closest to him.

Although very short, it's a superb ending to the album. It's appropriate lyrically to sum up a collection of love songs, and also orchestrally because of its mellow blending of strings, piano and stunning vocal – a combination that is the trademark of love songs.

Once again, Art received mixed responses from the critics. There were the usual comments that he was too lush, too heavily orchestrated. But Stephen Holden in *Rolling Stone* was one of those who enjoyed the album. '*Scissors Cut*, Art Garfunkel's finest solo album, easily justifies his unfashionable formal approach to pop music by its sheer aural beauty. With the aid of strong songs and heartfelt singing, plus exquisite arrangements, Garfunkel's artifactual approach works splendidly here. He hasn't sounded this good since the album *Bridge over Troubled Water*.'

In the autumn of 1981, both Paul and Artie turned forty. Both felt it was a significant point in their lives. Art told the press: 'Even though forty is only a symbolic number, somehow when you reach that age, you can't fool yourself into thinking you're still a kid. I know that if I tried to be a kid, I'd feel more than a little foolish.' And Paul told them: 'Once you get past the fear of being responsible, it feels good. At forty, it suddenly seems unattractive to be a boy, and very attractive to be a man. I feel that, given my place and my age, I have a responsibility. I don't know what I can do, but I feel I must do something.'

For Paul, becoming forty brought yet another honour. In late November, it was announced in New York by Sammy Cahn, President of the National Academy of Popular Music, that Paul was to be added to the Songwriters' Hall of Fame, in the following March. Others honoured included Jerry Herman, the composer-lyricist of *Hello Dolly*, and Paul's longtime peer, Bob Dylan.

Chapter Twenty-eight

EUROPEAN TOUR

`

On 10 February 1982, the ninety-minute video cassette of the Central Park Concert had its first showing on Home Box Office television, the rights of which were said to have cost around one million dollars. The special was directed by Michael Lindsay-Hogg, who had directed the Beatles' film *Let It Be*.

A couple of weeks later, the album of the concert was released: a lavish double album with a souvenir booklet packed with photographs and the song lyrics. Paul had his reservations about the album, in principle. 'I don't particularly like it. I don't think that Simon & Garfunkel as a live act compares to Simon & Garfunkel as a studio act.' But these aesthetic misgivings were put aside: it was a souvenir of a memorable moment in music history.

Ray Coleman reviewed both the televised concert and the album with a tribute to the duo: 'They are reaching a vast new audience while keeping the middle-aged happy with some of pop's finest golden oldies. And the duo who broke the golden rule, splitting at their peak, can theoretically remain together for as long as they wish. In the unpredictable world of pop music, it's an astonishing achievement and comeback.'

In *Stereo Review*, Noel Coppage wrote: 'The album is more than documentation. As live concert albums go, it shows unusual attention to detail, and reflects a great deal of care in the presentation. All these good songs gathered together will remind you that Simon has been one of the most important spokesmen for his generation.'

People Weekly commented: 'The voices sound as feathery, emotional and tight in harmony as ever. The backing is solid and the arrangements, happily, do not merely duplicate recorded versions, but add a vigorous live dimension.' Stephen Holden wrote in *Rolling Stone*: 'The new album has magic to spare, some of it rough. Though laboured over in the studio after the event, the tracks are far from 100 per cent polished. It's actually refreshing. If *The Concert in Central Park* is Paul Simon's valentine to the Big Apple, it is Art Garfunkel's voice that really tugs at the heartstrings and sends the message home.'

Paul and Art were discussing a tour of Europe and Japan, and perhaps even an American tour the following year. The press speculated on the massive financial bonus the reunion would be for the duo. But money wasn't the prime motivation for two men who were, by any standards, very wealthy. Moreover, these two men had calmly walked away from staggering financial profits eleven years earlier, in order to pursue their individual creative goals.

Paul summed it up: 'I don't think we'd get together if the potential for a joyous reunion weren't there. We'd never decide to grit our teeth just to make a couple of million dollars.' And later, he told *Playboy*: 'Well, hey – it was old material. But it wasn't cynically done. It wasn't hype. It was done because there was an overwhelming demand.'

They were pleased to be working together again, but both men were unwilling to say whether it would be permanent. They were just enjoying the creative boost it had given them. Paul told the press: 'Working with him will give me the opportunity to write the big ballad that I wouldn't write for myself.' And he admitted that he'd often thought of 'American Tune' as a Simon & Garfunkel song.

For Art too, due for a breathing space from films and albums, the bonus of Paul's composing talents was a great incentive to reunite for a while. As Ray Coleman wrote: 'Art Garfunkel sounds tremendously happy to be back, centre stage, with the best songs he ever sang.'

When asked what they had missed about each other during the solo years of the seventies, both men answered without hesitation. Paul said: 'Musically, the textures I have available when I have Art's voice to work with in my songs.' And Art replied concisely: 'The harmony and Paul's talent.'

In April, just two months later, Paul and Art came to London to promote their eighteen-concert tour that summer. It would include major cities in Europe and Japan and close in London. At the Carlton Tower Hotel, they gave an afternoon press conference that lasted over half an hour and was televised by Dutch, German and French cable crews. Later, the British press said how nervous Paul and Art seemed. It's no wonder. Once again, they were bombarded with questions about the reunion: was it permanent, was it motivated by cash, would there be a studio album to follow? These were questions they couldn't answer, because they didn't know.

Art told them: 'It's an option we always had and now choose to exercise.' Then he added: 'But neither of us see it as forsaking our individual careers. We never have a policy about what our status is now or next year. One improvises one's life as one goes along.'

So in June 1982, Paul and Art embarked on the tour that would announce and celebrate their reunion to the world. It was to be hugely successful, as a delight for veteran S & G fans who remembered the farewell concert at Forest Hills eleven years earlier, but also for a whole generation who had missed it in the sixties.

In one sense, Paul felt he was one of those people. He admitted that he expected to gain nothing creatively from this tour, but that he would gain something valuable emotionally from it. 'I felt I wasn't really present for Simon & Garfunkel the first time around. I wasn't home, the same way that I wasn't present for the concert in the park when it was happening. I mean, a phenomenon occurs, but because you're in the middle of it, you just think it's your life, until it's over.' It was, he felt, a chance to re-experience the feelings he hadn't absorbed the first time. He no longer had any interest in the hits of the sixties; musically he had passed them by. But he wanted to experience again how it felt to be half of the duo, to be the person who had written and sung those songs.

This emotional revisiting also had its negative side. While there can be no doubt that the tour was successful, a slight tension was starting up between the two of them on a personal level. Paul found himself reliving his past in the cities where he'd performed before, and remembering how he'd first realized that he no longer wanted to sing in a duo. In Germany, he recalled being there in the sixties. He realized he felt embarrassed about 'Homeward Bound' simply because he didn't want to sing it as half of Simon & Garfunkel.

He described the strain on his relationship with Artie during that European tour. 'We were hardly speaking to each other. I'm not sure why not. It wasn't my choice. I felt he wasn't speaking to me. When I asked, he'd say, "Oh look, don't be hurt by my behaviour. Don't think that I don't like you."' Paul and Art were in the unfortunate position of being compared all the time, to each other and to their past selves, the more so because of the close proximity of the tour. Paul explained his frustration with the reviews of those concerts: 'Simon was too pushy; Garfunkel sang out of tune; Simon sang out of tune; they didn't sing as well as they used to, they sing better now, but with less passion. Even when the comparisons are complimentary, it's too many comparisions for comfort.'

In Paris, the *International Herald Tribune* interviewed Paul and Art in their hotel rooms just before the concert. It was an interesting interview because it found both men in analytical moods. Both were, not surprisingly, fitting their present reunion into the framework of their solo careers, their friendship with each other, and their private lives.

That night, Paul was feeling particularly cheerful: 'These are the good times, these are the good old days. But even to use that term implies that there was something better about the past. I happen to be optimistic about the future.' It was perhaps a natural standpoint for a man with a nine-year-old son.

But Artie, four doors down the corridor, was seeing things differently: 'These are the bad days. The sixties were the good old days. I wonder what Paul thinks is so dynamic about today. Yes, I am very different from Paul.' He described his present life as reclusive, more so since Laurie's death, which still hurt him. 'The love of my life is gone. I've pulled back and I am no longer in touch with what others are doing,' he said.

He was spending his time consoling himself by reading a lot, taking long walks with his Walkman, thinking about his life and particularly about being Jewish. He told Michael Zwerrin about an experience he had had the day before, when they were performing in Stockholm. He had been taking one of his long walks to relax and a Jewish woman who was watering her garden had recognized him and said, 'I can tell by your face that you're Jewish.' This affected Artie profoundly. 'When I walked away, I thought about her, and her being Jewish and the fact that she seeks to share that sense with me. We share the same indoctrination, those synagogue experiences, speaking that language we didn't understand, a lot of those *meschugges*, and even though we didn't understand them, those are the things Jews share.'

He was also pondering on show business itself and the role of a performer in society. 'Can we do anything more than just soothe, console? Can't we make them go to sleep that night and wake up with a certain idea we planted that will make the world better?'

Art was very tense before the Paris concerts, and this wasn't just because he was performing for such a huge crowd. It stemmed more from his longing for perfection, his deeply rooted need to give his very best. 'I'm feeling the stress,' he admitted. 'There's something in me that makes me want to tear this hotel down. I'm a bit of a fanatic and obsessive when it comes to work. I'm very attached to the concept of doing a good job on stage, extremely attached to it.'

And they did a good job that night at the Hippodrome d'Auteuil Race Track. Fans rushed on to the field as soon as the gates were opened for the first day's concert on the 8th. On both the 8th and the 9th, they had full houses attracting 130,000 people, with a further 400,000 requests for tickets. Indeed, after the concert, 'Mrs Robinson' shot up to number 1 in the French charts. That was staggering for a song fifteen years after its original release.

It was a similar story in Zurich on the 10th, Rotterdam on the 12th, Dublin on the 15th and finally London on the 19th. The London finale was promoted by Harvey Goldsmith, who had hired Wembley Stadium for one night only, anticipating a full house of 72,000. The tickets were ten pounds. As one might expect, demand for tickets far exceeded the supply.

On the 19th, thousands of ardent fans flocked to Wembley to pay homage to the greatest duo of the age, and then sat spellbound as they listened to almost two hours of classic songs. Basically, the programme resembled the Central Park concert, with the addition of Mike Batt's 'Bright Eyes', Art's British hit.

Antony Thorncroft reviewed the show for *The Times*, describing the songs as remarkable 'not only for their melody and lyrics, their variety and the beautifully blended voices in performance, but their relevance to the history of the past fifteen years or more'. Alan King wrote: 'It was unashamed nostalgia. A journey back to innocence and hope, for both the performers and the vast majority of the crowd. After nearly two hours and double encores, the audience was totally under the spell. As darkness fell, hundreds lit candles and torches to add an extra emotional quality to "The Sound of Silence".'

After the London triumph, Paul and Art flew home, filled with enthusiasm and plans. They would do a tour of Australia and New Zealand, then a tour of the United States. And a studio album with new material. Surely this Simon & Garfunkel album would be the most eagerly awaited album ever.

Ironically though, this album, like *Bridge over Troubled Water*, would be fraught with tension and discord, almost from the first moment. For Paul and Artie, 1983 would have a distinct flavour of *déjà vu*.

Chapter Twenty-nine

THINK TOO MUCH

After the tour, Paul and Artie went into the studio with the intention of doing a duo album of new material. But Paul was far from content about it. From the beginning, he wasn't really sure whether he wanted Art to sing with him on the tracks. These particular songs were special for personal reasons. They were, he said, about Carrie and their relationship.

When he told Art how he felt, 'He had a good answer. He said, "Look, these aren't the events of my life but I understand the emotions you're dealing with. I understand what it is to be in love, to be in pain, to feel joy. I'm a singer. I'm able to interpret. That's what I do."'

So, with some reluctance, Paul agreed to a duo album. He did make one stipulation, however: he should produce it. In the Simon & Garfunkel days, Paul and Artie had had an equal vote on how things should be done. Now, he wanted to make the final decisions on the tracks and the overall production himself.

According to Paul, Art was disappointed: 'He said, "Well, you're dampening my enthusiasm because of your ambivalence." Anyway, that's how we began, with my sense of ambivalence about the project and his frustration at the rules of the game being stated.'

As the weeks passed, the tension grew between them. The situation was less than healthy for both artists. Paul was staunchly holding his ground about producing and supervising. 'I became even more rigid, even more the guardian of my music than I had been,' he said.

Art felt strongly that he couldn't work under these conditions. As Paul later said: 'Artie's a very powerful and autonomous person until he comes into contact with me on a professional level. Then he loses a great degree of power. And it makes him very angry, at me.'

The timing was a problem, just as it had been during *Bridge over Troubled Water*. Art wanted to follow more or less the routine they'd followed then. He insisted that he needed time to work out his harmony. He wanted to walk through Switzerland with his Walkman and write the parts. Then he wanted to come into the studio by himself and overlay his voice on to Paul's basic track.

Paul objected to this. These songs were harmonically very different from the sixties songs, less straightforward, and Paul wanted to control the working-out process. He wanted Art to go into the studio now, and to record his parts while Paul supervised. 'I knew that if what he did wasn't all right with me, I wasn't going to let it go. And that was the difference from the sixties. What we didn't realize at first was how big a difference it was. It was huge. As wide as his solo records are from mine.'

They found themselves confronting all the difficulties they had faced in the past, with one extra. Since their duo days, both men had matured and developed, emotionally and creatively. Throughout the seventies, they had pursued individual styles totally diverse from each other. Also, they had tasted autonomy now; neither artist could adjust to compromising to the extent that was needed.

Meanwhile, time was passing and production was infuriatingly slow for Paul. They had a time limit to consider. They had wanted to get the record on sale just prior to their tour in the spring of '83, which is the usual way. But the months passed and the situation worsened. Art wasn't happy with his performances; Paul wasn't happy with the delays. Relations became more and more strained, and it was now obvious that they were going to miss the spring release date.

In December, Art sang a small solo piece at a children's

concert. It was no more than that, but it would be expanded later into a full production with his longtime friend Jimmy Webb. This performance, strictly an amateur night, was in Jimmy's local church, St Mark's in Tuxedo Park, just north of New York City. It consisted of a children's choir accompanied by Jimmy on the piano.

The concert was a great success and received a standing ovation of ten minutes, which totally surprised all who took part. As Jimmy said: 'As far as I was concerned, the spirit of God was definitely in that church.' Art's part was quite short, but it would re-emerge just a year later in its expanded form, to provide another direction for him, in *The Animals' Christmas*.

The year 1983 opened with preparations for the Australasian tour which began in February. According to the promoters, demand for tickets was phenomenal: in Sydney, 28,000 were sold in only six days. In New Zealand too, demand far outstripped supply. They were travelling with an eight-piece band, taken from the Central Park group and featuring Steve Gadd, Richard Tee and Pete Carr. Unusually, they were on tour without the completed album to promote, but it simply wasn't ready.

On 18 February, Simon & Garfunkel appeared in the open air at Auckland's Carlaw Park, which had a seating capacity for 30,000. On 20 February, they performed at Athletic Park in Wellington. It was their first visit to New Zealand, and it smashed all box office records.

After the Australasian tour, recording continued on the album. By now, it had become a constant source of tension and frustration. They had decided on a title, *Think Too Much*, after one of its songs.

Art seemed to be taking the clashes in his stride. He told the press: 'In the studio, we tend to pull apart a fair amount. The best possible album is a healthy kind of pulling. It's as if we're pulling it so it will end up wider.' Paul was analytical: 'You have to work harder at the music than a friendship. You know if you're in the middle of a song and you haven't got a problem solved, you can't say, "So long, see you in six months." You can do that in a friendship.'

Clearly, what did emerge was that Paul was far from satisfied. He told the *Los Angeles Times*: 'I didn't want it to be a Simon & Garfunkel record because I felt it was my piece of work. I think, in a certain way, Artie improves my records. He makes the sound of them more agreeable to many, many people. But I don't care.'

The work had fallen far behind schedule. To save time, Art began to record his vocals in one studio with Roy Halee, while Paul mixed tracks with Russ Titelman in another. Now, the best they could hope for was an autumn release which would coincide with the completion of their next tour.

Then, at the beginning of June, Paul hit a run of personal problems. He split up with Carrie Fisher, ironically at the peak of her professional success. It was the opening of the eagerly awaited *Return of the Jedi*, the sequel to *Star Wars* and predicted to have similar box office success. The long separations, their mutual inability to make the commitment to marriage, the clashing of their separate and demanding careers, the confrontation of two creative egos – all had contributed to the split.

Carrie left Paul's New York apartment and went back to her modest, rustic log cabin in Laurel Canyon, Hollywood. She was broken-hearted and needed time to rest, collect her thoughts and re-assemble her resources. She had been shattered, a year earlier, by the death of her friend John Belushi, regular comedian on *Saturday Night*, with whom she had appeared in the cult movie *The Blues Brothers*.

She had been briefly involved with Dan Ackroyd, also starring in the movie and a regular on *Saturday Night*. The romance had, according to the press, come close to marriage. Since then, she had been trying to find out who she was in her own right. As Paul commented to the press: 'She drove herself to learn. She's gutsy and a real fighter.' And now, her nerves were raw, to say the least.

When the news of the split reached the press, it became

headlines. The ironic contrast between the happy romance of Princess Leia and the sorrows of Carrie was emphasized all the time. Paul and Carrie were inundated with questions. Throughout those weeks, both were tactful and professional in their statements.

'I will always be related to Paul,' Carrie stressed. 'How can I not be?' And Paul said: 'There is no animosity. We still care very much for each other. There is nobody else quite like Carrie. She's got one of the fastest, funniest minds I know. She is absolutely unique.'

But the show goes on. Also in June, Paul and Art announced to the press that they would be touring the United States during the summer. In some twenty cities they would perform a show, evocatively entitled *Summer Evening with Simon & Garfunkel*. This eagerly anticipated tour would take the duo right across the United States: Akron (Ohio) was the first stop, then Toronto, Pontiac (Michigan), Chicago, Milwaukee, Minneapolis, Pittsburgh, Clifton (New Jersey), Foxboro (Massachusetts), Flushing (New York), Baltimore, Atlanta, Houston, Dallas, Oakland, Vancouver, Los Angeles, San Diego and Boulder.

All the concerts were open air, in sport stadia. 'Music that's outside in the summer is special, it's nice,' Paul said. 'I used to go to concerts like that and I always thought there was something potentially magical about those shows. If you waited until we played a 3,000 seater, then most people couldn't get in to see it. It's American business. It's the old link of art and commerce.'

The programme, besides the usual Simon & Garfunkel hits, also included four or five new songs which were to feature on the album when it came out. Paul would be performing the tribute to John Lennon, 'The Late Great Johnny Ace', and 'Allergies' and 'Cars are Cars'.

Paul and Artie talked to the press and seemed optimistic, with some misgivings. 'We're skipping decades,' Paul said cheerfully. 'That seems to be the plan. Simon & Garfunkel were together in the '60s, took off the '70s. Don't expect anything from us in the

'90s. There's a big show coming in the year 2000. Let's hope we're all here.'

They were asked, predictably, how long the reunion was likely to last. Paul was guarded: 'If the tour and album turn out to be great, then the pressure on you to repeat it becomes greater. And if you enjoy doing it, you're more inclined to do it. I enjoyed the touring we've done abroad. But if it's an entire disaster, we won't repeat it. We've learned not to repeat disasters.'

There was an unmistakable undercurrent of tension. When asked what they would do after the tour, Paul replied with not a little sarcasm: 'Well, you know, here's a crazy thing. Simon and Garfunkel are actually two people. They do things separately. There is no Simon & Garfunkel after the tour. Simon & Garfunkel is a performing team. When the tour is over, I'm going on vacation.'

Paul shared some of his misgivings with the press. 'Don't be misled by this revival,' he insisted. 'I don't think we've resolved anything. I don't know if these problems can truly be resolved, but they can be put aside temporarily. And if you can extend temporarily, well, maybe they're resolved.' It was not the most encouraging beginning.

The tour was to commence on 19 July in Akron, Ohio. There they gave a large press conference, an occasion that provided some indication that things were now far from relaxed between them. With his characteristic dryness, Paul told the photographers: 'We're smiling now, so you can take our pictures.'

Speculations about the feasibility of the promised, eagerly sought duo album began to circulate. It was obvious that Paul and Artie were finding it difficult to be together. No one really doubted that the friendship was intact; it had come through too many storms to be in danger now. But many people were doubting that the partnership would remain.

Chapter Thirty

THE AMERICAN TOUR

It was an extravagant tour: they travelled with an eleven-piece band of Paul's favourite musicians, including, of course, Richard Tee. They took a breathtakingly inventive stage set, a painted drive-in theatre. They also used a huge screen of 700 square feet, 'the size of a two-storey house' according to the press release. On this, they showed a montage of pictures from their former duo days. Clearly, this was intended to give a feeling of intimacy in the midst of such vast arenas.

It didn't quite work. Throughout the tour, the press followed the concerts closely. In the reviews, journalists praised the skill of the band, the new and updated arrangements, some of the song renditions and the solo performances of both Paul and Artie. But most felt a sense of disappointment, of having been let down. The reason for this was clear enough: it was becoming obvious that the two artists were no longer pulling as a team. In different cities on different nights, that was the message that pervaded the reviews.

At the first stop in Akron, they appeared at the Rubber Bowl to a full house of 40,000 and sang twenty-six songs, beginning with 'Cecilia' and closing on a third encore of 'The Sound of Silence' two hours later. The reception was ecstatic, everything they could have hoped for. Paul told the crowd: 'It's good to be home.'

Only a couple of days later at the Silverdome in Pontiac, Michigan before 33,000 people, the *Detroit Times* ran the headline 'Two Tired Troubadours'. Jim McFarlin pointed out that the two men were actually more comfortable as solo acts these days: 'Each singer displayed his best work alone. Garfunkel's "I Only Have Eyes for You" took on a disarming pop-folk wistfulness, while Simon turned his wry genius loose on "Fifty Ways to Leave Your Lover". At the end, Simon borrowed a fan's sign to hold aloft which read "We love you". That may be true, but they don't seem to love each other, and that love is essential in making their music work.'

Their New Jersey concert on 31 July took place in the huge Giants Stadium in East Rutherford. They overcame the vastness with a superb quality 400-unit speaker system. Stephen Holden wrote in the *New York Times*: 'The blend of both voices was uneasy toward the start of the concert, but as the evening wore on, the singers subtly accommodated each other's moods.'

Of the same concert, Michael Hill wrote for *Village Voice*: 'The audience, their memories untampered with, sang along enthusiastically and unselfconsciously. Heading toward the Jersey Turnpike afterward, it wasn't hard to feel like a young Simon did when he was in the same place: empty and aching and not knowing why.'

On 13 August, they performed at Laurel Race Course in Washington. Originally the concert had been planned for Baltimore, but all three proposed locations were rejected because there wasn't enough room for the huge crowd anticipated. Richard Harrington wrote for the *Washington Post*: 'The singers don't seem to like each other. They hardly exchanged glances during the program. By the time Simon & Garfunkel drifted into the sweet melancholy pathos of "Old Friends", there was very little passion. In their heyday, Simon & Garfunkel suggested shared dreams and experiences, a serial that never ended except in stages of growth. This time around, it was painfully obvious that they were just passing through a one-night stand.'

After Washington, Paul flew back to New York. He wanted to see Carrie and they sat down to talk seriously about their relationship. Neither of them was satisfied. Throughout the years, there had been a great deal of friction between them and constant periods of separation. But they still loved each other and had felt the recent loss very acutely.

Perhaps it was time to make a definite commitment, to get married? She said: 'Let's do it. Let's agree that we'll solve our problems. We don't leave when we're frustrated or angry.' Paul felt nervous at the prospect of another marriage. With a painful divorce behind him, he was reluctant to let history repeat itself.

Then suddenly, after watching a triumphant baseball game in his home town on one of the few nights off from the tour, he changed his mind. 'I was feeling very secure on my second beer. And I thought, "Well, come on, Paul. You're going to do it." I'd always loved her, even when we were most separated.' And Carrie told the press: 'Maybe we're not good room-mates, but I love Paul.'

Pausing only to do a concert in Atlanta, Paul and Carrie applied for their wedding licence and planned a whirwind wedding. No one, they thought, could be that surprised after all their years of living together.

They were married at a private Jewish ceremony in Paul's apartment on 16 August. It was attended by relatives and close friends. An all-star guest list included Art Garfunkel with Penny Marshall, Lorne Michaels, Randy Newman, Charles Grodin, Mike Nichols, George Lucas, Robin Williams, Kevin Kline, Teri Garr and Christie Brinkley with Billy Joel.

Teri Garr flew in especially from Paris for the wedding, telling the press: 'I wouldn't have missed it for the world.' Billy Joel gave the couple a very special wedding present: a jukebox filled with 1950s records. After the ceremony, he bashed on the piano in a jam session with Harper, now ten, who played three chords on the guitar and sang.

Paul's parents attended from their home in New Jersey. Carrie's brother Todd was there, grinning delightedly and escorting his mother, Debbie Reynolds and his grandmother, Maxine.

There was, in this mood of romance and optimism, some anxious speculation about the reunion of Debbie Reynolds and Eddie Fisher, who had been estranged for the past twenty-five years, since their bitter divorce in 1958 when Fisher left his wife for Elizabeth Taylor. His subsequent autobiography had been less than flattering to Debbie Reynolds.

She arrived first and it was whispered, according to the *Globe*, that Eddie was expected to bring a girlfriend. Everyone was nervous about how Debbie would react. In fact, he strode in with his 81-year-old mother, Kate. He kissed his daughter, congratulated Paul, then went across to Debbie. Their reunion was touching and emotional. After the ceremony, he raised his glass of champagne in a toast to 'A beautiful, wonderful woman – Debbie Reynolds'.

It was a joyous occasion for the bride and groom. Carrie said happily: 'Let's just say we've had a stormy romance and the storm's finally over.' And Paul later said: 'We were married, and immediately, I felt a sense of relief.'

The press made much of the event. It was headline news in most of the newspapers on both sides of the Atlantic – and generally, the headlines and leading paragraphs reported that Paul Simon was marrying Princess Leia. Even that couldn't dampen the spirits of the couple. They were obviously glowing with happiness and very much in love. So maybe there was, after all, a strong fairy-tale element in this match.

The so-called honeymoon began the following day, when the couple flew to Houston, Texas for the next Simon & Garfunkel concert. Then on the 20th, at Oakland Coliseum, Carrie joined her husband on stage briefly in front of 30,000 fans. Characteristically, she was witty: 'I'd like to thank you all for joining us on our honeymoon,' she said. 'We couldn't have done it without you.'

Joel Selvin reviewed the concert, harshly, perhaps, but echoing the general feelings about the tour. 'Both performers appeared decidedly ill at ease – with the audience, with the repertoire, and most obviously with each other. Even Princess Leia, the new Mrs Paul Simon, who was introduced to the crowd during the encore, couldn't save this enterprise.'

The next day, Paul flew north to a concert in Vancouver. Carrie flew to her log cabin in Los Angeles to start work as Thumbelina in Shelley Duvall's series of fairy tales for *Showtime*. Shelley, a close friend of Carrie's, could take the credit for introducing the couple to each other in 1978 at the LA Film Critics Awards.

Paul joined his wife there straight after Vancouver and had a few days' rest until the LA concert on the 27th. There he was interviewed by *Weekend*. He talked candidly about the past and about Artie: 'We didn't quit because it wasn't working. We quit because it wasn't any fun to work together.' And he spoke about the present, somewhat ominously. It was clear that he had come to realize the reunion with Artie wasn't going to last. 'Art and I have known each other for so long. We have a very good friendship but we don't have a very good partnership. At least we know when you decide you don't want to be in the partnership, you're not walking away from a friendship.'

On the subject of the forthcoming album, he reiterated his earlier claim: 'This is probably as personal as I've ever gotten.' He compared it to his award-winning, starkly personal album *Still Crazy after All These Years*. 'Except it's a jump of a few years. This is back to telling stories about people. Overall, it's about relationships and love.'

The Los Angeles concert at the Dodger Stadium had an audience of 45,000. Dennis Hunt commented: 'Simon & Garfunkel should stay together. They work better together than as soloists. They obviously bring out the best in each other. The Dodger Stadium audience, in ecstasy most of the time, would certainly agree.'

The following night they were at the Jack Murphy Stadium in San Diego. They were growing tired. They still had the problems of the album to resolve, and that time was getting closer. Despite all the success of this tour, both men knew that difficult decisions were waiting to be confronted.

The tour closed on 30 August at Folsom Stadium in Boulder, Colorado. There 35,000 fans gathered to see them. The three video cameras followed their movements on stage, instantly replaying to the audience on the huge screen behind the stage. There was a sense of relief for both Paul and Artie – and also, perhaps, a sense of sadness.

Jackie Campbell wrote in *Rocky Mountain News*: 'For old time's sake. For one last summer evening with the double rainbow just before sunset and lightning on the horizon. There was never a wrong note between the two of them. The relationship was back on for one night, anyway.'

Chapter Thirty-one

HEARTS AND BONES

Immediately after their US tour, Paul and Art set off on some European dates. This had been arranged to promote the duo album, which of course was still not released. Nevertheless, these concerts did have the effect of making the public even more eager in their anticipation of the album. In Europe, the public swarmed out to see them. In Nice, they sang to a crowd of 50,000 fans and became headline news.

The climax of the tour, on 24 and 25 September was two benefit concerts in Tel Aviv, Israel. Over 50,000 people arrived to see them perform their final concerts, at fifty dollars a seat. The profits were going to charities through the Variety Club of Israel.

Simon & Garfunkel had never performed there, though Paul had appeared solo in 1978. As Americans never very far from their Jewish heritage, this affected Paul and Art profoundly. It was a joyous occasion, as the ecstatic Israeli audience cheered wildly in appreciation. The performers were emotional in the face of this response. Struggling to hold back tears, Paul told them: 'I want to say so much, but I can't. I'm so happy to be here. I love you all.' And Art added: 'We should have done this a long time ago.'

They arrived back in America and still the world awaited the arrival of the new Simon & Garfunkel album. Press and fans alike were curious about the songs, the arrangements, the style of harmony. Art talked to the press about Paul's writing for the album: 'I think it's his best music ever.'

Meanwhile, Paul set off with Carrie on a belated honeymoon, cruising down the Nile. While he was away, the press were given the news that the new album would be a Paul Simon solo, not a duo release. It was alleged that Paul had ordered Art's voice to be electronically erased from the album, though Paul later said this wasn't true because Artie hadn't actually got down to much recording; most of the work he had done was thinking about harmony, writing his part. Paul's prepared statement explained that the songs were, after all, too personal to be sung with another voice.

A spokesperson told the *LA Times*: 'Paul simply felt the material he wrote is so close to his own life that it had to be his own record. Art was hoping to be on the album, but I'm sure there will be other projects that they will work on together. They are still friends.' It was something of an understatement to say that Art was hoping to be on the album, since Art had worked for months on his singing parts and had been deeply committed to making it a success.

The news was apparently no surprise to those people nearest to the duo. Co-producer Russ Titelman told the press: 'Paul never really decided if he wanted the record to be his or Simon & Garfunkel's. I'd imagine it would strain their personal relationship.'

Indeed, it would. Essentially, it meant that Art had worked for over a year on a project that was now a Paul Simon solo; moreover, he had spent the past summer on an exhausting tour which would now merely promote a Paul Simon album. To Artie, it not only seemed like a betrayal, it had also been a terrible waste of time and energy.

He gave no comment to the press, which did him credit. It was evident from the news releases that the press were in sympathy with Artie and were baffled by Paul's sudden decision and the way in which it had been carried out. In a sense, even the press seemed disappointed.

And not only the press: fans throughout the world felt a sense of loss. After a series of Simon & Garfunkel concerts which had started triumphantly in the autumn of 1981 with Central Park, and had come to a stupendous climax in Israel just weeks ago, it came as a shock that the duo had once again shattered into pieces. There was a feeling that it had all been for nothing.

On a business level, the news was far from welcome to Warner Brothers. It was said they had suffered a poor year financially and were counting on the Simon & Garfunkel album to boost their profits. The reunion album of a well-loved duo was obviously a better prospect than a solo album by either performer. For Warner Brothers too, it was a crashing disappointment.

Nevertheless, Paul felt he had made the right decision, based on his own strong instincts. He regretted the difficulty and embarrassment of Artie's predicament, but he remained firm. 'I would be willing,' he told *Playboy*, 'to do almost – that word is important – almost anything to make Art happy. I care about our friendship. The only thing I feel I won't do is change the essence of my work. That was the crux of our problem on this new album.'

The album was renamed, but would still be given the title of one of its songs. In a sense that also seems significant, as if in Paul's mind *Think Too Much* was the album he worked on with Artie, but *Hearts and Bones* was entirely his own.

Hearts and Bones was finally released in October '83. It opens with the upbeat 'Allergies', the song Paul wrote after his first visits to his analyst. It's a cry for help, underlined by Al Di Meola's furious staccato solo. Sam Sutherland in *High Fidelity* wrote: 'This is Simon at his articulate best: spirited and eclectic, droll but serious, balancing careful poesy with flashes of conversational realism.'

The title track explores the wide gap between thinking and feeling, between what is ideal and what is real. It traces the journey, both geographical and emotional, of two lovers, clearly Paul and Carrie, described as one and a half wandering Jews, as they try to come to terms with their relationship. It's a sad, evocative song, which wistfully blends the past and the present – and leaves the future unresolved. The *New York Times* described it as: 'nothing less than a finished musical poem'.

'When Numbers Get Serious' is a playful, syncopated song which reminds us of 'Kodachrome' and 'Mother and Child Reunion'. Like those songs, it has some darker undertones woven into the tongue-in-cheek flippancy.

The first version of 'Think Too Much' is more sombre musically and lyrically than the second, and explores the conflict between intellect and emotion, symbolized in the left and right sides of the brain. Again, it is inspired by Paul's relationship with Carrie. With wry humour, he dismisses the press as 'the smartest people in the world' who gather to analyse the love affair and get them unscrambled.

'Song about the Moon' describes the writer's block and the solution, returning to simple themes and imagery, which are, after all, more potent than complex intellectualizing. It's foot tapping and catchy with some homage to doo-wap in the vocal backing.

The second 'Think Too Much' is a lighter treatment of the same theme of conflict. The vocal backing is layered to produce a counterpoint to his own vocal, and handclapping and percussion give this song a sharp, caustic edge.

'Train in the Distance' similarly uses voices and percussion to produce the sound of a moving train. It's the story of Paul's relationship with Peggy, the birth of Harper, the divorce and subsequent friendship. It's a wistful, plaintive narrative underlined by the sustained metaphor – the closer we get to things, the more profound our disenchantment becomes. At the end of the song, Paul steps out from the narrative to make the comment that it's only our indomitable feelings of hope that get us through the pain, let us survive.

'Réné and Georgette Magritte with Their Dog after the War' is a modified waltz which surrealistically depicts two immigrants, the famous modern painter and his wife, who dance naked in their hotel room to the rhythm and blues songs which take them back to easier, more peaceful times. It traces their gradual coming to terms with the new life and the ultimate hiding away of their sense of the past.

Stephen Holden wrote: 'Like a Magritte painting, the images are presented as a sequence of unexpected visual tableaux with impossible juxtapositions. With its translucent layers of sound, the cut is also a kind of aural time capsule in which rock 'n' roll becomes a magical, spiritual and erotic source that Mr Simon offers as the purest expression of the American dream.' The backing is sung appropriately by the Harptones who create a melancholy doo-wap counterpoint to Paul's poignant vocal which is woven, in a somewhat unlikely combination, with the traditional string orchestration.

'Cars Are Cars' is another upbeat, syncopated track. It's witty, skips along and makes the point that cars are cars all over the world, but people vary and quarrel about their differences. There isn't much more to it than that.

The album closes with the mournful tribute to John Lennon, 'The Late Great Johnny Ace'. From the fifties death of Johnny Ace, a shocking gun death while playing Russian roulette, it moves to 1964, to the idyllic England days just after the gun death of John Kennedy. Here the change in musical style captures the flavour of the Beatles and the Rolling Stones, the sounds which dominated those happy times. The narrative closes sombrely in New York on a cold December night, with the news of John Lennon's death. The three deaths are thus linked in a cyclical structure which unifies the song thematically. It ends with a quiet woodwind and string coda by Philip Glass, which evokes 'Eleanor Rigby'.

The entire album is a thematic unity. To a greater or lesser extent, the songs explore the tragic gap between thinking and feeling, intellect and emotion, wanting and having, hope and disillusionment. The major songs are narrative episodes which trace relationships from their simple beginnings to their restless questioning, to wistful yearning and a sense of loss.

The album received great acclaim from the critics. Whatever their reactions had been to the news that Artie's voice had been erased from the recordings, having heard the album, they were almost unanimous in their unstinting praise.

Robin Denselow wrote in the *Guardian*: 'Simon allegedly removed his partner's voice from the tapes. If that is so, it is certainly understandable, for no other vocals are needed on this exquisitely crafted set. Gently tuneful and rhythmic, Simon's songs mix the introspection with a welcome sense of humour. Simon has obviously taken this album very seriously.'

In *Audio*, Michael Tearson wrote: 'Simon's writing has never been better or more literate. The production of the album is stunning. I really do believe that *Hearts and Bones* is very possibly the best album Paul Simon has ever done, solo or not. There is commitment, maturity, intelligence and artistry here in abundance.'

Sam Sutherland in *High Fidelity*: 'This is Simon at his articulate best. *Hearts and Bones* is a stunning piece of work.' Similarly, in *Options*: 'Simon proves more subtle and elusive than ever on *Hearts and Bones*, an album which is literate and craftsmanlike.' *High Fidelity* called it 'Paul Simon's best album in nearly a decade'.

The *San Francisco Chronicle*: 'Simon, one of pop music's most accomplished writers, keeps getting better and better. His songs are all staggering creations, each crafted within an inch of its life and produced with pristine fidelity to the composer's demanding vision.'

Stephen Holden wrote in the *New York Times*: 'The most ambitious songwriting on *Hearts and Bones* has a visionary beauty and eloquence that go beyond anything Mr Simon has done before.' The review in *Time* also acclaimed Paul: '*Hearts and Bones*, an album of old and lost love, shattered dreams and delicate possibilities, is rueful, mature, self-mocking and hauntingly melodic.' And in England, the *Sunday Times*: 'Simon's album is nothing less than genius.'

Paul came back from his honeymoon with Carrie filled with optimism, determined to make the marriage work. He needed time with her, he decided. 'I would like to take a year off and just try to live happily with Carrie. That's what we're planning to do. It does have a happy ending.'

But it didn't. In November, Carrie suffered a miscarriage following an ectopic pregnancy. She was devastated by the loss. She had been very excited at the realization she was pregnant and very much wanted to be a mother. Only hours before being rushed to hospital, she had been laughing delightedly about the baby with her father. Carrie's mother, Debbie Reynolds, broke down in tears when she heard the news.

In December, Paul and Carrie travelled to London and were photographed walking through the park. Carrie was putting on a brave face but seemed – understandably – depressed. Paul, too, looked disappointed. As well as being shattered by the loss of the baby, he was also upset that the sales of *Hearts and Bones*, despite the acclaim from the critics, were his lowest so far. He had hoped for more.

December was a busy month for Art Garfunkel. He came to London to appear at the Royal Festival Hall on the 21st in Jimmy Webb's British premiere of *The Animals' Christmas*, a cantation for children's voices. The conductor was Carl Davis with the Wren Orchestra and the Finchley Children's Music Choir. Art was the soloist, along with Jimmy Webb's sister, Susan. Jimmy accompanied on piano.

The entire venture was for charity, with all profits going to Capital Radio's Help a London Child appeal. Art explained his reasons for doing it: 'I love beautiful notes, so I wanted to be involved in Jimmy Webb's *Animals' Christmas*. London has always been good to me, so I felt I'd like to do something for it. And why did I choose to do it in aid of Help a London Child? If we don't look after the children of this generation, heaven help the future.'

It was a good show. Art arrived on stage dressed immaculately in a black suit and gave an impassioned performance. Whatever his personal disappointments were in his relationship with Paul, they didn't interfere with his work. I was at the concert, and the applause was amazing; Art was clearly very welcome in London.

The next day, I went to the Roundhouse Recording Studio in north London and watched Artie, Jimmy Webb and Roy Halee prepare the tapes of the previous night for a radio concert to be broadcast on Christmas Day. They worked hard, obviously striving for the best sounds. The atmosphere in that tiny studio was one of friendship, shared motivation and trust.

During his visit to London I soon got used to Artie's dry, caustic sense of humour, something that doesn't often come across in his work. Articulate, measured and thoughtful, he talked to me about the strange world of show business. We spoke of books, music, writing. At no time did he mention *Hearts and Bones*. I felt he simply didn't want to discuss it. It was clear to everyone that Simon & Garfunkel, apart from an occasional nod to nostalgia in the form of one-off concerts, were a duo no more. They had separate ideas of the way ahead; they had misgivings about their feelings towards each other; they had collected various scars along the route, both solo and together. A chapter in their lives was definitely closed. What had happened in the recent months had happened and Artie, for one, didn't intend to dwell on it. He was, at the end of 1983, looking firmly towards the future.

Chapter Thirty-two

AFTER THE END

In spite of Paul's optimistic vow at the close of 1983 that he would take a year off and live happily with Carrie, the next year was far from happy. In April '84, Carrie walked out of the marriage and moved in with a friend a few blocks away from the apartment where she had lived with Paul.

There was much speculation as to why the couple had split after just eight months of marriage. Carrie had very much wanted a family life and children, but had been very depressed after losing her baby; naturally, this had made her want to throw herself back into her work. She was due to fly to London to act in a new version of *Frankenstein* with Sir John Gielgud.

Recently, with all the emotional strain, Paul and Carrie had been quarrelling. Some people said this was because Paul had never wanted Carrie to have a career. Who knows? Perhaps they had waited too long to be married, to start a family, to reconcile the differences that had kept them apart for so long. By July, the couple were officially separated. Carrie was back on the West Coast and Paul was getting ready for a summer tour of the US to take place in August.

The tour received good reviews; in Saratoga, Stephen Leon wrote: 'This was Simon at his best.' And Michael Hochanadel wrote: 'It was a masterly performance, a chance to see the songwriter exposed on stage alone, with just his guitar, his feelings and his memories.'

There was a sense of *déjà vu* because Paul had been on tour a year earlier – only with Artie – and had taken a couple of days off to get married. Now, in August, Carrie celebrated their first wedding anniversary without Paul, by throwing a large party for her friends. She was house-hunting in Beverly Hills, having decided her log cabin was no longer large enough.

This was a fruitful period for Artie. In October, his single 'Sometimes When I'm Dreaming' came out, another Mike Batt composition, a wistful and romantic ballad. In December, he released a greatest hits compilation, *The Art Garfunkel Album*, which included all his well known songs such as 'Bright Eyes', 'All I know', 'Breakaway' and 'I Only Have Eyes for You', remixed to create a richer sound.

Art came to London in December to promote the album and stayed at St James's Club. I went to see him there, and he read me some of his poetry, which he was considering publishing in the near future. We talked about the loneliness of show business and he told me how much he wanted to have a family.

He also talked about marriage to Trudi Pacter of the *Sunday Mirror*. 'I'm beginning to think the two great areas of fulfilment are work and love,' he said. 'If you have only one, you have less than a full life. The other night I was having dinner with a friend in London. As I walked out afterwards, I thought, gee, I feel like going home to my wife and kids. But I don't have a wife and kids. Do you know, for a moment, it was something I really yearned for.'

For Paul, 1985 began in a very positive way, when he took part in the USA for Africa recording of 'We Are the World' in a Los Angeles studio on 28 January. Inspired by Bob Geldof's efforts to raise money for Africa, and set in motion by screen star Harry Belafonte, the project was to record a song composed by Lionel Richie and Michael Jackson. A host of megastars, forty-five in all, took part: among them, Bob Dylan, Diana Ross, Stevie Wonder, Bette Midler – and Paul Simon.

In the early months of 1985, the song was a hit, selling over a million copies in the first week. It was followed by money-making spin-offs such as a video documentary of the recording. In July, a Live Aid concert was broadcast on worldwide television, featuring some forty-five acts and including Paul.

Paul's interest in Africa was firmly established by now, though it was said to have started when he heard a bootleg tape in 1984. But in his solo years, he had shown a passion for different kinds of music, as well as an insistence on being authentic. By late summer '85 he was working on a new album which would clearly indicate that African music was to be his new direction.

He worked on the album for the next year and in August '86 released a single, 'You Can Call Me Al', with 'Gumboots' on the B side. His first single in three years, this was to herald the forthcoming album, to be entitled *Graceland*. The name was taken from Elvis Presley's magnificently and opulent estate, which Paul went to visit with Harper. So, as well as being a tribute to African music, this album was also a tribute to Paul's lifelong hero, Elvis.

The album came out in September, after taking two years and elements from several continents to make. It featured South African artists General M.D. Shirinda and the Gaza Sisters and Ladysmith Black Mambazo. Paul had also attempted to wed the African sounds to American ones and included contributions from Rockin' Dopsie, Los Lobos and the Everly Brothers.

It caused a stir in the press for its political implications. Many people disapproved of Paul for going against the United Nations' resolution not to go to South Africa, and not to work there. Paul was disdainful of this. He gave a plush press conference at London's Mayfair Theatre and invited the press to fire questions at him about his reasons for choosing to work in South Africa.

He defended his actions by saying he paid his musicians $190 per hour, triple the US Musicians Union rate, and that he had given them full royalty credits. Furthermore, he insisted he had turned down a lucrative offer to perform at Sun City – and had done no performing at all in South Africa. He was, he said, just eager to see that 'such rich music' should be introduced to the rest of the world.

However, Jerry Dammers, the ex-Special who wrote 'Free Nelson Mandela' and helped start Artists against Apartheid, was furious. Of Paul, he said: 'He's helping maybe thirty people and he's damaging solidarity over sanctions. He's doing more harm than good.'

Robin Denselow reviewed the conference and the album in the *Guardian*. 'Judged in purely musical terms, *Graceland* is a pleasantly intriguing, immaculately crafted and produced piece of work. In spite of his doubtless honest desire to promote African styles, this is much more a Paul Simon LP than an African LP . . . even so, this odd fusion does produce some interesting effects.' The political fracas inevitably cast a shadow over the album's release and Paul's fans took sides. Paul's closing comment at the press conference was: 'Next I might look at the music of New York City.' Drily, Robin Denselow commented: 'The Anti-Apartheid campaigners might find that a very good idea.'

That same month, the release of the movie *Good to Go* with Artie in the starring role also led to press speculation. A thriller, set in the go-go ghettos of Washington DC, it had Artie playing a hard-drinking journalist who has fallen on hard times. As a background, the movie featured a soundtrack of go-go music by Troublefunk, Chuck Brown and the Soul Searchers, Redds and the Boys. Some mixed reviews followed. Deanne Pearson wrote: 'It's a good story, unfortunately let down by weak characterization.' And Lucy O'Brien in *NME* wrote: 'Rape is used as a kneejerk device . . . life is a bitch, basically, and then you die.' *Rolling Stone*: 'Art Garfunkel is believable as a guilty, white, liberal reporter.' And *UK Mix*: 'As it turns out, the now middle-aged ex-folk singer turns in a remarkably good performance . . . one of the best things about Blaine Novak's film.'

In the autumn of '86, Paul's album *Graceland* was doing very well; despite the political disagreements, it was being hailed as brilliant. This brought Paul immense satisfaction, professionally and personally.

Then, quite suddenly, Art's father died and Paul went to offer condolences to the family. It was the first meeting between Paul and Art since the fateful tour, but Paul told the press: 'I've known him since the age of ten and I'm with him to the end. Real life puts those things in perspective.'

In December Paul did a *Whistle Test Extra* for BBC television, to celebrate his amazing success with *Graceland*, his first solo number 1 album. His new single 'The Boy in the Bubble' was also at the top of the charts. At forty-five, Paul was riding high. In a review of the year's albums that month, Robin Denselow called *Graceland* 'an exquisite collaboration with African musicians'.

But his troubles weren't over. In 1987 the criticism was revived when Paul announced a world tour in the spring, to be backed by the African musicians who had appeared on the album. He planned to begin in February in Europe, then cover Zimbabwe and the United States, before ending in Britain in April. At the same time, he was honoured by another Grammy Award for *Graceland*, which clearly delighted him. He said: 'I hope the African National Congress will be as happy as I am. We both certainly want the same thing.'

The tour was a hugely successful sell-out with thousands of disappointed fans unable to get tickets. There was some Anti-Apartheid Movement picketing outside the concert at the Albert Hall, but that wasn't disruptive to the concert in any way. John Peel summed up the audience reaction in the *Observer*: 'During the finale, Paul Simon moved to the side of the stage where he stood smiling and playing percussion. He had enabled us to see and hear performers that otherwise we might not have seen and heard.'

The year 1988 was fairly uneventful for both Paul and Art, but for the release of one album each. For Art it was *Lefty*, a collection of romantic ballads, not particularly well received by the critics; the title takes its name from Art being left-handed and the album carries a picture of Art, poised for baseball, the bat in his left hand. Paul's album was a greatest hits compilation, *Negotiations and Love Songs*, which was well received by critics and the public. It served as a statement that Paul was definitely a solo artist now; indeed, the body of his solo work was now larger than that of Simon & Garfunkel.

Art's long-considered book of poetry appeared in 1989. Simply entitled *Still Water*, it contained a collection of deeply personal prose poems. That same year he also married former model Kathryn Cermak, nicknamed Kim. He was introduced to her by a photographer friend and had known her for some time.

Artie had liked her instantly. He told *Hello*: 'She clearly has a wonderful goodness of heart that I respond to. Before I knew it, she was definitely my favourite person to spend time with. I was falling in love with her.' It was a huge turning point in Art's life and he recognized it as such. Some years earlier, upon marrying Linda, his first wife, he had remarked that timing is the most important factor in the decision to get married. And though that marriage had not lasted, he had clearly been ready to be married. This time it was different. Instinctively, he felt everything was right, not just the timing but also the woman.

For Paul, the summer of 1990 brought some nostalgia with it. In August, the brewery company Harp sponsored a series of plaques to be placed at important rock music sites in Britain. The first was at Widnes Station to honour Paul's creation of 'Homeward Bound' which Paul is said to have written while waiting for a train. Of course, he didn't actually write it there, as Geoff Speed took Paul to the station and saw him board the train on that famous day. But this was showbiz, and the spirit of the thing was what mattered. It was entirely appropriate that Geoff Speed was asked to do the unveiling, though Geoff told me he was chosen only because the organizers were unable to locate Kathy, Paul's English girfriend in the sixties. It is doubtful that Kathy would have wanted to unveil the plaque, as she has consistently shunned the limelight.

September '90 saw the release of Paul's new album, *Rhythm of the Saints*, which incorporated the music and rhythms of West Africa and Brazil. Paul found the mix of the two cultures very satisfying, and recorded Brazilian musicians live in the streets. 'We just set up microphones in a cobbled square in the city of Salvador,' he said. 'We hung the microphones from the windows of buildings and telephone poles. Hundreds of people gathered. It was an amazing day – an extraordinary recording experience.'

The album was very well received. David Jenson wrote in *Sunday People*: '*Rhythm of the Saints* could do for Brazilian music what *Graceland* did for African. This album is exotic and emotional and will grow and grow with each hearing.' Michael Cowton in the *Daily Express*: 'Effective and melodious, it is an incarnation of rhythms, primitive in style and infectious in their delivery.' Marcus Berkmann called it 'a splendid record'.

Once again, there was some controversy about Paul's ethics in recording artists from the Third World. At the press conference to launch the album, a journalist asked him why he had not shared more of the songwriting royalties with his South American collaborators. He replied: 'Before *Graceland*, people never credited or paid anybody a royalty. The idea that one was automatically entitled to be credited as a songwriter for playing the drums was unheard of. When I recorded "Fifty Ways to Leave Your Lover" and Steve Gadd made up that famous drum lick which drives the whole song, he was just doing his job, to be a creative drummer and he charged a commensurate salary.'

In December 1990, Artie's wife Kim gave birth to a healthy baby boy. 'He's gorgeous, he's fabulous,' Art told the press. Artie was present at the birth and later explained how it affected him: 'Nothing's ever been quite so gorgeous or so poignant.' He embraced fatherhood immediately as it suddenly put his life into perspective: 'I've had the adventure of trying to sing and get popular and have fame, but what could possibly be more interesting than to produce a live human being that is the embodiment of our love?' The baby, James, was clearly the child Artie had longed for.

The year 1991 opened for Paul with his *Born at the Right Time* tour which received wonderful reviews. In Oakland, California in March, Michael Goldberg wrote that the concert carried the details and rich sounds of both *Graceland* and *Rhythm of the Saints*. Jonathan King saw the concert at Nassau: 'It is brilliant. My old friend has really reached his peak. The sound in the giant Nassau Colliseum was crystal clear and the band were marvellous.'

By May, the tour had reached Britain, opening at Wembley. Paul was feeling reflective about his life. 'I've been living on my own for a long time now,' he told the *Daily Mirror*, 'and I am very comfortable.' Though he confessed to wanting another marriage and more children, he was content with his work: 'When I write a great line, I am out of myself, the way you are when you make love.'

He was spending more and more time at his seafront house in Long Island and was looking forward to returning there after the tour. He told *Radio Times*: 'All of this is about finding peace. I know I have been on a journey. I have to take the elements from that and, sooner or later, I have to say well, this is home.'

Britain welcomed Paul and his band as it had always done. David Cheal wrote in the *Daily Telegraph* described 'an evening which had been dominated by one man's thoughtful quest for new and different musical experiences. It had been absorbing, intriguing and, occasionally, compelling.' In *Today*, David Seymour wrote: 'It was an extraordinary performance from quite an extraordinary musician. You'll still be crazy about Paul Simon after all these years.'

On 17 August, Paul did a free concert in Central Park and three-quarters of a million people turned out to see it. Ten years earlier, Paul had performed there with Artie; now, as a solo artist backed by his seventeen-piece band, he treated his fans of all ages to over two hours of non-stop hits.

One face missing from the crowd was Artie; despite speculation that Paul would ask his old partner to perform a couple of
numbers with him, it didn't happen. 'I just sensed he wasn't going
to ask me,' Art said. Furthermore, his disappointment was evident
when he told the press in New York: 'I'm not good enough to be
invited. My guess is that it would hurt his sense of stature.'

The world tour continued, reaching China by October. Paul
had now been on tour for months and was getting tired. He was
looking forward to some time off in the next year. But 1992
opened with more controversy. Paul's plans to take his *Born at
the Right Time* tour to South Africa in January were met with
protest and indignation from the Anti-Apartheid Movement. This
was despite the fact that Paul had received approval this time. The
trip was certified as politically correct by the ANC who extracted
pledges to coach workshops of young black musicians in return.
The United Nations also lifted the ban so that Paul could perform
there. 'I wouldn't say I felt vindicated exactly,' Paul said. 'But I'm
glad that everyone has now come around to the position we had
all along.'

The reason for the trip to South Africa was musical, he
stressed; he was doing a lot to promote black music and absolutely
nothing to comfort South African white people. 'The boycott was
designed to inflict pressure or pain on the white community, but
it unnecessarily inflicted it on blacks as well,' Paul said.

Despite threats of violence, the tour went ahead. Only seven
hours after Paul flew in from New York, a radical anti-apartheid
group bombed the offices of a Johannesburg firm supplying
equipment for the tour. More attacks were threatened. Paul
remained steadfast in his resolve to complete the tour. 'I should
not give way to a handful of extremists. We are here to make
music and have fun.'

All the same, security was very tight for the concerts; in the
hours before the shows, dogs sniffed for bombs inside the stadium
while the police set up barricades on the nearby roads. With a

team of 800 security officers and bodyguards, this was the biggest ever security operation for a musical event.

Nelson Mandela, the ANC president, joined the crowd of welcome for Paul. 'This is a very happy day for South Africans,' he said. 'Please feel comfortable because you are among friends.' Nevertheless, the crowds who flocked to see Paul were mostly middle-class white fans, and it seemed clear that black people were boycotting the concerts. At Johannesburg's Ellis Park Stadium which seats 70,000, fewer than 20,000 people turned up. This was a disappointing second day of the tour.

Though he had responded with admirable courage to the threats, Paul was naturally aware of the danger he was in while he performed. Later, he admitted: 'Whenever I was singing and closing my eyes to get into the song, I'd think, I may never open them again.'

The controversy continued in the press. For some time, Paul was dogged with questions about visiting South Africa, payment of royalties to musicians on the album, his motives for using music from other countries. He grew tired of the argument. 'You don't erect barriers between cultures,' he said in despair, 'you tear them down.'

One music critic accused Paul of mercenary motives in promoting South African music: 'He waltzes into town, takes the catchiest thing he can find, brings it back and it's his hit.' But the brilliant Soweto guitarist Ray Phiri defended Paul: 'We, as South African musicians, were using him more than he was using us. We were isolated and trying hard to get involved in the international community, but it wasn't happening. And suddenly there was this guy who was known for writing beautiful words and I thought, "Maybe if we mix our rhythms with his thoughts, we might get some kind of musical osmosis."' Joseph Tshabalala of the Ladysmith Black Mambazo added: 'It came into my mind that Paul Simon was sent by God to South Africa, because that was my dream – to promote our culture.'

In May, Paul and Artie were reunited for one night at the Brooks Atkinson Theater in New York in a benefit for Friends in Need, a new organization set up to provide non-medical needs for AIDS sufferers and their families.

Also in May, Paul married Texas rock singer-songwriter Edie Brickell. Now fifty, Paul made his vows to Edie, twenty-five, at his Long Island home in a secret civil ceremony. They intended to start a family right away, they told the press. Edie had already won many fans in 1988 with her debut album *Shooting Rubber-bands at the Stars*. Her hit song was 'What I Am', performed with her band the New Bohemians before she became a solo performer. Close friends remarked how much in love the two of them were.

The close of 1992 saw Artie bathing in love and family life, with baby James now an active one-and-a-half-year-old. The marriage and fatherhood were giving him infinite joy and pride. He told *Hello* magazine: 'I feel pretty young, if you want to know the truth.' He allowed photographs to be taken of him and his family in his New York apartment – and it was clear that Artie was no longer reclusive or soul-searching. He had found, at fifty, the happiness of family life that he had always wanted.

In the early months of 1993, Paul was also enjoying the delights of fatherhood – in his case, for the second time around. His first son, Harper, was now grown up and very much a musician like his father. The birth of this second son, Adrian, who weighed 7 lb 2 oz, seemed like a good omen to Paul. 'Like anybody, I love the feeling of being in love – and Edie and I are wonderfully happy together.'

In August, Paul recorded a ninety-minute edition of the prestigious *South Bank Show*, written and presented by Melvyn Bragg. The programme was a detailed profile of Paul's career and contained footage from the long *Born at the Right Time* tour. It also showed Paul preparing to team up again with Artie on a temporary basis for a series of concerts in New York's Madison Square Garden in October.

This was a good time for Paul; he was thinking about his

career and how lucky he had been. 'A lot of talent is a gift,' he told the press, 'but a lot is also luck. I'm very aware of that. I was born in the right place at the right time. I am also blessed because I've never been a sex symbol. I'm spared the embarrassment of acting young.'

Now he was content to be his age, to enjoy the fruits of family life in his home at Montauk, Long Island. He had come to terms with the fact that, compared to the huge success of *Graceland*, *Rhythm of the Saints* had been a disappointment. He was now able to shrug it off and not look too far forward. 'I don't think I'm ready to get back into writing,' he said. 'There are too many things happening in my life. I'm married again with a baby and there are a lot of things that are so important. I'm in my life now, not in my imagination.'

Nevertheless, he was working hard. He and Edie were in a New York studio most days making an album together and producing Edie's third solo album. After a day spent deep in productivity, they would escape each evening to the peace and tranquillity of their Montauk home overlooking the Atlantic Ocean.

For Paul, in those late days of 1993, life was looking good. It was third time lucky in terms of his marriage and he had another child who was absorbing him just as much as Harper had always done. In a moment of characteristic humour, he told the press: 'The older I get, the better I feel about myself. I even get better looking.'

Again in a striking parallel, the first years of the nineties brought for both Paul and Art a time of relaxing and re-evaluating the past. For both of them, it was a time to be with their families, to devote energy to their new sons, their marriages. It was a time to count their blessings.

EPILOGUE

Logically, there can be no end to a biography of two people who are still alive. On the other hand, there is an end to the duo of Simon & Garfunkel, which is, after all, the subject of this book. Most people would agree that Simon & Garfunkel ended after their world tour and just before the release of *Hearts and Bones* as a solo album. With that release, Paul Simon settled the matter, if there was still any doubt.

The two artists have solo careers which are very different. From time to time, despite periods of reclusive silence or domestic preoccupation, they produce something to indicate that they are still alive and well: an album, a film, a documentary, an exclusive interview. From time to time, we hear from Paul Simon and Art Garfunkel.

But that is not the same as Simon & Garfunkel. We will not, I believe, hear from them again in any permanent way. There will be an occasional reunion, perhaps a song, a charity performance, a momentary journey into nostalgia in which the audiences will light candles, solemnly mouth the words to 'The Sound of Silence' or 'The Boxer' and enjoy the divine indulgence of remembering where they were when they first heard that song, what it meant to them, what memories it evokes.

Other than that, we have the albums and the video recordings. Although the duo spanned only a few years, it represents a generation, a time that is history now. Like most great artists, Simon & Garfunkel are unique and also part of their own time.

They gave us a feeling of optimism, a faith in the strength of friendship, that unity and harmony were, after all, possible – if only for a few short years.

Nevertheless Paul Simon's perceptive, beautifully crafted lyrics, the melodies he matched them to, and the faultless, flawless harmonies of Paul Simon and Art Garfunkel are enough. Simon and Garfunkel remain, as possibly the greatest and best loved duo in musical history.

DISCOGRAPHY

SIMON & GARFUNKEL
Albums

Wednesday Morning 3 am (CBS, US April 1964, UK Oct 1968)
'You Can Tell the World'
'Last Night I Had the Strangest Dream'
'Bleecker Street'
'Sparrow'
'Benedictus'
'The Sound of Silence'
'He Was My Brother'
'Peggy-O'
'Go Tell It on the Mountain'
'The Sun is Burning'
'The Times They Are A-Changing'
'Wednesday Morning 3am'

Sounds of Silence (CBS, April 1966)
'The Sound of Silence'
'Leaves That Are Green'
'Blessed'
'Kathy's Song'
'Somewhere They Can't Find Me'
'Anji'
'Homeward Bound' (on UK album only)
'Richard Cory'
'A Most Peculiar Man'

'April Come She Will'
'We've Got A Groovy Thing Goin''
'I Am a Rock'

Parsley Sage Rosemary and Thyme (CBS, Nov 1966)
'Scarborough Fair/Canticle'
'Patterns'
'Cloudy'
'The Big Bright Green Pleasure Machine'
'The 59th Street Bridge Song (Feeling Groovy)'
'The Dangling Conversation'
'Flowers Never Bend with the Rainfall'
'A Simple Desultory Philippic'
'For Emily Whenever I May Find Her'
'A Poem on the Underground Wall'
'7 o'clock News/Silent Night'

('Homeward Bound' is on the US version)

Simon and Garfunkel (Pickwick Jan 1967 – later deleted)

'Hey Schoolgirl'
'Our Song'
'That's My Story'
'Teenage Fool'
'Tia-juana Blues'
'Dancin' Wild'
'Don't Say Goodbye'
'Two Teenagers'
'True or False'
'Simon Says'

The Graduate (CBS, June 1968)
'The Sound of Silence'
'Mrs Robinson' (instrumental)
'Scarborough Fair/Canticle'
'April Come She Will'
'The Big Bright Green Pleasure
   Machine'
'Mrs Robinson'
'The Sound of Silence'

(Also contains incidental music by
   Dave Grusin)

Bookends (CBS, June 1968)
'Bookends Theme'
'Save the Life of My Child'
'America'
'Overs'
'Voices of Old People'
'Old Friends'
'Bookends Theme'
'Fakin' It'
'Punky's Dilemna'
'Mrs Robinson'
'A Hazy Shade of Winter'
'At the Zoo'

Bridge over Troubled Water (CBS,
   Feb 1970)
'Bridge over Troubled Water'
'El Condor Pasa'

'Cecilia'
'Keep the Customer Satisfied'
'So Long, Frank Lloyd Wright'
'The Boxer'
'Baby Driver'
'The Only Living Boy in New
   York'
'Why Don't You Write Me?'
'Bye Bye Love'
'Song for the Asking'

*Simon & Garfunkel's Greatest
   Hits* (CBS, June 1972)
'Mrs Robinson'
'For Emily, Whenever I May Find
   Her'
'The Boxer'
'The 59th Street Bridge Song'
   (Feeling Groovy)
'The Sound of Silence'
'I Am a Rock'
'Scarborough Fair/Canticle'
'Homeward Bound'
'Bridge over Troubled Water'
'America'
'Kathy's Song'
'El Condor Pasa'
'Bookends'
'Cecilia'

*The Simon & Garfunkel
   Collection* (CBS, Dec 1981)
'I Am a Rock'
'Homeward Bound'
'America'
'The 59th Street Bridge Song'
'Wednesday Morning 3am'
'El Condor Pasa'
'At the Zoo'
'Scarborough Fair/Canticle'
'The Boxer'
'The Sound of Silence'

'Mrs Robinson'
'Keep the Customer Satisfied'
'Song for the Asking'
'A Hazy Shade of Winter'
'Cecilia'
'Old Friends'/'Bookends Theme'
'Bridge over Troubled Water'

The Concert in Central Park
   (Geffen/CBS, Feb 1982)
'Mrs Robinson'
'Homeward Bound'
'America'
'Me and Julio down by the
   Schoolyard'
'Scarborough Fair'

'April Come She Will'
'Wake Up Little Susie'
'Still Crazy after All These
   Years'
'American Tune'
'Late in the Evening'
'Slip Slidin' Away'
'A Heart in New York'
'Kodachrome'/'Maybelline'
'Bridge over Troubled Water'
'Fifty Ways to Leave Your
   Lover'
'The Boxer'
'Old Friends'
'The 59th Street Bridge Song'
'The Sound of Silence'

Singles

'Hey Schoolgirl'/'Dancin' Wild'
   (Big Records, 1957)(Tom &
   Jerry)
'Our Song'/'Don't Say Goodbye'
   (Big Records, 1957)(Tom &
   Jerry)
'That's My Story'/'Two
   Teenagers' (Hunt, 1957)(Tom
   & Jerry)
'The Sound of Silence'/'We've Got
   a Groovy Thing Goin'' (CBS,
   1965)
'Homeward Bound'/'Leaves That
   Are Green' (CBS, 1966)
'I Am a Rock'/'Flowers Never
   Bend with the Rainfall' (CBS,
   1966)
'The Dangling Conversation'/'The
   Big Bright Green Pleasure
   Machine' (CBS, 1966)
'A Hazy Shade of Winter'/'For
   Emily Whenever I May Find
   Her' (CBS, 1966)

'At The Zoo'/'The 59th Street
   Bridge Song' (CBS, 1967)
'Fakin' It'/'You Don't Know
   Where Your Interest Lies' (CBS
   1967)
'Scarborough Fair'/'April Come
   She Will' (CBS, 1968)
'Mrs Robinson'/'Old Friends'/
   'Bookends'(CBS, 1968)
'The Boxer'/'Baby Driver' (CBS,
   1969)
'Bridge over Troubled Water'/
   'Keep the Customer Satisfied'
   (CBS, 1970)
'The Sound of Silence'/'The 59th
   Street Bridge Song' (CBS, 1970)
'Cecilia'/'The Only Living Boy in
   New York' (CBS, 1970)
'America'/'For Emily Whenever I
   May Find Her' (CBS, 1972)
'Mrs Robinson'/'Bookends
   Theme' (Hall Of Fame Series)
   (CBS, 1973)

'The Boxer'/'Baby Driver' (CBS, 1975)

'Bridge over Troubled Water'/'Cecilia' (CBS, 1975)

'Scarborough Fair'/'Canticle'/'I Am a Rock' (CBS, 1975)

'Mrs Robinson'/'Old Friends'/'Bookends' (CBS, 1975)

'The Sound of Silence'/'Homeward Bound' (CBS, 1975)

'The Sound of Silence'/'Homeward Bound' (CBS, 1976)

'Bridge over Troubled Water'/'Keep the Customer Satisfied' (CBS, 1978 and 1969)

'Homeward Bound'/'The 59th Street Bridge Song' (CBS, 1981)

'Mrs Robinson'/'Late in the Evening' (Geffen, 1982)

'Mrs Robinson'/'Bridge over Troubled Water' (CBS, 1982)

'Wake Up Little Susie'/'The Boxer' (Geffen, 1982)

'Bridge Over Troubled Water'/'Keep the Customer Satisfied' (CBS, 1984)

Extended Play Records

'Bleecker Street'/'Sparrow'/'Wednesday Morning 3am'/'The Sound of Silence' (CBS, 1965)

'I Am a Rock'/'Flowers Never Bend with the Rainfall'/'The Sound of Silence'/'Blessed' (CBS, 1966)

'The 59th Street Bridge Song'/'The

Big Bright Green Pleasure Machine'/'Homeward Bound'/'A Hazy Shade of Winter' (CBS, 1967)

'Mrs Robinson'/'April Come She Will'/'Scarborough Fair'/'Canticle'/'The Sound of Silence' (CBS, 1968)

PAUL SIMON

Albums

The Paul Simon Songbook (CBS, Aug 1965)
'I Am a Rock'
'Leaves That Are Green'
'A Church is Burning'
'April Come She Will'
'The Sound of Silence'
'A Most Peculiar Man'
'He Was My Brother'
'Kathy's Song'

'The Side of a Hill'
'A Simple Desultory Philippic'
'Flowers Never Bend with the Rainfall'
'Patterns'

Paul Simon (CBS, Feb 1972)
'Mother and Child Reunion'
'Duncan'

'Everything Put Together Falls
     Apart'
'Run That Body Down'
'Armistice Day'
'Me and Julio Down by the
     Schoolyard'
'Peace Like a River'
'Papa Hobo'
'Hobo Blues'
'Paranoia Blues'
'Congratulations'

There Goes Rhymin' Simon (CBS,
     May 73)
'Kodachrome'
'Tenderness'
'Take Me to the Mardi Gras'
'Something So Right'
'One Man's Ceiling is Another
     Man's Floor'
'American Tune'
'Was a Sunny Day'
'Learn How To Fall'
'Saint Judy's Comet'
'Loves Me Like a Rock'

Live Rhymin' (CBS, March 1974)
'Me and Julio Down by the
     Schoolyard'
'Homeward Bound'
'American Tune'
'El Condor Pasa'
'Duncan'
'The Boxer'
'Mother and Child Reunion'
'The Sound of Silence'
'Jesus is the Answer' (Jessy Dixon
     Singers)
'Bridge over Troubled Water'
'Loves Me Like a Rock'
'America'

Still Crazy After All These Years
     (CBS, Oct 1975)
'Still Crazy After All These Years'
'My Little Town'
'I Do It For Your Love'
'Fifty Ways to Leave Your Lover'
'Night Game'
'Gone at Last'
'Some Folks' Lives Roll Easy'
'Have a Good Time'
'You're Kind'
'Silent Eyes'

Greatest Hits etc. (CBS, Nov
     1977)
'Slip Slidin' Away'
'Stranded in a Limousine'
'Still Crazy After All These Years'
'Have a Good Time'
'Duncan'
'Me and Julio Down by the
     Schoolyard'
'Something So Right'
'Kodachrome'
'I Do It For Your Love'
'Fifty Ways to Leave Your Lover'
'American Tune'
'Mother and Child Reunion'
'Loves Me Like a Rock'
'Take Me to the Mardi Gras'

One Trick Pony (Warner
     Brothers, Sept 1980)
'Late in the Evening'
'That's Why God Made the
     Movies'
'One Trick Pony'
'How the Heart Approaches What
     It Yearns'
'Oh Marion'
'Ace in the Hole'
'Nobody'

'Jonah'
'God Bless the Absentee'
'Long Long Day'

Hearts and Bones (W. B., Oct
  1983)
'Allergies'
'Hearts and Bones'
'When Numbers Get Serious'
'Think Too Much'
'Song About the Moon'
'Think Too Much',
'Train in the Distance'
'Réné and Georgette Magritte
  with their Dog after the War'
'Cars Are Cars'
'The Late Great Johnny Ace'

Graceland (W. B., Sept 1986)
'The Boy in the Bubble'
'Graceland'
'I Know What I Know'
'Gumboots'
'Diamonds on the Soles of her
  Shoes'
'You Can Call Me Al'
'Under African Skies'
'Homeless'
'Crazy Love Vol 2'
'That Was Your Mother'
'All Around The World' or 'The
  Myth of Fingerprints'

Negotiations and Love Songs
  1971–86 (W.B., Oct 1988)
'Mother and Child Reunion'
'Me and Julio Down by the
  Schoolyard'
'Something So Right'
'St Judy's Comet'
'Loves Me Like a Rock'
'Kodachrome'

'Have a Good Time'
'Fifty Ways to Leave Your Lover'
'Still Crazy After All These Years'
'Late in the Evening'
'Slip Slidin' Away'
'Hearts and Bones'
'Train in the Distance'
'Réné and Georgette Magritte
  with their Dog After the War'
'Diamonds on the Soles of Her
  Shoes'
'You Can Call Me Al'
'Graceland'

Rhythm of the Saints (W.B., Oct
  1990)
'The Obvious Child'
'Can't Run But'
'The Coast'
'Proof'
'Further to Fly'
'She Moves On'
'Born at the Right Time'
'The Cool Cool River'
'Spirit Voices'
'The Rhythm of the Saints'

Paul Simon's Concert in the Park
  (W.B., Aug 1991)
'The Obvious Child'
'The Boy in the Bubble'
'She Moves On'
'Kodachrome'
'Born at the Right Time'
'Train in the Distance'
'Me and Julio Down by the
  Schoolyard'
'I Know What I Know'
'The Cool, Cool River'
'Bridge over Troubled Water'
'Proof'
'The Coast'

'Graceland'
'You Can Call Me Al'
'Still Crazy After All These Years'
'Loves Me Like A Rock'
'Diamonds on the Soles of Her
    Shoes'
'Hearts and Bones'
'Late in the Evening'
'America'
'The Boxer'
'Cecilia'
'The Sound of Silence'

The Paul Simon Anthology (W.B.,
    Aug 1993)
'The Sound of Silence'
'Cecilia'
'El Condor Pasa'
'The Boxer'
'Mrs Robinson'
'Bridge over Troubled Water'
'Me and Julio Down by the
    Schoolyard'
'Peace Like a River'
'Mother and Child Reunion'
'American Tune'
'Loves Me Like a Rock'

'Kodachrome'
'Gone At Last'
'Still Crazy After All These Years'
'Something So Right'
'Fifty Ways to Leave Your Lover'
'Slip Slidin' Away'
'Late in the Evening'
'Hearts and Bones'
'Réné and Georgette Magritte
    with their Dog after the War'
'The Boy in the Bubble'
'Graceland'
'Under African Skies'
'That Was Your Mother'
'Diamonds on the Soles of her
    Shoes'
'You Can Call Me Al'
'Homeless'
'Spirit Voices'
'The Obvious Child'
'Can't Run But'
'Thelma'
'Further to Fly'
'She Moves On'
'Born at the Right Time'
'The Cool, Cool River'
'The Sound of Silence'

Singles

'He Was My Brother'/'Carlos
    Domingues' (Oriole 1964 – as
    Jerry Landis)
'I Am a Rock'/'Leaves That Are
    Green' (CBS 1965)
'Mother and Child Reunion'/
    'Paranoia Blues' (CBS 1972)
'Me and Julio Down by the
    Schoolyard'/'Congratulations'
    (CBS 1972)
'Take Me to the Mardi Gras'/
    'Kodachrome' (CBS 1973)

'Loves Me Like a Rock'/'Learn
    How to Fall' (CBS 1973)
'American Tune'/'One Man's
    Ceiling is Another Man's Floor'
    (CBS 1974)
'The Sound of Silence'/'Mother
    and Child Reunion' (live
    versions) (CBS 1974)
'Something So Right'/'Tenderness'
    (CBS 1975)
'Gone At Last'/'Tenderness' (CBS
    1975)

'My Little Town'/'You're Kind' (CBS 1975)

'Loves Me Like a Rock'/ 'Kodachrome' (CBS 1975)

'Mother and Child Reunion'/'Me and Julio Down by the Schoolyard' (CBS 1975)

'Fifty Ways to Leave Your Lover'/ 'Some Folks' Lives' (CBS 1976)

'Still Crazy After All These Years'/ 'Silent Eyes' (CBS 1976)

'Slip Slidin' Away'/'Something So Right' (CBS 1977)

'Stranded in a Limousine'/'Have a Good Time' (CBS 1978)

'Late in the Evening'/'How the Heart Approaches What It Yearns' (WB 1980)

'One Trick Pony'/'Long Long Day' (WB 1980)

'Oh Marion'/'God Bless the Absentee' (WB 1981)

'Allergies'/'Think Too Much' (WB 1983)

'Hearts and Bones'/'Think Too Much' (WB 1983)

'When Numbers Get Serious'/'The Late Great Johnny Ace' (WB 1983)

'You Can Call Me Al'/'Gumboots' (WB 1986)

'Graceland'/'Crazy Love Vol 2' (WB 1987)

'Under African Skies'/'I Know What I Know'/'Homeless' (WB 1987)

'Under African Skies'/'I Know What I Know' (WB 1987)

ART GARFUNKEL

Albums

Angel Clare (CBS, Sept 1973)
'Travellin' Boy'
'Down in the Willow Garden'
'I Shall Sing'
'Old Man'
'Feuilles-Oh/Do Space Men Pass Dead Souls on their Way to the Moon?'
'All I Know'
'Mary was an Only Child'
'Woyaya'
'Barbara Allen'
'Another Lullaby'

Breakaway (CBS, Oct 1975)
'I Believe (When I Fall In Love With You It Will Be Forever)'

'Rag Doll'
'Breakaway'
'Disney Girls'
'Waters of March'
'My Little Town'
'I Only Have Eyes For You'
'Looking for the Right One'
'99 Miles from L.A.'
'The Same Old Tears on a New Background'

Watermark (CBS, Mar 1978)
'Crying in my Sleep'
'Marionette'
'Shine It On Me'
'Watermark'
'Saturday Suit'

'All My Love's Laughter'
'What a Wonderful World'
'Mr Shuck'n'Jive'
'Paperchase'
'She Moved Through the
    Fair'
'Someone Else'
'Wooden Planes'

Fate for Breakfast (CBS, May
    1979)
'In a Little While'
'Since I Don't Have You'
'And I Know'
'Sail on a Rainbow'
'Miss You Nights'
'Bright Eyes'
'Finally Found a Reason'
'Beyond the Tears'
'Oh How Happy'
'When Someone Doesn't Want
    You'
'Take Me Away'

Scissors Cut (CBS, Oct 1981)
'Scissors Cut'
'A Heart in New York'
'Up in the World'
'Hang On In'
'So Easy to Begin'
'Can't Turn My Heart Away'
'The French Waltz'
'The Romance'

'In Cars'
'That's All I've Got to Say'

The Art Garfunkel Album (CBS,
    Dec 1984)
'Bright Eyes'
'Breakaway'
'A Heart in New York'
'I Shall Sing'
'99 Miles From L.A.'
'All I Know'
'(What A) Wonderful World'
'I Only Have Eyes For You'
'Watermark'
'I Believe (When I Fall In Love
    With You It Will Be Forever)'
'Scissors Cut'
'Sometimes When I'm Dreaming'
'Travellin' Boy'
'The Same Old Tears on a New
    Background'

Lefty (CBS 1988)
'This is the Moment'
'I Have a Love'
'So Much in Love'
'Slow Break-Up'
'Love is the Only Chain'
'When a Man Loves a Woman'
'I Wonder Why'
'King of Tonga'
'Love Takes You Away'
'The Promise'

Singles

'All I Know'/'Mary Was an Only
    Child' (CBS, 1973)
'I Shall Sing'/'Feuilles-Oh' (CBS,
    1974)

'Second Avenue'/'Woyaya' (CBS,
    1974)
'Travellin' Boy'/'Old Man' (CBS,
    1974)

'I Only Have Eyes For You'/
'Looking for the Right One'
(CBS, 1975)
'My Little Town'/'Rag Doll' (CBS, 1975)
'Breakaway'/'The Same Old Tears on a New Background' (CBS, 1976)
'I Believe (When I Fall In Love With You It Will Be Forever)'/'Waters Of March' (CBS, 1976)
'We Are Going'/'Second Avenue' (CBS, 1976)
'Crying in My Sleep'/'Mr Shuck'n'Jive' (CBS, 1977)
'I Only Have Eyes For You'/'Looking for the Right One' (CBS, 1978)
'Marionette'/'All My Love's Laughter' (CBS, 1978)
'What a Wonderful World'/'Wooden Planes' (CBS, 1978)
'Bright Eyes'/'Keehaar's Theme' (CBS, 1979)
'Since I Don't Have You'/'And I Know' (CBS, 1979)
'A Heart in New York'/'Is This Love?' (Epic, 1981)
'Scissors Cut'/'So Easy to Begin' (CBS 1981)
'Bright Eyes'/'Keehaar's Theme' (CBS 1984)
'Sometimes When I'm Dreaming'/'Scissors Cut' (CBS 1984)
'When a Man Loves a Woman'/'King of Tonga' (CBS 1988)

For supplying much of the data here, I am indebted to Chris Stanbury, Managing Director of Cravenplan Computers Ltd, publishers of *RockBase Plus* (CD-ROM discography). This contains details of some 400,000 tracks on 120,000 albums and 100,000 single releases by 40,000 artists – on vinyl, cassette and CD. I thank him for helping me through such a staggering amount of data and modern technology with so much patience.

I also thank CBS/Columbia Records (now Sony) and Warner Brothers Records, both in London.

INDEX

Note: entries with inverted commas denote the name of a single